Dick Simpson is a former Chicago alderman, an associate professor of political science at the University of Illinois at Chicago, an ordained minister, executive director of Metro Chicago Clergy and Laity Concerned, and the author of seven books. In *The Politics of Compassion and Transformation* he offers a vision of the personal and social transformation our times require.

THE POLITICS OF COMPASSION AND TRANSFORMATION

THE POLITICS OF COMPASSION AND TRANSFORMATION

DICK SIMPSON

SWALLOW PRESS/OHIO UNIVERSITY PRESS
ATHENS

Swallow Press books are published by
Ohio University Press

Swallow Press/Ohio University Press books are
printed on acid-free paper.∞

Library of Congress Cataloging in Publication Data

Simpson, Dick W.
   The politics of compassion and transformation/Dick Simpson.
     p.   cm.
   Bibliography: p.
   Includes index.
   ISBN 0-8040-0903-1 (alk. paper). ISBN 0-8040-0904-X (pbk. : alk.
paper)
   1. Political ethics.   2. Religion and politics.   I. Title.
JA79.S56 1989
172—dc19   88-29445
                                       CIP

For Sarajane, Kate, and August

Contents

Part I

CRISIS

Chapter 1
A NEW BEGINNING

And he told this parable: "A man had a fig tree planted in his vineyard; and he came seeking fruit on it and found none. And he said to the vinedresser, "Lo, these three years I have come seeking fruit on this fig tree, and I find none. Cut it down; why should it use up the ground?"

And he answered him, "Let it alone, sir, this year also, till I dig about it and put on manure. And if it bears fruit next year, well and good; but if not, you can cut it down."
Jesus of Nazareth
Luke 13: 6-9

To my fellow humans who will face the coming time of troubles, greetings. I have chosen to address those in my own time who can understand me and those who will come after us and will know the results of our struggles all too well. Now we see only dimly the darkly lit present and nearly inevitable future. In William Butler Yeats's phrase, "the blood dimmed tide is loosed." Our civilization, nearly twenty-five centuries in the making, slides into decadence and decline. Rather than creating a more glorious civilization, we fall deeper into a dark age from which the birth of a better society remains, as yet, only a hope.

Echoing Yeats, we have the dark sensation that an ominous Second Coming is at hand. That Brave New World will be peopled not by angels and saints but by the "rough beast" and demons of the Book of Revelation. Like many seers and common citizens, I share a nightmarish premonition of our potential future.

I fear "limited" nuclear wars in the 1990s, which will have devastating effects upon the earth. In my nightmare, Jerusalem is conventionally bombed from the air by Arabs. Israelis respond with a single nuclear bomb destroying the capital of the Arab nation that attacked them. Although the Arabs are forced to sue for peace, terrorist groups, with the help of Arab governments, build nuclear devices which they plant strategically throughout Israel, and a few years after the original war they detonate these bombs, destroying both Israel and much of the life in Europe, the Middle East, Africa, and North America.

The first bomb would pollute the Mediterranean Sea with radioactivity, extend the desert in North Africa because of climate changes, and directly kill

1

millions of people. The series of bombs used in retaliation would extend the catastrophe to a global scale depopulating much of the planet, destroying the remaining institutions of our civilization, and wreaking havoc upon the earth itself.

But I also have a positive dream. Before the nuclear and environmental catastrophes occur, I see a network of people connecting around the globe, winking on like lights on a map. These individuals blaze like lights in the darkness. As they begin to interconnect in continental and planetary webs, a sphere of light and peace is gradually extended as more and more life is protected and enhanced. These people of this network have new talents, abilities, skills, and powers. And they are connected together as a single community despite distances. They are the remnant who survive the coming holocaust, able to give birth to a future race. A marvelous people will live in the new civilization to follow. They will have greater physical, psychic, and intuitive abilities, and an enlarged capacity to love.

As a final image, I see the shell of a huge building collapsing, like in a bombing raid. From the rubble rises a pristine, crystal energy structure looking like an ancient Greek temple. In the future every community will have such a temple at the center of its life. This image represents the collapse of our outmoded institutions and the emergence, from destruction, of the new structures of the coming Aquarian Age.

This vision of the future, which is widely shared in different forms, confronts us with the question: How shall we live in such a world? What must we oppose and what must we affirm in order to sustain ourselves in these difficult times? To what must we say "No" and to what must we say "Yes"? Will we have the courage in these seductively easy times at the height of our civilization and in the more painful, deadly years of the coming collapse to stake our reputations, our cultural inheritance, and our lives on our choice to create a better future? If we fail to act because of cowardice, twenty billion years of cosmic evolution and thousands of years of human struggle will be for nought. If we act to prevent crises which do not come to pass, we will be labeled fanatics who mistook our nightmares for reality. We will be said to have had so little faith in God and in our fellow humans that we wasted our lives in vain.

In our scientific era of "progress," we might expect to look with confidence to the "scientific" disciplines of political science, sociology, and economics to solve the problems of our civilization. We might also look to the older disciplines of religion and ethics to determine our values and to tell us what we ought to do. If science can reveal so much about the physical universe and if technology can eliminate so many of the historical problems of human society, then should not the developing social sciences and humanities successfully guide our future?

The sad truth is that the dominant paradigms, methods, and conclusions of the social sciences and humanities are inadequate to this task. It is critical that we know what is to be done and that we do our tasks unflinchingly. This will allow us to save our lives, and also give our lives meaning. We cannot count only on visions to dictate the steps we must take. We need social sciences, ethics, and religions adequate to guide us through these fateful times. And a more certain knowledge of politics, ethics, and religion is available to us.

We are faced with a number of political, ethical, and religious dilemmas that demand a single solution. I believe that what is required is a particular politics of compassion involving personal as well as social transformation. But before deciding how to resolve them, it is necessary to delineate our worst crises. We face a series of interconnected crises that cannot be solved by our existing institutions because they spring from the very values and structures that undergird our civilization. Since only personal and social transformation can forestall the coming disasters, we can only trust that the collapse of some aspects of our civilization will force the necessary transformations before sentient life is destroyed.

Forecasting the Future

My vision, like other negative forecasts, might be dismissed as simply a bad dream. After all, prophesies are more often wrong than right, and it is hard to tell those which are divinely inspired from personal, psychological projections. But rational forecasts of the future confirm the likelihood of at least five potential catastrophes before the turn of the century. Arguably, we might escape any one of them, but it seems hard to believe that we will escape them all. In fact, they are already having an impact on our lives.

The five great crises are (1) overpopulation/starvation, (2) war, (3) resource depletion/pollution, (4) inflation/unemployment, and (5) the demise of democracy. Spiritual and religious crises both cause and are engendered by these other crises, and it is only by spiritual/religious transformation that we will be able to resolve them.

Overpopulation/Starvation

The world's population is now about five billion people and would grow to between eight and fifteen billion by the middle of the next century if we were able to avoid the worst catastrophes. Unfortunately, under any technology that can be reasonably forecast for the near future, the world cannot feed even eight billion people.[1] The number of hungry or malnourished people currently on the planet is as high as two billion, at least twelve million of whom live in the United States.[2] One-third of the dog food sold in grocery stores in the low-income areas of the United States is eaten by humans.[3] Worst of all, as many as thirteen to eighteen million people currently die hunger-related deaths each year on the planet.[4]

Even if we were able to feed eight to fifteen billion people through the heavy use of fertilizers, hydroponic farming, and farming the seas, the energy costs would be too great to bear.[5] Thus, we can only conclude that "the ravages of overpopulation will . . . be experienced in many parts of the world during our lifetimes and the lifetimes of our children, bringing us horrors of famine and malnutrition and poverty."[6]

Nuclear and Conventional Wars

There are currently as many as forty or fifty conventional wars around the globe in countries such as Afghanistan, Lebanon, Iran-Iraq, and countries of Central America, such as El Salvador and Nicaragua. Since World War Two there have also been numerous "police actions" such as Hungary, Korea, and Vietnam. Many efforts at "destabilizing" Third World countries are undertaken by the CIA of the United States and the KGB of the Soviet Union. Whatever the source of these wars and police actions, the costs in life and property have been staggering. Altogether there have been 120 "wars" since World War Two, resulting in 22 million deaths. Neither treaties nor United Nations peace-keeping efforts are currently capable of preventing the recurrence of similar wars in the future. The effects of these continuing wars are millions of deaths; millions of injured combatants and civilians; millions of homes, farms, and businesses destroyed; and continued suffering.

Because of our inability to curb war, because of the continuance of the institutions that beget war, nuclear war seems likely, perhaps, even inevitable. And preparations for nuclear war are imposing a terrible cost upon the world. The escalating arms race between the superpowers has caused the United States to *increase* military spending by $1.6 trillion from 1981 to 1985, and our military spending was already enormous. In Third World countries military spending has increased five times since 1960 so that even the least developed countries spend at least 5 percent of their Gross National Product on the military. Some, like Pakistan, spend 50 percent of their government budget on defense. Military spending is a major cause of inflation. It does not produce the food, goods, and services needed by a hungry and desperate world. Instead, scarce planetary resources are used to build the instruments of death and destruction.

The supposed purpose of this arms race is nuclear deterrence—to prevent nuclear war by the threat of retaliation against potential aggressors—but, in fact, the existence of ever more bombs and ever more complex defense systems, poised ever closer to "enemy" nations, makes nuclear war by accident, if not by decision, ever more likely. Because of the placement of

Cruise missiles in Europe and the moving of Soviet missile submarines closer to the U.S. coasts, nuclear attack is less than ten minutes away. Any human errors or technical malfunctions have only a few minutes to be rectified before we would be at nuclear war with the Soviet Union. The signing of the recent Intermediate Nuclear Forces treaty between the U.S. and the U.S.S.R. in 1987 will only slightly lengthen the decision-making time by eliminating the closest missiles.

Nuclear war is also made more likely because the superpowers do not use these weapons only for purposes of deterrence. As Jonathan Schell concludes in *The Fate of the Earth,* nations use these frightful weapons to serve national interests as well.

> For the fact is that the nuclear powers do *not,* as the statesmen so often proclaim, possess nuclear weapons with the sole aim of preventing their use and so keeping the peace; they possess them also to defend national interests and aspirations—indeed, to perpetuate the whole system of sovereign states. But now, instead of relying on war for this enforcement, as nations did in pre-nuclear times, they rely on the threat of extinction. . . . [Thus,] one prepares for extinction in order to protect national interests.[7]

Because nuclear weapons are used to protect the nation-state system and to advance the material interests of the superpowers, nuclear disarmament requires more than a simple policy change or the adoption of a different law. In the forty years since their creation, nuclear weapons have become interwoven into the national and international political systems.

Nuclear holocaust is likely, not just because the superpowers have armed for deterrence and pursue their own nationalistic interests. Small nations such as Israel now possess, and terrorist groups will soon possess, these fearful weapons which they will be able to use for international blackmail. Robert Heilbroner has written:

> Many small or relatively poor nations, even though they possess no fully developed industrial base or highly skilled labor force, can gain possession of nuclear weapons . . . Nuclear weaponry for the first time makes [possible] . . . "wars of redistribution" . . . [as] the only way by which the poor nations can hope to remedy their condition.[8]

Thus, a "limited" nuclear war between Third World nations is an all too frightening possibility. As overpopulation brings famine conditions to many parts of the world, some smaller nations may well be tempted to try to gain the food and resources they desperately need from more developed nations by the threat or use of nuclear weapons. Moreover, wars between Third World nations or their "wars of retribution" against wealthy nations could begin nuclear war without participation by the superpowers. As the number of nations with nuclear arsenals grows from seven to more than twenty by the end of the century, some form of nuclear war becomes ever more likely.

As if the much-documented effects of nuclear war were not horrific enough, scientists have recently developed a theory of even more profoundly destructive results. It is called "nuclear winter." A nuclear war could result in a months-long global climate of subfreezing cold, nighttime darkness, and intense radiation. In a 1983 article in *Science* magazine, scientists summarized the phenomenon of nuclear winter as follows:

> Significant hemispherical attenuation of the solar radiation flux and subfreezing land temperatures may be caused by fine dust raised in high-yield nuclear surface bursts and by smoke from city and forest fires ignited by airbursts of all yields. For many simulated exchanges of several thousand megatons, in which dust and smoke are generated and encircle the earth within one to two weeks, average light levels can be reduced to a few percent of [normal levels], and land temperatures can reach -15 to -25 degrees C. The yield threshold for major optical and climatic consequences may be very low: only about 100 megatons detonated over major urban centers. . . . When combined with the prompt destruction from nuclear blast, fires, and fallout and the later enhancement of solar ultraviolet radiation due to ozone depletion, long-term exposure to cold, dark, and radioactivity could pose a serious threat to human survivors and to other species.[9]

In sum, a nuclear war would obliterate many species of life, possibly including human beings. Among animals only such hardy "pests" as rats and cockroaches would probably survive and even proliferate.[10]

Resource Depletion/Pollution

The third dire prospect, if we survive overpopulation/starvation and the threat of nuclear war, is resource depletion and pollution brought about by continued industrialization. By current estimates, many critical energy and mineral resources will be depleted in the next twenty-five to fifty years because of an exponential increase in energy and mineral consumption. This exponential increase in demand is created, in part, by the increasing world population and, in part, by the industrialization of more and more countries. In the Third World, a "revolution in rising expectations" demands machine-made, resource-intensive products just as in the industrialized Western nations the lower socioeconomic classes now demand more of the "good life." This ever-increasing demand is met by building more factories and by producing more products but this, in turn, uses up "cheap" energy and mineral resources at an ever faster rate. Gold is already scarce and selling at incredibly high prices. Despite momentarily cheaper prices, another oil crisis looms in the future (like the one we experienced in the 1970s) as more automobiles and an ever-increasing number of factories burn oil and gasoline for fuel. Making new plastic products from petroleum also uses up scarce oil supplies.

Increased consumption of energy and minerals within the next twenty-five years may eventually force us to adopt "alternative" technologies that are both renewable and nonpolluting. But, by then, it may be too late to save the environment. For the other inevitable effect of massive industrialization, ruled only by the profit motive, is pollution. We already know of the general dangers of air pollution (seen as smog in many cities of the world), of water pollution, and of toxic solid wastes. One of the worst pollution problems is disposing of radioactive "spent" fuel. And pollution hazards continue to appear in ever more lethal and subtle forms such as acid rain and nuclear accidents like the one in Chernobyl in the Soviet Union.

We are also destroying natural habitats at such a rate that more than one million species of animals, plants, and insects are expected to be extinct by the year 2000. Already more than 1,000 species a year are disappearing from the planet. And all these destructive developments are tied directly to industrialization. Our ever-growing worldwide industrial civilization is destroying rain forests in the tropics even as suburbanization destroys prairies and farm lands in the United States.

Still more subtle dangers of industrialization remain ahead:

> According to current scientific estimates, the amount of CO_2 in the air is expected to double by the year 2020. This addition to the "window pane" within our atmosphere would be sufficient to raise surface temperatures on earth by some 1.5 to 3 [degrees centigrade]. . . . Among the projected effects of [such] a rise in temperatures . . . in our planetary greenhouse would be the future unlocking of vast amounts of water still congealed in our polar ice caps. This could eventually bring sea levels above the level of land in the populous delta areas of Asia, the coastal areas of Europe, and much of Florida. Long before that it is feared that the rise in temperature would have irreversibly altered rainfall patterns, with grave potential effects.[11]

Needless to say, if the ice caps melted, such cities as Chicago on the Great Lakes and New York on the eastern seaboard would also be flooded unless a massive system of dikes like those in Holland was erected. Many scientists are predicting a one-foot rise in sea level that will drive the ocean shorelines back from 100 to 1,000 feet in the next forty years. Lake Michigan is predicted to rise at least five feet. Some meteorologists counter that the greenhouse effect might be less of a problem as the earth is scheduled to move back into its normal colder climate pattern leading to the next ice age in a few thousand years. But the most likely scenario is for the greenhouse effect to hit first and the ice age to follow by a few thousand years with some of the worst possible results. In any case we are certain that 2.3 percent of the ozone has been destroyed in the upper atmoshpere over the Northern Hemisphere and that this will soon begin to affect crops and increase cases of skin cancer in humans. Some futurists believe either that we will find new technological solutions before the atmospheric pollution becomes too severe or that the warming trends will prove beneficial.[12] However, these subtle forms of air pollution are more likely to have devastating effects and are unlikely to be prevented unless our form of industrialization is changed.

It is important to realize what vast forces we have loosed upon the planet with the full advent of worldwide industrialization. We humans are profoundly altering global patterns. Unfortunately, we are not acting with care and forethought concerning how we might best protect and preserve life. We seem to act only from our desire for a short-term profit as individual entrepreneurs, corporations, and nations. We are currently destroying species of life that can never be replaced. We are using up, at a prodigious rate, minerals and fuels we will desperately need in only a few years. We are thoughtlessly interfering in the planetary ecology with our pollution and resource destruction.

It is essential to understand that just as the dangers of war may be rooted in the human condition, or at least in the conditions of our civilization, just as nuclear war becomes more likely because of the nation-state system which is the building block of our world order, resource depletion and ecological crises are rooted in industrialization itself. Industrialization destroys nature in order to produce as efficiently as possible artificial "products" that soon wear out and need to be replaced. Efficient industrial production moves as rapidly as possible from the world of nature to the junk heap. Our resource and ecological crises can be solved only by first slowing industrialization and then by switching to alternative technologies that use renewable energy sources, generate less heat, and decrease all forms of pollution. In the phrase of the American Indians and the ecologists, we must learn "to live lightly upon the earth." But that will require a major cultural transformation. And although we can manipulate businesses by governmental regulations, we cannot change the nature of industrialization that has developed over four centuries merely by adopting a new law outlawing air pollution or a new regulation requiring experimentation with alternative technologies.

Inflation/Unemployment

The fourth worldwide crisis, inflation and intolerable levels of unemployment, is brought about in large part by the nature of the three preceding crises and by the business ethic governing our industrial civilization. Overpopulation brings increasing demands for food, goods, and products. The continuing wars and preparations for wars siphon off scarce resources for "defense" rather than produce the economic multiplier effect necessary to create a thriving economy. Advancing industrialization brings resource depletion, which makes the price of "raw" materials and finished products ever greater, and results in pollution, which wantonly destroys the planetary ecology. In this escalating economic crisis, there is justifiable fear that the world may be headed for a universal depression, repeating the tragic pattern of the 1930s. There is no longer any confidence that the market, regulatory agencies, or international financial institutions would be able to prevent such a calamity. The stock market crash of October 1987 illustrates how fragile our international economy has become.

The other global crises make an economic crisis almost inevitable. First, there is overpopulation and resource depletion: "The growth of population, from 3 to 4 billion in the last generation, [and the rise to five billion in our generation] means a massive rise in world demand, while the rapacious environmental policies of nation states and powerful corporations have contributed to a decline in the supply of resources."[13]

Added to population growth, which creates ever greater demand, and rapid industrialization, which produces a greater scarcity of the necessary resources, is wasteful military expenditures. These are increased by an escalating arms race and by the many "conventional" wars around the world. Building military weapons may provide a profit for some corporations and jobs for some workers, but many more companies would be aided and many additional jobs would be provided by other uses of these funds. If farm implements are produced, for example, they can be used to produce future harvests, whereas military expenditures do not have this "multiplier effect." Thus, military expenditures naturally tend to be inflationary because they use scarce capital, raw materials, and natural resources for noneconomic expenditures. Unless there are, at the same time, price and wage controls imposed, price increases fueled by military spending and competition for capital and resources produce an inflationary spiral—driving up interest rates and costs to such an extent that many companies are forced to declare bankruptcy and many workers become unemployed. So population growth, the nuclear arms race, and resource depletion exacerbate our economic problems. As a result, we are faced with an unstable world economy alternately marked by high rates of inflation and high rates of unemployment.

One index of how serious economic problems have become is the global debt crisis. According to the World Bank, developing nations had a foreign debt of $1.19 trillion in 1987 that was expected to rise to at least $1.25 trillion in 1988. At the end of 1987 Argentina owed $49.4 billion and needed to spend 33 percent of its export revenues just to cover interest payments; Brazil owed $114.5 billion and needed to spend 30 percent of its export revenues; and Nigeria owed $27 billion and needed 12 percent of its exports to cover interest payments. The story for most other developing nations was similar.

The causes of inflation and unemployment are endemic to the industrial society, which is subject to business cycles of boom and bust—of inflation and recession. Even with governmental regulations and international financial agreements to regulate these cycles, they can not be controlled entirely as long as the economy is tied to supply and demand as calculated by profits. The ever-closer connections in the global economy make inflation or recession more likely on a worldwide scale.

The Demise of Democracy

The preceding crises, which are expected to worsen considerably, make a governmental crisis more likely. Democracy cannot flourish under such conditions. It can only be maintained in difficult circumstances by heroic efforts on the part of both a determined populace and their leaders. As the general worsening conditions bring on sharp crises such as food and race riots, wars, ecological disasters of various types, runaway double-digit inflation, massive unemployment and stock market crashes, there will inevitably be a demand for strong leaders to cope with these crises. A "leader on a white horse" will be sought to rescue people from the despair they face in their daily lives. It was just this type of situation in the Weimar Republic that led Germans to accept and follow Adolf Hitler. Even a democratic leader, like Abraham Lincoln in the Civil War, was forced to resort to martial law and to suspend First Amendment rights essential to a democracy.

Thus, as the crises begin to unfold in the years to come, a more authoritarian government becomes almost inevitable. Advantages of a more authoritarian government include quicker and stronger responses to crises, and an ability to rally the citizenry to combat problems by coercion as well as exhortation. There are, of course, great disadvantages to such a government. It would be more likely to make major errors because freedom of discussion and criticism would be strictly limited. Its desire to expand to gain more resources could cause it to war with other nations. And such a government would soon eliminate the freedoms a democracy protects, thereby reducing the population to a mindless mob instead of individual, thinking citizens able to come up with creative responses to new crises.

The Religious Crisis

Behind the social, economic, and political crises at both the local and international levels looms an even more basic religious crisis. Religion has been a necessary aspect of every civilization, and a sure sign of a civilization's decay has been the corruption and irrelevance of its religious life. Religion expresses the values and goals of a people and is necessary to motivate citizens to act in an orderly, predictable fashion, to perform their duties as expected, and to make those individual sacrifices essential to preserve civilization. Religious values and sentiments undergird and support the other major institutions of a society.

There are, of course, major differences among civilizations in the relationships between religion and other institutions. For instance, ancient Greece did not create the clear separation between religion and political/social institutions we have developed in modern times. The Greek gods, including the patron god or goddess of a city, provided religious sanctions for the particular *polis* or city-state, and government officials provided for and conducted the many religious ceremonies and holidays. Even Athenean drama began as morality plays to reinforce religious and moral teachings.

To take another example of religion's importance to civilization, Christianity in the Middle Ages supported the feudal system, kept learning and culture alive, blessed the Crusades, and supported the "divine right of kings." And religion has an effect on economic life as well. Social theorists like Max Weber maintain that the Protestant Reformation gave rise to the Protestant work ethic which helped to make possible the Industrial Revolution which created, in turn, the current era of capitalism.

To be sure, the links between a culture and its religion are subtle. Yet to consider these connections leads us to think about religion in our own time. Given the great crises we face, which may lead to either the collapse or radical transformation of our civilization, we must ask: Is our religion adequate to sustain us through this period?

Major world religions such as Judaism, Christianity, Islam, Buddhism, and Hinduism are at least two thousand years old. They have survived several civilization shifts already. This suggests that they are founded on enduring truths. Judaism, for instance, survived the Babylonian Exile, and Christianity survived Roman persecution. These earlier crises are analogous in many ways to the crises we face.

However, religions have been secularized in modern society and often linked to nationalist ideology. On the other hand, national ideology has been raised to the status of religion. Thus, communism in the Soviet Union or Mao Tse Tung's communist philosophy in China have become state religions performing most of the symbolic and practical functions of other religions.

Both secularized traditional religions and modern state religions are linked to the chief institutions of our society—the business firm (whether capitalist or socialist), the nuclear family (however constructed and maintained), and the nation-state. All modern religions assume abundance, not scarcity; success, not adversity; and, most of all, a continuation of the status quo. The crises of overpopulation/hunger, nuclear war, resource depletion/pollution, inflation/unemployment, and the rise of autocratic government are, for the most part, not considered in their teachings. This is not to say that there are no relevant teachings in the traditional religions on these subjects. However, the religions as they are practiced in our modern civilization give more emphasis to preserving the status quo than to the transformations necessary to adjust to the dire crises that threaten.

Perhaps for our current situation the most relevant passages of the Hebrew Scriptures come from the prophets predicting the destruction of the Northern kingdom of Israel, the later destruction of the Southern kingdom of Judah, and the Exile in Babylon which followed. Hosea predicted the fall of Israel in these terms:

> Ephraim is like a dove,
>   silly and without sense,
>   calling to Egypt, going to Assyria.
> As they go, I will spread over them
>   my net;
>   I will bring them down like birds of the air;
>   I will chastise them for their wicked deeds.
> Woe to them, for they have strayed from me!
>   Destruction to them, for they have rebelled
>   against me!
> I would redeem them, but they speak lies against me. . . .
>
> O Death, where are your plagues?
> O Sheol, where is your destruction?
>   Compassion is hid from my eyes.
> Though he may flourish as the reed plant,
>   the east wind, the wind of the Lord, shall
>   come,
>   rising from the wilderness;
>   and his fountain shall dry up,
>   his spring shall be parched;
>   it shall strip his treasury of every precious thing.
> Samaria shall bear her guilt
>   because she has rebelled against her God;
>   they shall fall by the sword,
>   their little ones shall be dashed to pieces,

and their pregnant women ripped open.
(Hosea 7:11-13; 13:14-16)

Jeremiah's prediction of the fate of the Southern kingdom, Judah, was equally graphic:

And the dead bodies of this people will be food for the birds of the air, and for the beasts of the earth; and none will frighten them away. And I will make to cease from the cities of Judah and from the streets of Jerusalem the voice of mirth and the voice of gladness, the voice of the bridegroom and the voice of the bride; for the land shall become a waste.
(Jeremiah 7:33-34)

Nor is the prophesy of Isaiah any less explicit:

Your country lies desolate,
  your cities are burned with fire;
  in your very presence aliens devour your land;
  it is desolate, as overthrown by aliens.
(Isaiah 1:7)

There is with all the Jewish prophets also a message of hope, a pleading as it were. If Israel or Judah would only turn back to the Lord they would be saved. They would not be destroyed. And after they were destroyed, if the remnant that remained would only return to the Lord, all would be restored. Thus, the second prophet called Isaiah proclaims the return after the Babylonian Exile:

Comfort, comfort my people, says your God.
Speak tenderly to Jerusalem, and cry to her
that warfare is ended, that her iniquity is pardoned,
that she has received from the Lord's hand
double for all her sins.

A voice cries:
In the wilderness prepare the way of the Lord,
make straight in the desert a highway for our God.
every valley shall be lifted up, and every mountain and hill
be made low;
the uneven ground shall become level, and the rough
places plain.
And the glory of the Lord shall be revealed . . .

Get you up to a high mountain . . .
Behold, the Lord God comes with might . . .
God will feed his flock like a shepherd,
God will gather the lambs in his arms,
God will carry them in his bosom
and gently lead those that are with young.
                              (Isaiah 40:1-5, 9, 10-11)

In the same way, when the folly of this civilization and the failure of our religion shall have been reaped, there may yet be salvation. There may be a "rebirth of wonder" if there is, again, a reunion between God and humans. After destruction of Israel there was a refounding of "The Chosen People of God." The prophets in the Hebrew scriptures predicted the collapse of the northern and southern kingdoms, but they also offered a vision of hope. As we now face serious crises in our civilization we need to remember these earlier crises and the advice of the prophets as to how such crises should be faced.

The Christian scriptures also carry an apocalyptic message. Thus, reads the final book, the Book of Revelation:

Now the seven angels who had the seven trumpets made ready to blow them.

The first angel blew his trumpet and there followed hail and fire. mixed with blood, which fell on the earth; and a third of the earth was burnt up, and a third of the trees were burnt up.

The second angel blew her trumpet, and something like a great mountain burning with fire, was thrown into the sea; and a third of the sea became blood, a third of the living creatures in the sea died, and a third of the ships were destroyed.
                              (Revelation 8:7-8)

Like the Hebrew scriptures, Christian scriptures also have a message of salvation. For example, the Gospel of Luke, chapter 15, offers parables of the lost sheep, lost coin, and the prodigal son which promise that when we turn back to God, we will be saved.

These passages from the Hebrew and Christian Scriptures could describe our plight. We are faced with great international crises which also manifest themselves in our daily lives. To prevail in these crises or to rebuild society after its collapse, we must have a valid religion—a value center around which civilization can be built and sustained.

My vision of the future at the beginning of this chapter also has the same element of promise. After a limited nuclear war, I see a shell of a building collapsing and falling to rubble. But then I see arising from its center a crystal temple. The temple looks a lot like the ancient Greek Parthenon. It has pillars front and back and along the sides. It is open except for the roof and floor. It is aglow with energy.

Towns and cities of the future will have to be built around a single temple—there can not be competing sects or denominations but only a common faith. The problems of survival will demand this unity of purpose. In each crystal temple, there will be an altar bathed in light and energy. People will come to the temple to worship, but their worship will involve sharing their energy with the community and taking from the community the energy they need. Throughout the world there will be these temples of faith to sustain the people in the hard times of scarcity and turmoil.

Such visions have always motivated religion. Christianity has wanted to see a world of peace in which the Kingdom of God arrived. Judaism has believed that Israel would be a light to the other nations and that the "chosen people" were chosen to lead the way to God. Such a millennium has never occurred for either Christians or Jews. But such visions of a better world have allowed religion to remain the center and core of society. Our secular culture, in foreship religion, has given up an essential mainstay of the civilization itself.

Institutional churches as we know them are not an adequate religious center for people facing crises, just as our current political institutions are inadequate to eliminate war, prevent starvation, or limit resource depletion. But the teachings of religion can provide hope in the times ahead until the crystal temples are built and we can experience religion in its future form.

The central religious element, running through all the great world religions, is *compassion*. Narrower religious laws and injunctions will not prove enduring in the coming times, but a religion based upon compassion can be the bedrock on which to reform this civilization or to found a better one. Joe Holland, a Catholic theorist has written, "I would now argue that *our whole Western civilization has entered into a profound and irreversible crisis. . . .* Increasingly the energies of our civilization are pointed toward destruction . . . " He writes that Pope John Paul II also concluded that "we have come to an *inescapable crisis of modern civilization.*" If the "destructive energies are allowed to continue they will destroy humanity and the earth . . . On the positive side, new energies are emerging to create a fresh . . . 'civilization of love.'"[14] Only love and compassion can create this new civilization and unleash the positive energies necessary to cope with our current crises.

Facing the Crises of our Civilization

Sigmund Freud, in *Civilization and Its Discontents,* suggests that there is a fundamental, enduring struggle between Eros and Thanatos, between the basic instincts of love and death, between our efforts to achieve simple happiness and the structures and mores of civilization that we have erected in order to achieve happiness. Freud wrote that the

> meaning of the evolution of civilization is no longer obscure to us. It must present the struggle between Eros and Death, between the instinct of life and the instinct of destruction as it works itself out in the human species. . . . The evolution of civilization may therefore be simply described as the struggle for life of the human species.[15]

The impulse for destruction, instinctive aggressiveness, and even human sexual desires must necessarily be curbed by civilization. We cannot simply follow our impulses to fulfill every desire without limitation. Freud concludes that "the fateful question for the human species seems to me to be whether and to what extent their cultural development will succeed in mastering the disturbance of their communal life by the human instinct of aggression and self-destruction."[16]

Thus, our civilization serves as a partial shield against aggression. But, at the same time, our human nature and our civilization create a series of fundamental crises that threaten life itself. To achieve happiness we need civilization to provide both necessities and comforts. We also need civilization to protect us from our own and from others' baser instincts. Yet, the very civilization upon which we must depend inevitably creates crises.

To face these crises can be psychologically very painful, for they are depressing and often lead to despair. We seldom want to voice them to our family, friends, and, least of all, to our children. The truth is that we don't even want to admit them to ourselves. Yet, facing the crises empowers us and liberates us from their tyranny. Joanna Macy, in *Despair and Personal Power in the Nuclear Age,* maintains "that everyone in this planet-time, by the simple fact of being threatened with horrors too vast to contemplate, is a victim of the Bomb. '"The very existence of nuclear weapons . . . is an assault on the human heart.'"[17]

Macy advocates that we face the crises directly because of five psychological principles. She writes that (1) feelings of pain for our world are natural and healthy, (2) this pain is morbid only if denied (when we disown our pain for the world the pain becomes dysfunctional), (3) more information about our plight alone is not enough, (4) unblocking repressed feelings releases energy and clears the the mind, and (5) unblocking our pain for the world reconnects us with the larger web of life. "By recognizing our capacity to suffer with our world, we are drawn to wider dimensions of being . . . and there is a new kind of power."[18] Macy argues that we must face the crises and experience the pain of recognizing the potential catastrophes in order to experience the power of our connection with others and with life.

Two other psychologists, Robert Jay Lifton and Nicholas Humphrey, in their anthology *In a Dark Time: Images for Survival,* also advocate facing the threat of nuclear war in order to discover hope beyond the inevitable despair. Nicholas Humphrey writes:

> Just as despair can be a self-fulfilling prophecy, so can its opposite. Hope, too, will create its own object—by giving us the strength of mind and voice to tackle our own embarrassment, our helplessness, our own dark images of death, and come through to a world not merely of our making but of our choosing. . . . The bomb is not an uncontrollable automaton, and we are not uncontrolling people. Our control lies—as it always has done *whenever it has been tried*—in the force of public argument and public anger.[19]

Robert Jay Lifton, like Joanna Macy and Nicholas Humphrey, stresses the importance of the psychological breakthrough that comes from confronting these crises:

> In confronting the threat rather than numbing ourselves to it, we experience greater vitality. We feel stronger human ties. We turn to beauty, love, spirituality, and sensuality. We touch the earth and we touch each other.
>
> In struggling to preserve humankind we experience a renewed sense of human possibility in general. We feel part of prospective historical and evolutionary achievements. We feel not only ourselves but our species, and relationship to the species, to be newly alive.[20]

Humphrey and Lifton also quote Freud's *Civilization and Its Discontents* as a sign that Eros may yet overcome the instincts of death and destruction. They write that we

> have gained control over the forces of nature to such an extent that with their help [we] would have no difficulty in exterminating one another to the last [person. We] know this, and hence comes a large part of [our] current unrest, [our] unhappiness and [our] mood of anxiety. And now it is to be expected that the other of the two "Heavenly Powers," eternal Eros, will make an effort to assert [itself] in the struggle with [its] equally immortal adversary [Thanatos].[21]

The insights of modern psychology echo the wisdom of ancient Hinduism. There are sublime and wonderful gods such as Krishna in the Hindu pantheon. However, there are also terrible dark gods such as the goddess Kali. In *The*

Sword and the Flute: Kali and Krsna: Dark Visions of the Terrible and the Sublime in Hindu Mythology, David Kinsley quotes ancient texts that describe Kali as follows:

> Of terrible face and fearful aspect is Kali the awful. Four-armed, garlanded with skulls, with disheveled hair, she holds a freshly cut human head and a bloodied scimitar in her left hands and makes the signs of fearlessness-assurance and the bestowing of boons with her right hands. . . . She is dark and naked.

Kali is a goddess who confronts us with death yet who grants us a boon. "To worship the dark goddess, to meditate upon her terrifying presence, to invoke her name in the cremation ground [where she is worshiped most of all by her devotees] is . . . to confront the painful, sorrowful dimensions of the world that are summed up in death." By meditating upon the reality Kali represents, the devotee is able to penetrate the meaning of life and gain release from fear. As Kinsley puts it, to the person who has discovered his or her eternal destiny:

> the cremation ground represents the gateway to complete liberation. . . . From this point of view Kali's overall presence may be understood as benign. Her raised and bloodied sword suggest the death of ignorance, her disheveled hair suggests the freedom of release, and her girdle of severed arms may suggest the end of grasping. As death or the mistress of death she grants to [those] who see truly the ultimate boon of unconditioned freedom, release from the cycle of *samsara,* release from pain, sorrow, and not-knowing. . . . It is a freedom based upon a release from ignorance, a freedom that comes to one who knows [oneself] to be mortal, a freedom that enables [us] to revel in the moment, to accept the fullness of life as a gift to be reveled in rather than as a curse to be gotten rid of.[22]

Whether we understand the psychological challenge as one to be reconnected to the web of life, or simply to be released to revel in the moment, both modern psychoanalysis and ancient religions teach us that we must confront the terrible potential end, not only of our individual lives but also the destruction of all life, if we are to be freed to act effectively. It is in this spirit that we confront honestly the crises of our time. As we do, we soon recognize that the roots of the crises of starvation, war, resource depletion, economic misery, and autocracy lie deeper than any single crisis. Only when we have faced the true nature of these crises can we begin to consider what we can do about them. To be freed from our despair and paralysis is the first step.

The End of Civilization

I am not alone in foreseeing a negative end to the twentieth century. Many Christians in their reading of the prophesies of Daniel, Ezekiel, and Revelations concluded that the final apocalypse would arrive at the end of the first millennium after the birth of Christ. When these expectations were not fulfilled, it was concluded that the apocalypse would arrive at the end of the second millennium. Although the prediction of an eventual apocalypse may be correct, there is no guarantee from this evidence alone that it will occur in our time.

Still many prognosticators have predicted calamities from the time of Halley's Comet in 1986 to the year 2011. The most famous predictions are those of Michel de Nostradamus who, in the sixteenth century, predicted a Third World War would occur during the period from 1986 to 1999. Nostradamus predicted the arrival of a third "Antichrist" from Asia (the first two "Antichrists" he predicted correctly were Napoleon and Hitler). This war started by the Antichrist from Asia will involve nuclear weapons and will, more or less, end human life. This coming period, according to Nostradamus, will also witness the final eclipse of the papacy and many terrible wars in the Middle East. All these events are interrelated. As a current commentator on Nostradamus explains, "to Nostradamus the final decline of the Vatican was an indication of the end of the old spiritual order as he understood it, and worse, the indication of future anarchy. In short, the end of civilization as he comprehended it."

> Nostradamus's general predictions of the fate of the world are to be found in several different quatrains. Quatrain II.46 has the following prophecy: "After great misery for [humankind] an even greater one approaches as the great cycle of the centuries starts to renew itself. It will rain blood, milk, famine, war and disease. In the sky will be seen fire, dragging a great trail of sparks."

This general prediction of great evil from the time of Halley's Comet (the fire in the sky dragging a great trail of sparks) until the end of the second millennium (as the great cycle of the centuries starts to renew itself) seems to include nuclear fallout pictured in the vivid image of raining blood and milk, followed by famine, war, and disease. In any case, we have already experienced massive famines, such as the Ethiopian famine, many wars, and terrible, seemingly incurable diseases such as AIDS. These disasters would worsen greatly in a nuclear war. Nostradamus's quatrains X.72 and IX.55 express the similar themes.

> In the year 1999 and seven months from the sky will come the Great

King of Terror. He will bring back the Great King of the Mongols. Both
before and after this, war reigns unrestrained. . . .

The dreadful war is being prepared in the West, the following year
will be followed by the pestilence: so very horrible that young, nor old,
nor animal [will survive]. Blood, fire, Mercury, Mars, Jupiter in
France.[23]

As Nostradamus's commentator concludes: "One cannot but feel that
Nostradamus' vision of the twentieth century was one of war, brutality,
famine and disaster."[24] Other modern prognosticators such as Jeane Dixon
come to similar conclusions.[25]

Since the beginning of the century, the sense of the impending collapse of
civilization has been echoed by our best poets and authors. Thus, William
Butler Yeats declared in "The Second Coming":

> Things fall apart; and the center cannot hold;
> Mere anarchy is loosed upon the world,. . . .
> And what rough beast, its hour come at last,
> Slouches towards Bethlehem to be born?[26]

Currently it has become very popular to write about the coming collapse of
our civilization. Dozens of science fiction books, films, and television
programs take this as an accepted theme. They describe in considerable detail
the coming catastrophes and potential new civilizations, either glorious or
merely survival oriented, which might be born from the rubble of the current
civilization.[27] The imagination of our time, much like the imagination of the
people in the Dark Ages approaching the first millennium, seems fixed upon
coming apocalyptic events. Although our world may not come to an end,
there is a common foreboding that disasters will occur in the years
immediately ahead. Unless we act to relieve the pending crises, these
unconscious beliefs in the apocalyptic time ahead will become self-fulfilling
prophecies.

Even scholars who do not necessarily foresee an end of civilization in the
last years of this century see inevitable, historical cycles culminating in major
crises. Arthur M. Schlesinger, Jr., in *The Cycles of American History*
concludes that there is a roughly thirty year generational cycle in American
political life between an emphasis upon conservatism and reform or
capitalism and democracy. After the turbulent '60s with Kennedy as an
activist president and the civil rights, student, and antiwar movements came
the Reagan "counterrevolution" of privatization and conservatism. Of the
years immediately ahead Schlesinger writes:

We may conclude that the public purpose will have at least one more chance. At some point, shortly before or after the year 1990, there should come a sharp change in the national mood and direction—a change comparable to those bursts of innovation and reform that followed the accessions to office of Theodore Roosevelt in 1901, of Franklin Roosevelt in 1933, and of John Kennedy in 1961. The 1990s should be the turn in the generational succession for the young men and women who came of political age in the Kennedy years. . . .

Still let us not be complacent. Should private interest fail [in the 1980s to solve our national and international problems] and public purpose fail thereafter [in the 1990s], what rough beast, its hour come round at last, may be slouching toward Washington to be born?[28]

Physicist Fritjof Capra makes positive predictions for the time immediately ahead. He quotes the ancient Chinese book the *I Ching* to describe the time of change at which we have now arrived:

After a time of decay comes the turning point. The powerful light that has been banished returns. There is movement, but it is not brought about by force. . . . The movement is natural, arising spontaneously. For this reason the transformation of the old becomes easy. The old is discarded and the new is introduced. Both measures accord with the time; therefore, no harm results.[29]

Capra goes on to assert:

I have come to believe that today our society as a whole finds itself in . . . crises. . . . We have high inflation and unemployment, we have an energy crisis, a crisis in health care, pollution and other environmental disasters, a rising wave of violence and crime and so on . . . [These] are all different facets of one and the same crisis . . . The gravity and global extent of our current crisis indicate that this change is likely to result in a transformation of unprecedented dimensions, a turning point for the planet as a whole.[30]

Capra believes that the social movements of the 1960s and 1970s represent the "rising culture, which is now ready for the passage to the solar age" when patriarchy will be overturned by feminism, fossil-fuel technology will be replaced by renewable energy sources, and a paradigm shift will occur when we change from a view of the universe as a mechanical system to a view of the universe as a dynamic interconnected web of relations. While these interrelated cultural and social transformations are taking place, "the declining culture refuses to change, clinging ever more rigidly to its outdated ideas; nor will the dominant social institutions hand over their leading roles to the new cultural forces. But they inevitably go on to decline and disintegrate while the rising culture will continue to rise and eventually will assume its leading role."[31]

Finally, even historians such as Paul Kennedy who do not automatically subscribe to a theory of cyclical decay, do believe that the United States faces a crisis in the balance between military armaments and its domestic economy that must be met by wise leadership if we are not to fall as previous great powers have. In *The New York Times Book Review* Michael Howard summarized Kennedy's thesis in *The Rise and Fall of the Great Powers* as follows:

> The more states increase their power, the larger the proportion of their resources they devote to maintaining it. If too large a proportion of national resources is diverted to military purposes, this in the long run leads to a weakening of power. The capacity to sustain a conflict with a comparable state or coalition of states ultimately depends on economic strength; but states apparently at the zenith of their political power are usually already in a condition of comparative economic decline, and the United States is no exception to this rule.[32]

In short, if we continue our overexpenditures for defense and if we become engaged in wars like the Vietnam War, we will fall just as European powers have fallen from power over the last 500 years.

George Gallup in his book *Forecast 2000* confirms that a majority of experts and "national opinion leaders" concur on the most serious problems facing the United States today and believe that they are likely to worsen by the turn of the century. The trends these "experts" foresee are the same ones reported here: wars, terrorism, and the threat of nuclear war; overpopulation, inflation, and unemployment; pollution; crime, violence, and the decline of the family. These leaders look to education and religion to provide answers to these dilemmas even though they recognize that formal education and organized religion are inadequate today. Of the 1,346 opinion leaders surveyed, more tend to be optimistic than pessimistic about the future of the country and our world, but all agree about the seriousness of the crises that we will face in the years immediately ahead.[33]

We do not need to decide whether the particular predictions of the seers, scholars, or national opinion leaders are correct. What is important is the convergence of such different thinkers and leaders on the common proposition that ours is a time of crisis and, inevitably, a time of change and transformation.

A New Politics

We are faced with crises in our civilization for which our institutions are inadequate. We should not be surprised that these crises require both a new politics and a new political science just as they require new ethical norms and new religious institutions. Political Science used to describe politics as "who gets what, where, when, and how." A more adequate definition of politics is that it is the struggle for the power to determine governmental outcomes. Politics is important because governments determine war and peace, the way taxes are collected, how tax money is spent, and the laws that control our lives. But now we must also come to understand that politics includes the power to create, maintain, or destroy institutions.

If a broadened understanding of religion, ethics, and politics is needed in our time, then it is obvious that neither behavioral political science, fundamentalist religion, nor formalistic ethics can provide it. It also becomes obvious that the tactics of elections, interest group politics, lobbying, and policymaking must now be understood within the broader context of the creation, maintenance, or destruction of political and governmental institutions themselves.

We need a new "politics of compassion and transformation" based upon a clear understanding of political action and its consequences.[34] "Politics of Compassion" at first seems an oxymoron, a clash of irreconcilable concepts. But it is now necessary to act politically on deeply held religious values.

As in the past, politics today is often founded upon greed and self-interest, not compassion. Our starting point in personal ethics, religious faith, and social transformation must be compassion. Yet the most difficult step is to develop a new politics of compassion. Politics leads to action just as political science can lead to thoughtful reflection upon political acts. So both the practice and study of politics are essential to a politics of compassion and transformation in which we act from our compassionate desire to protect and enhance life rather than from narrow self-interest alone and in which we are ready to seek radical change.

Because we face serious crises, we must decide which of our institutions to save, which to modify, and which are to be allowed to collapse. More than this, we must know how to maintain those institutions that should be preserved. We must learn how to build new institutions adequate to meet our goals. In our politics of compassion and transformation, we must be guided in making political decisions by our religious values. Our politics and religion must be knit together more closely than they have been in our secular society. We must practice a religious politics and a political religion in which religious values are dominant. Only a profoundly religious politics can provide a sound foundation on which to make a new beginning, to build a more humane civilization. Only a fully conscious and a deeply compassionate people would dare to try.

Chapter 2
RESOLVING THE DILEMMAS IN RELIGION, ETHICS, AND POLITICS

The conditions are difficult. The task is great and full of responsibility. It is nothing less than that of leading the world out of confusion back to order. But it is a task that promises success, because there is a goal that can unite the forces tending in different directions.

Now is the time of struggle. The transition must be completed. We must make ourselves strong in resolution; this brings good fortune. All misgivings that might arise in such grave times of struggle must be silenced. It is a question of a fierce battle to break and to discipline . . . the forces of decadence. But the struggle also has its reward. Now is the time to lay the foundations of power and mastery for the future. . . . And just as the sun shines forth in redoubled beauty after rain, or as a forest grows more freshly green from charred ruins after a fire, so the new era appears all the more glorious by contrast with the misery of the old.

I Ching
Hexagram 63: "Before Completion"

Religion, ethics, and politics have engendered philosophical and practical arguments for thousands of years around such questions as: How are we to define them? What ideals should we strive to achieve? What are we required to do in our religious, ethical, and political life?

We now confront these three realms afresh in light of the great pending crises of our civilization. We must ask anew what religion, ethics, and politics is adequate in these perilous times. I maintain that our politics and ethics must be guided by our religion, that we must explicitly adopt a politics and an ethics of compassion and transformation. But this will require us to discard previous understandings of religion, ethics, and politics that are inadequate. We will have to forego religion as merely individual feelings about the divine, or as an abstract participation in the ultimate, and accept, in the last analysis, religion as acts of compassion and personal transformation. We will have to forego understanding ethics as merely a set of obligatory rules, or as a set of goals to be achieved, and accept ethics as actions by which we reveal ultimate reality in daily life. We will have to forego understanding politics as merely individual political behavior, or as only believing in philosophical goals, and understand it as political acts by many people to create, maintain, or destroy institutions and civilizations.

The three disciplines of religious studies, ethics, and political science currently face a similar intellectual crisis. Attempts to achieve positivist or "scientific" definitions of religion, ethics, and politics yield only personal subjective experiences, restricted moral rules, and individual "behavior." These modern approaches are too limited to include the collective, societal, and intersubjective elements necessary to comprehend religion, ethics, and politics. On the other hand, the traditional or classical alternative of creating abstract, universal definitions of these fields of study yield only abstract definitions of God, ethical goals, and philosophical principles which are too bloodless to apply to real world problems. A politics of compassion and transformation must incorporate both the concrete and intersubjective aspects of these disciplines while transcending them. It must unite the concrete with the abstract in a more comprehensive understanding. It will bridge the gap between theory and action because compassion inevitably compels action to alleviate shared pain and suffering, and transformation requires both personal and institutional change. Compassion drives a politics intent upon nothing less than the birthing of a new civilization.[1]

To move to a politics of compassion and transformation, which is simultaneously religious, ethical, and political, we must move away from both individualistic and abstract definitions into the realm of praxis and action. There we discover through our own direct experience and involvement the truths we seek. As we reflect upon our experience, as well as the wisdom from the experiences of human beings over thousands of years, we gain the necessary judgment to act effectively. This is not to deny the power of thought, theology, science, Scripture, history, or philosophy but to say that their conclusions must be tested and proven in our own experiences if they are to live within us. Neither revelation nor wisdom ended with the saints or thinkers of years ago; rather, they await us in the world today.

Religion

Religion has been defined in many different ways. Its etymology is from the latin *religare*, to bind again, and refers to a binding back to one's faith or ethics.[2] It also refers to being bound by vows to a certain style of life. But such definitions are insufficient to indicate the range of institutions and experiences we call religious. They are also insufficient definitions on which to base the field of religious studies. Ken Wilber, in *A Sociable God: Toward a New Understanding of Religion,* provides nine different definitions of religion which differ according to the level of an individual's psychological development.[3] Religion is experienced very differently according to an individual's spiritual development, cultural background, and personal experiences. With many different definitions of religion, it is not surprising that the field of religious studies includes many different subjects such as theology, history of religions, comparative religion, scriptural studies, the sociology of religion, pastoral counseling, Christian education, hymnology, and sermon writing. The study of religion is not a coherent academic discipline.[4]

But religion and the study of religion do have this in common. They have to do with God and with our relationship to God. As Langdon Gilkey puts it in *Naming the Whirlwind: The Renewal of God-Language:*

> Religious language is fundamentally referent to the ultimate, the unconditional, and the holy or sacred as these manifest themselves in human experience. Religious discourse has three characteristic features: (1) multivalent, referring both to the finite world and to the sacred, (2) concerned with existential, ultimate issues of life, and (3) crucial models or norms by which life is directed and judged.[5]

Thus, the problem in defining religion has to do with how we know God, what we know about God's relationship to us, and how we are to live our life in relationship to God and our fellow humans. As we have fundamentally different ways of understanding God and our relationship to God, approaches to religion and religious studies are often diametrically opposed.

Religion as Feeling

One fruitful and, at least partially, empirical definition of religion was offered by William James in his lectures published as *The Varieties of Religious Experience:*

> Religion, therefore, as I now ask you arbitrarily to take it, shall mean for us *the feelings, acts, and experiences of individual men [and women] in their solitude, so far as they apprehend themselves to stand in relation to whatever they consider the divine.* Since the relation may be either moral, physical, or ritual, it is evident that out of religion in the sense in which we take it, theologies, philosophies, and ecclesiastical organizations may secondarily grow.[6]

For James, the religious experience is an individual experience of a relationship to the divine. Religious people, whatever the particular church or religious group to which they belong, share similar experiences in which they feel themselves to be in a direct relationship to God. From this felt experience, indeed, spring the theologies, churches, temples, synagogues, and ashrams.

James's approach to religion as an individual religious experience or feeling is similar to the more specific feelings reported by the Christian theologian Friedrich Schleiermacher who wrote in *The Christian Faith:*

> The immediate feeling of absolute dependence is presupposed and actually contained in every religious and Christian self-consciousness as the only way in which, in general, our own being and the infinite Being of God can be one in self-consciousness. . . . We assert that in every religious affection, however much its special contents may predominate, the God-consciousness must be present and cannot be neutralized by anything else, so that there can be no relation to Christ which does not contain also a relation to God. . . .
>
> The feeling of absolute dependence, in which our self-consciousness in general represents the finitude of our being is therefore not an accidental element, or a thing which varies from person to person, but is a universal element of life; and the recognition of this fact entirely takes the place, for the system of doctrine, of all the so-called proofs of the existence of God.[7]

Like James's, Schleiermacher's view is that religion is a feeling or experience, specifically the "feeling of absolute dependence." This feeling is engendered by a consciousness of our relation to "the infinite Being of God." Schleiermacher claims that this is not a particular experience of a single sect but an experience of all religious people. As with James, the very universalism of Schleiermacher's definition recommends it. But neither definition accounts for the corporate religious experience except as an amalgam of individual experiences. And they don't provide a basis for acting in crises except to guarantee that there is a God upon whom we are ultimately dependent. Such definitions tend to be too private and, strangely, to render us inactive because we are dependent upon divine intervention or revelation in order to act religiously.

Religion as Symbols

In opposition to individual experiences as the sole basis of religion, the modern theologian David Tracy has tried to correct and to advance the definitions of James and Schleiermacher. In *Blessed Rage for Order,* he begins with the admission that "there is no universally agreed upon single definition for the human phenomenon called 'religion.'"[8] On the other hand, he recognizes as valid the retort, "I can't define religion, but I know it when I see it."[9] After reviewing various theological alternatives, Tracy considers the "functional" definition of Clifford Geertz who argues that religion is "(1) a system of symbols which acts to (2) establish powerful, pervasive, and long-lasting moods and motivations in [people] by (3) formulating conceptions of a general order of existence, and (4) clothing these conceptions with such an aura of factuality that (5) the moods and motivations seem uniquely realistic.[10] There are, of course, advantages to a definition that focuses upon symbols that provide motivation for people. But Tracy concludes that not just any moods and motivations are religious but only those that imply "a limit-experience, a limit-language, or a limit-dimension."[11] This is because we face limits in our life, including the final limit of the meaning of our existence. Religious language speaks about these limits in terms of a concept of "God" who is unlimited. Because of our limits, Tracy concludes that religion involves "some kind of participation in the whole [of existence], however construed."[12] Religion is the experience of creation beyond our personal limitations.

In Tracy's view, the study of religion requires a hermeneutic, or interpretive, approach to religious experiences. Because religious consciousness cannot exist without symbols, expressing that consciousness requires that the symbols be interpreted. The "unknown and ineffable" must be interpreted to be understood. Religion in this approach is not just an individual feeling but an experience of the "whole" or the "divine" expressed in the shared symbols of a community.

David Tracy develops this idea of God-experience further when he speaks of participation in the whole of life because this participation reveals our finitude and our limits as we recognize that we are not the whole. Through this experience, we then encounter the "divine," the "sacred," the "ultimate," the "whole." Paul Tillich, another academic theologian, similarly defined "God" as the "Ground of Being." Tillich says: "The name of this infinite and inexhaustible depth and ground of all being is *God* . . . the source of your being, of your ultimate concern. . . . The name of this infinite and inexhaustible ground of history is God."[13] Thus, for Tillich, we sense that beyond our limited selves we are upheld by a life force that allows us "to be." This leads us back to Schleiermacher's "feeling of absolute dependence" because we must depend upon a life force that is beyond our limited physical self and our psychological ego.

Civil Religion

Robert Bellah in *The Broken Covenant* speaks of religion quite differently. He argues that all societies possess a set of "religious" beliefs that provide the moral justification for their institutions. As he puts it,

> It is one of the oldest of sociological generalizations that any coherent
> and viable society rests on a common set of moral understandings about
> good and bad, right and wrong, in the realm of individual and social
> action. It is almost as widely held that these common moral
> understandings must also in turn rest upon a common set of religious
> understandings that provide a picture of the universe in terms of which
> the moral understandings make sense. Such moral and religious
> understandings produce both a basic cultural legitimation for a society
> which is viewed as at least approximately in accord with them and a
> standard of judgement for the criticism of a society that is seen as
> deviating too far from them.[14]

Bellah goes on to argue that America has developed a particular "civil
religion" that includes minimal agreement upon four premises: (1) the
existence of God, (2) life after death, (3) reward of virtue and punishment of
vice, and (4) exclusion of religious intolerance. This same "civil religion" in
America includes such rhetorical themes drawn from Judaism and Christianity
as Exodus, Chosen People, Promised Land, New Jerusalem, Sacrificial
Death, and Rebirth. Bellah thus follows very closely Jean-Jacques Rousseau's
list of essentials in a "civil religion": "The existence of a powerful, intelligent,
benevolent, foreseeing and provident Divinity, the life to come, the happiness
of the righteous, the punishment of the wicked, the sanctity of the social
contract and the positive law."[15]

Many authors have written about the important role of religion in society.
In addition to Clifford Geertz, Jean-Jacques Rousseau, and Robert Bellah we
might include Georg Wilhelm Friedrich Hegel, Emile Durkheim, and Peter
Berger. Hegel maintained that "religion is the place where a people defines
itself. . . . From this point of view religion is the closest of relationships with
the state."[16] Durkheim argued that not only was religion social but that
people must celebrate their unity and cement their society by religious rituals
and commemorations.[17] Peter Berger completes these sociological views by
pointing out the primary social function of religion: "Religion legitimates
social institutions by bestowing upon them an ultimately valid ontological
status, that is, by *locating* them within a sacred and cosmic frame of
reference."[18] Thus, an understanding of religion as civil religion would
define it as a set of moral understandings or basic premises that allow a
society to define itself and celebrate its unity through rituals and rhetoric
providing a sacred justification for societal institutions.

Civil religion undergirds our societal institutions and our politics. In
America, our civil religion evolved from Puritan images of God's new
"chosen people" founding a "city on a hill" to serve as a beacon and example

to all nations. This self-righteous understanding led to manifest destiny and to "just wars" throughout two centuries in which we sought "to make the world safe for democracy." Some figures such as President Lincoln offered a more profound civil religion. In his Gettysburg Address, Lincoln sought to refound our republic on Jefferson's "proposition" that all people are created equal. In his second inaugural address he sounded an even more biblical judgment:

> Yet, if God wills that [the Civil War] continue, until all the wealth piled by the bondman's two hundred and fifty years of unrequited toil shall be sunk, and until every drop of blood drawn with the lash, shall be paid by another drawn with the sword, as was said three thousand years ago, so still it must be said "the judgments of the Lord, are true and righteous altogether."
>
> With malice toward none; with charity for all; with firmness in the right, as God gives us to see the right, let us strive on to finish the work we are in; to bind up the nation's wounds; to care for him who shall have borne the battle, and for his widow, and his orphan—to do all which may achieve and cherish a just, and a lasting peace, among ourselves, and with all nations.[19]

But civil religion has not always included this broad vision. Consider the much more limited rhetoric of President Nixon discussing the Vietnam War in 1969.

> Our greatness as a nation has been our capacity to do what had to be done when we knew our course was right. . . .
>
> I know it may not be fashionable to speak of patriotism or national destiny these days. But I feel it is appropriate to do so on this occasion. . . . The wheel of destiny has turned so that any hope the world has for the survival of peace and freedom will be determined by whether the American people have the moral stamina and the courage to meet the challenge of free world leadership.
>
> Let historians not record that when America was the most powerful nation in the world we passed on the other side of the road and allowed the last hopes for peace and freedom of millions of people to be suffocated by the forces of totalitarianism. . . .
>
> Let us be united for peace. Let us also be united against defeat. Because let us understand: North Vietnam cannot defeat or humiliate the United States. Only Americans can do that.[20]

President Nixon's rhetoric, echoed by President Reagan during the United States invasion of Grenada, attack on Libya, and covert war in Nicaragua, has been based upon a shallow form of civil religion. But both shallow and profound civil religions, like all religions, still make assumptions about the existence of God, God's purposes, and our relationship to our God. These assumptions and moral understandings provide a foundation for our national institutions and determine many critical political decisions.

In the United States today, we face a crisis in our civil religion. As Americans, we have come to doubt that we are necessarily God's "Chosen People" with a preordained national destiny. But the crisis in our civil religion is only a part of an even larger crisis in our civilization. Not only is civil religion being undermined but all forms of religion are also being eroded. Secularization since the time of the Enlightenment has created a profound religious crisis of doubt sometimes known as the "Death of God." Michael Harrington has said that the

> Greek-Judeo-Christian notion of God was an ideological basis of Western civilization from at least the time of Constantine to the twentieth century. As such, it helped express individual and collective identities. This more than millennium of theological-political interrelationship is not an accident, or an experience which can be easily abandoned as one searches for new gods, or new definitions of the old God. For that old God was a political figure of great importance and people trusted him, usually because he counseled patience and obedience, occasionally because he was a revolutionary. . . .
>
> God defined by the most serious Protestant and Catholic theologians of the twentieth century is obviously incapable of playing the political and social role of the God whom they rightly declare obsolete. He is too problematic, subjective, existential for that. . . .
>
> This has meant . . . the loss of
> - that philosophy for nonphilosophers that made an intolerable life tolerable for the great mass of the people and thus contributed both to civil peace and to the passive acceptance of injustice;
> - God, the conservative, who legitimized established institutions, and that much rarer persona, God the radical, who legitimized the overthrow of those institutions;
> - the transcendent symbols and sacraments of human community;
> - a spiritual dimension for the pursuit of daily bread;
> - a major source of personal and social identity.[21]

The "Death of God" or the rendering of God as "problematic, subjective, existential" has made our very lives seem meaningless. In its worst forms, this loss of traditional religions has spawned Nazism, Stalinism, and the cheapening of human life to the point that "winning" a nuclear war could be discussed by policymakers in both the United States and the Soviet Union. Our social and political crises in the United States are made worse by the underlying religious crisis in all of Western civilization.

God is Compassion

Various modern definitions of religion as based in feelings and experiences, as participation in existence, as the ground of our being, and as a common set of moral understandings point to different "truths" about religion. But these understandings cannot help us in the crisis-filled times in which we live. Religion may well be an encounter with the "divine," may engender a "feeling of absolute dependence," may be "some kind of participation in the whole," may provide the values upon which other institutions depend, and may need to be interpreted through symbols. But the central religious questions for us must be, What is our actual relationship with "God," what is it we learn from our relationship, and what does this relationship require us to do?

Here a radical affirmation is required. Many religions, and especially Judaism and Christianity, declare that God is a compassionate God who calls upon us also to be compassionate. This is not to say merely that one aspect of God is compassion but that the very essence of God is compassion. Meister Eckhart, the fourteenth-century Dominican mystic, proclaimed:

> You may call God love
> You may call God goodness
> But the best name for God is compassion.[22]

Because of this, we who would be religious are required to be compassionate as well.

Before we can evaluate whether God is compassion, we must better understand the term. First, definitions. In Latin and English the word means to feel "sorrow for the sufferings or trouble of another" or "suffering together with another."[23] In various religions, the term "compassion" has a stronger meaning. In the Christian scriptures Jesus' compassion is expressed by the greek word *splagchnizomai* which means literally a wrenching of one's guts. Similarly, compassion in the Hebrew scriptures is expressed as *rachum,* meaning God's special compassion or mercy. It comes from the Hebrew root, *rachem,* or womb, and it might be translated "womb mercy"—the feeling of a mother for a child in her womb. Whether it means a wrenching of the guts, a mother's feeling for a child in her womb, or the intimate sharing of passions and sorrows, compassion in religion is known to be a powerful emotion leading to action as well as to personal and societal transformation.

If compassion is to be religiously central, we must be clear that it cannot be understood to be mere sentimentality, charity, or emotion. The Roman

Catholic theologian Matthew Fox has said of compassion that it is not sentimentality but making justice and doing works of mercy.[24] On a caravan taking illegal Guatemalan refugees from Chicago to sanctuary in Vermont, Filipe, a Guatemalan catechist, suggested the word "solidarity" is a better term to express true compassion. He said that "compassion [understood as charity] is giving someone who is hungry a crust of bread. Solidarity is going on the journey with them to get the bread and sharing their experiences along the way."

Given the frequent confusion, maybe the way to begin to understand compassion is to consider what it is not. Matthew Fox has argued that compassion is not pity but celebration, not private, egocentric, or narcissistic but public; not altruism but self-love and other-love at once.[25] Mere sentimentality causes us to wallow in our own emotions and self-pity, but compassion leads us to understanding, empathy, and *action*. Compassion bears the fruits of justice-making and deeds of mercy.

The problem in defining compassion is that it is, indeed, many things, and the term has many meanings to people of different traditions. Compassion is an emotion—the feeling of passions (whether of sorrow or joy) of another human being. It is often an immediate response to unquestionable pain. But when we say that God is compassion, we are saying that compassion is a state of being, a way of being in the world. This form of compassion inevitably leads to justice and social transformation. As Matthew Fox has written: "Compassion is about justice-making as much as it is about celebration for the very same reason, that 'What happens to another, whether it be a joy *or* a sorrow, happens to me.' Another's pain is my pain; my pain is another's pain. To relieve another's pain is to relieve one's own, and to relieve the pain of God, who shares in all the pain in the universe."[26]

But compassion is not known merely to the religions of the West. *Karuna* or compassion is also central to Buddhism. In Buddhism, ethical conduct is explicitly based upon *karuna* and includes at least three aspects of the Noble Eightfold Path: Right Speech, Right Action, and Right Livelihood.

> Right Speech means abstention from (1) telling lies, (2) from backbiting and slander . . . (3) from harsh, rude, impolite, malicious, and abusive language, and (4) from idle, useless, and foolish babble and gossip. . . .
>
> Right Action . . . admonishes us that we should abstain from destroying life, from stealing, from dishonest dealings, from illegitimate sexual intercourse, and that we should also help others to lead a peaceful and honourable life in the right way.
>
> Right Livelihood means that one should abstain from making one's living through a profession that brings harm to others such as trading in arms and lethal weapons, intoxicating drinks, poisons, killing animals,

cheating, etc., and should live by a profession which is honourable, blameless, and innocent of harm to others.

Even Buddhist meditation, which might seem the most unworldly, is to be focused upon compassion and particularly upon the four Sublime States.

1. extending unlimited, universal love and goodwill to all living beings without any kind of discrimination, "just as a mother loves her only child";
2. compassion for all the living beings who are suffering, in trouble and affliction;
3. sympathetic joy in other's success, welfare, and happiness; and
4. equanimity in all vicissitudes of life.[27]

There is a long and honorable tradition in Buddhism, from Siddhartha Guatama, that after enlightenment one should return to civilization, to the marketplace to save all sentient beings.[28] Even in this most contemplative of religious traditions, enlightenment brings compassion which demands action for the sake of others.

Like Judaism, Christianity, and Buddhism, Islam believes God is compassionate and Islam requires believers to act so as to establish justice in the world. As Alfred Guillaume has written, "The Quran shows us what [Muhammed's] conception of God was."

> The formula "compassionate and merciful" is familiar to almost everyone, and though the sufferings of the damned are painted in sombre colours, divine mercy and forgiveness are strongly emphasized. God's power is infinite, as is [God's] knowledge. Though transcendent and above all similitude, [God] is nearer to [us] than the vein of our [neck]. Again, though not bound by [our] ideas of justice and equity, God hates injustice and oppression, and requires kindness to orphans and widows and charity to the poor.[29]

Often we in the West believe that Islam only advocates holy warfare and is not centered upon compassion. The Islamic concept of *Jihad,* which is normally translated as a holy war against unbelievers implies, first of all, a struggle against the bad part of oneself. It thus means to struggle against evil, including the effort to purify and cleanse oneself and to make our own life compatible with our faith. The commandment to struggle against evil does not automatically require violence. Moreover, the need to struggle against injustice includes the need to take care of the poor. Thus, a Muslim is required to pay a *Zakat* (a tithe or tax on the wealthy) whose funds are used to help the poor, orphans, and widows.

It is important to remember that every chapter of the Quran but one begins, "In the name of Allah, the Compassionate, the Merciful," and that prayers in the Mosque always include:

> Praise belongs to God, Lord of the Worlds,
> The Compassionate, the Merciful,
> King of the Day of Judgement,
> 'Tis Thee we worship and Thee we ask for help.[30]

The Arabic word *Rahem* used to refer to the compassionate aspects of God is related to the Hebrew word *Rachem,* which tells of God's mercy in Hebrew scriptures.

Finally, one particular branch of Islam needs to be mentioned, the Sufi tradition, which is the Islamic version of mysticism. The Sufis follow a mystical path to attain an ecstatic union with God. One of the leaders of the many Sufi orders, Hallaj, was executed in A.D. 922 for claiming, as Jesus had, union with the Divine. The mystical path of the Sufis involves "abandoning the delights of the flesh and getting rid of all evil thoughts and desires so that the mind could be cleared of everything but the thought of God."[31] This is the wisdom taught by Sufis:

> Love is a quality of the Creator.
> Lover, and love, and beauty—three, yet One
> Creator and sustainer, only God . . .
> In perfect loveliness [God] was revealed,
> Giving to spiritual [individuals] the power
> Of love. [God's] manifesting attributes
> Found housing in the lover; power from Power,
> Knowledge from Knowledge, hearing from Hearing,
> Sight from Sight, speech from Speech divine informed:
> Will grew from Will, and life from Life was born,
> Beauty from Beauty glowed, continuance
> Of love in [God's] continuance increased,
> In [our] affection God's affection shone,
> And of [God's] love revealing, [our] love sprang.[32]

Buddhists and Sufis provide us an additional clue as to the enigmatic nature of compassion that makes definition so difficult. Religiously speaking, compassion is a *way,* a *path,* not a completed thing. It is dynamic, not static. In interpreting the works of Meister Eckhart, Matthew Fox has concluded that "creation-centered spirituality" that leads to compassion is a fourfold path. The first path is the positive path of creation, the second is the negative path of letting go and letting be in which we empty our life in order to be filled, the third is the path of personal breakthrough and birthing, and the fourth is the path of transformation and social justice. In all these paths we learn *the way of compassion.*

The first path to compassion is the positive path in which we identify with creation and with life itself. Meister Eckhart in one of his sermons says:

> This I know.
> That the only way to live
> is like the rose
> which lives
> without a why.
> You may ask life itself over a period of a thousand years the
> following question: "Why are you alive?" And still the only
> response you would receive would be: "I live so that I may
> live."
> Why does this happen?
>   Because life rises from its own foundation
> and rises out of itself.
> Therefore,
> life lives without a reason—
> life lives for itself.[33]

Eckhart's fellow mystic Hildegard of Bingen also tells of a compassionate God of creation.

> Thru animate eyes
> I divide the seasons
> of time.
>
> I am aware of what they are.
> I am aware of their potential.
>
> With my mouth
> I kiss my own chosen creation.
>
> I uniquely,
> lovingly,
> embrace every image
> I have made
> out of the earth's clay.
>
> With a fiery spirit
> I transform it

into a body
to serve
all the world.[34]

On this positive path the sense of life boils over, wells up, and floods itself with itself. It is a joyous path but not the only one. There is also a negative path which profoundly lets us know ourselves, know others, and know compassion. Meister Eckhart describes the negative path this way:

We become a pure nothing by an unknowing
knowledge which is
        emptiness
        and solitude
        and darkness
        and remaining still.[35]

Another mystic, Mechtild of Magdeburg, declares that if "you wish to have love, then you must leave love." And she advises further that to follow this path you must:

Love the nothing,
flee the self
Stand alone.
Seek help from no one.
Let your being be quiet,
Be free from the bondage of all things.
Free those who are bound.
Give exhortation to the free.
Care for the sick
but dwell alone.
When you drink the waters of sorrow
you shall kindle the fire of love
with the match of perseverance—
    This is the way
        to dwell in the desert.[36]

What we learn on the negative path is to let go of societal and personality structures that block our way to God. The supreme task of this path, according to Meister Eckhart, is to let go:

Think of the soul as a vortex or whirlpool
  and you will understand how we are to
Sink eternally from negation to negation

into the one.
And how we are to
Sink eternally from letting go to letting go
  into God.

On this path "God is not found in the soul by adding anything but by a process of subtraction." We find God by ridding ourselves of what is not God. By experiencing pain we are able empathetically to experience the pain of others. Eckhart describes the purpose of emptying like this:

If a cask is to contain wine,
  you must first pour out the water.
The cask must be bare and empty.

  Therefore,
if you wish to receive divine joy and God
first pour out your clinging to things.

Everything that is to receive
must and ought to be empty.[37]

The dialectical tension established between the positive, creation-centered path, which overflows with life, and the negative, interior path, by which we empty ourselves, often leads to the third path of personal awakening and breakthrough. It is a path of birthing and creativity. Mechtild describes the awakening this way:

As soon as the soul
  begins to grow
  the dust of sin
    falls away
  and the soul becomes
    a god with God.
Then,
  what God wills
    the soul wills.[38]

And Meister Eckhart says of this birthing:

Let me express myself in even a clearer way.
The fruitful person
gives birth
out of the very same foundation

from which the Creator begets the eternal Word
or Creative Energy
and it is from this core
that one becomes fruitfully pregnant.
And in this power of birthing
God is as fully verdant
and as wholly flourishing in you
and in all honor
as he/she is in him/herself.
The divine rapture
is unimaginably great.
It is ineffable.[39]

This path of awakening, birthing, and personal breakthrough cannot stay exclusively private if it is to lead to compassion. From the high mystical experience the wise Buddha returned to teach humanity. Therefore, the fourth path to compassion is the path of social transformation and social justice. The first step on this path is described by Hildegard of Bingen.

Humankind demonstrates two aspects:
  the singing of praise to God,
  and doing of good works.

God is made known through praise,
and in good works
  the wonders of God can be seen.

In the praise of God
a person is like an angel.
But in the doing of good works
that is the hallmark of humanity.

This completeness
makes humankind the fullest creation
  of God.

It is in praise and service
that the surprise of God is consummated.[40]

Thus, to complete the cycle of compassion we must enter the fourth path. Meister Eckhart says that if we were in a rapture even as Saint Paul experienced on the road to Damascus "and learned that [our] neighbor were in need of a cup of soup, it would be best to withdraw from the rapture and give the person the soup she needs." The end result of our compassionate action, our work at creating social justice, is this:

> And those who follow compassion
> find life for themselves,
> justice for their neighbor,
> and glory for God.[41]

How can a religion based upon compassion be adequate to the crises we face in our time? First, a people of compassion love life dearly. Because they cherish life, they make every effort to save the life of all creatures on the planet. Second, they experience the pain of starvation, war, scarcity, unemployment, and repressive regimes as their own pain so they will act to relieve suffering. Third, a people of compassion are creative and able to conceive of new forms, structures, and solutions to crises. And fourth, a people of compassion so love justice, so need to do justice and mercy, that they will work unceasingly to transform the society and the world. The claim of the mystics is that in this process they will be aided by their connection to God—they will breathe God's breath, know God's thoughts, and do God's deeds upon earth. This will give them the strength, energy, and courage needed to face these crises.

People of compassion see vividly the connection between their religion and the crises of the world. Filipe Excot, the Guatemalan refugee who spoke on the caravan to sanctuary, compared the situation in Guatemala to Jesus' passion. He said that Christ did not just die two thousand years ago. No, today, Christs are still crucified in Central America. Instead of the stripes from a whip that Jesus received, the Christs of Central America have their fingernails torn out. Instead of a crown of thorns, the Christs of Central America have their feet cut open and salt and lemon applied to their wounds. Instead of a wooden cross, the Christs of Central America face the flying crucifixes of U.S. helicopters dropping napalm bombs on their villages. Thus, for the people of compassion, the individual feelings and experience of the divine and the older religious symbols are transformed to vivid calls to action.

Ethics

Ethics extends the personal dimension of religion. Both religious and philosophical ethics try to answer the pressing human question, "What shall I do?" Those concerned with "social ethics" enlarge this to the corporate issue of "What shall we do?" These simple, straightforward questions about how people should act are not easy to answer.

Philosophical Ethics

Philosophically speaking, there are two kinds of answers and, thus, two basic types of ethical systems although there are many versions of each type.

Deontological ethical theories.

These theories maintain that either acts themselves or our moral obligations make an action, or a rule of action, obligatory. Deontological ethical systems are usually identified by a set of rules such as the Ten Commandments or the Deuteronomistic Laws of the Hebrew scripture for guiding ethical and religious conduct.

Teleological ethical theories.

These theories, on the other hand, suggest that nonmoral ends such as the "good" or pleasure to be achieved is the standard of what is morally right.[42] Teleological ethical systems are usually identified with particular goals and lead to purposive action to achieve those goals rather than a specific set of rules to be followed. Thus, Rabbi Hillel and Jesus of Nazareth taught that the essence of all the Jewish law is to love God and to love your neighbor. In an effort to maximize these values, therefore, Jesus is recorded as breaking the law forbidding work on the Sabbath, so as to heal individuals, and as violating social norms by running money changers out of the temple in Jerusalem.

Both deontological and teleological ethical systems turn out to be inadequate. The attempt to reduce all ethical systems to these two types makes philosophical ethics today appear to be interested only in labeling actions in a manner reminiscent of the old-style biology in which the effort to classify plants and animals into their proper genus and species was the chief preoccupation. The classification of actions as either deontological or teleological doesn't really answer the question "What am I/we to do?" The process of classification may help clarify the basis upon which decisions might be made or may suggest an alternative basis for future decisions, but these guidelines seem to answer easily only the simplest issues like whether or not I should steal or cheat. More complex individual ethical problems are not so easily resolved, and what we should do about planetary crises can not be effectively posed within these formal ethical systems.

Choosing between rival systems of philosophical ethics is even more difficult. As Alasdair MacIntyre wrote in *After Virtue: A Study in Moral Theory,* "There seems to be no rational way of securing moral agreement in our culture." In moral debates today, there is a "conceptual incommensurability of rival arguments . . . Every one of the arguments is logically valid or can be easily expanded so as to be made so; the conclusions do indeed follow from the premises. But the rival premises are such that we possess no rational way of weighing the claims of one as against another."[43]

According to MacIntyre, classical ethics such as Aristotelianism involved a three-fold structure "of human nature-as-it-happens-to-be, human nature-as-it-could-be-if-it-realized-its-*telos* [or purpose] and the precepts of rational ethics."[44] The rejections by the enlightenment of both theology and *telos* made this ethical framework untenable and reason could no longer evaluate competing ethical principles. Without an agreement upon the purpose of human beings no rational decision between competing deontological rules or teleological goals is possible. Ethics becomes a matter of emotivism in which "This is Good" becomes the equivalent of "Hurrah for this" or "I approve of this; do so as well."[45] The end result has been a total breakdown of philosophical ethics in our time.

Theocentric Ethics

There are, of course, many ethicists who move beyond mere classification to attempt to provide substantive ethical guides to conduct and who continue to assert a purpose or goal for us to seek to achieve. Many Christian ethicists, for instance, begin with Jesus' premise that "all humans are brothers and sisters because they are created by one God." Such a premise then means that rules like the Ten Commandments are automatically in effect. The same general premise that all beings are of value leads to similar rules in other religions such as the Buddhist requirements of ethical conduct in Right Speech, Right Action, and Right Livelihood. This leads to the lay Buddhist's minimum moral obligation not to destroy life, not to steal, not to commit adultery, not to tell lies, and not to take intoxicating drinks."[46] But these premises can lead beyond mere rules. Saint Augustine paraphrased Christian ethics as "Love God and do as you please." For if we love God, then we will want what God wills, and we need not simply follow rules. Instead, we will act as our love of God and our love of our fellow humans dictates.

A standard way of expressing ethical injunctions is "to do good and avoid evil." This assumes, however, that one knows what is good and what is bad either from a "moral faculty," conscience, societal norms, or religious teachings. But the German Christian martyr Dietrich Bonhoeffer in his unfinished manuscript on ethics has questioned this ethical standard.

> If the ethical problem presents itself essentially in the form of enquiries about one's own being good and doing good, that means that it has already been decided that it is the self and the world which are the ultimate reality. The aim of all ethical reflection is, then, that I myself shall be good and that the world shall become good through my action. But the problem of ethics at once assumes a new aspect if it becomes apparent that these realities, myself and the world, themselves lie

embedded in a quite different ultimate reconciler, namely the reality of God, the Creator, Reconciler, and Redeemer. What is of ultimate importance is now no longer that I should become good, or that the condition of the world should be made better by my action, but that the reality of God should show itself everywhere to be the ultimate reality.[47]

With this perspective on ethics it is not enough to memorize a set of religious rules like "thou shalt not kill." For instance, Bonhoeffer decided to join an underground effort whose purpose was to assassinate Hitler. According to Bonhoeffer, we must analyze our concrete situation and, moved by our compassion and by our understanding of God's will, decide what to do. Bonhoeffer's own formulation was "what can and should be said is not what is good once and for all, but, 'how Christ is formed in us today and here.' "[48]

Because Bonhoeffer expects to encounter Christ in reality—in the very concrete reality of our work and our relations with others—this world, and not some spiritualized heaven, is key. He opposed religious "other-worldliness" with "this-worldliness" even in the midst of painful circumstances such as his imprisonment in Nazi Germany. He wrote from his prison cell just before his execution in 1944:

> I discovered later, and I am still discovering right up to this moment, that it is only by living completely in this world that one learns to have faith. . . . By this-worldliness I mean living unreservedly in life's duties, problems, successes and failures, experiences and perplexities. In so doing we throw ourselves completely into the arms of God, taking seriously, not our own sufferings but those of God in the world—watching with Christ in Gethsemane. That, I think, is faith, that is metanoia [transformation]; and that is how one becomes a [human being] and a Christian.[49]

In looking for Christ and God in the concrete reality of everyday life, we become fully religious—not by fleeing this world in ascetic contemplation but by being fully part of it.

Bonhoeffer's approach to ethics is echoed in the "Theocentric Ethics" of James Gustafson. After rejecting traditional deontological and teleological theories of ethics as focusing too narrowly upon the purely human point of reference, Gustafson suggests that "God, rather than [the human], ought to be the measure of all things." This principle leads, for instance, to the biblical ethics recorded in the Scriptures: "Morality was to be governed by the law of the Deity, not by the customs of [society]." The switch from an anthropocentric to a more theocentric focus has major consequences. Not only must one move away from a personalized God but traditional pious religious expectations of personal salvation are also overturned. For if the human is not the center of the universe and the "chief end of creation," then the "chief end of God may not be the salvation of [the individual]."[50]

Theocentric ethics develops a different moral imperative from philosophical ethics. "The practical moral question in a theocentric construal of the world is . . . 'What is God enabling and requiring us to be and to do?' The most general answer is that we are to relate ourselves and all things in a manner appropriate to their relations to God." Theocentric ethics, rather than following a set of rules or striving after abstract goals, asks "What is God enabling and requiring us to be and to do?"[51]

E. Clinton Gardner in *Biblical Faith and Social Ethics* attempted to combine theocentric and philosophical ethics by acknowledging that "while Christian ethics recognizes a legitimate place for aspiration after the good [teleological ethics] and for law as a guide to the discovery of God's will [deontological ethics], its method is best understood as that of [the human's] response to the activity of God."[52] The practical problem remains of how to know God's will which Gardner asserts "can be most adequately understood in terms of [God's] creative, ordering and redeeming purposes."[53] Being responsive to God and to God's love is not simply a sentiment but requires decisions and action. As Gardner concludes,

> Praise and gratitude to the Creator are not . . . simply feelings; rather, they are to be understood in terms of the personal encounter of [an individual] with God in specific moments of decision in which by one's deeds one either shows praise and gratitude or one dishonors God and unthankfully rejects [God's] creative intent.[54]

Theocentric ethics uses the goal of love and the laws set forth in the Bible and in philosophical ethics as guides to God's will but, ultimately, concrete actions must be taken in which we must respond directly to the love of God as best our own compassion lets us discern it.

Ethics of Caring

We do not have to accept theocentric ethics to transcend traditional deontological and teleological theories. A philosophical alternative is feminist ethics. Carol Gilligan, in her influential book, *In a Different Voice: Psychological Theory and Women's Development,* opposes male models of psychological development and ideal ethical decision making. Although her model is primarily associated with women's development, it is shared by some men as well. Feminist ethics is a morality based upon responsibility and relationships rather than formal rights and abstract moral reasoning. As Gilligan puts it,

> In this conception, the moral problem arises from conflicting responsibilities rather than from competing rights and requires for its resolution a mode of thinking that is contextual and narrative rather than formal and abstract. This conception of morality as concerned with the activity of care centers moral development around the understanding of responsibility and relationships, just as the conception of morality as fairness ties moral development to the understanding of rights and rules.[55]

The "ethics of care" which Gilligan formulates is further developed by Nell Noddings in *Caring: A Feminine Approach to Ethics and Moral Education.* She argues there that

> Ethics, the philosophical study of morality, has concentrated for the most part on moral reasoning. . . . Ethical argumentation has frequently proceeded as if it were governed by the logical necessity characteristic of geometry. It has concentrated on the establishment of principles and that which can be logically derived from them. One might say that ethics has been discussed largely in the language of the father: in principles and propositions, in terms such as justification, fairness, justice. The mother's voice has been silent.

Nodding rejects the ethics of principles and rules "as ambiguous and unstable." She says that "wherever there is a principle, there is implied its exception and, too often, principles function to separate us from each other. We may become dangerously self-righteous when we perceive ourselves as holding a precious principle not held by the other." Instead of being located in rules, the ethics of caring has as its goal to be in a relationship of caring.

> The relation of natural caring will be identified as the human condition that we, consciously or unconsciously, perceive as "good." It is that condition toward which we long and strive, and it is our longing for caring—to be in that special relationship—that provides the motivation for us to be *moral* in order to remain in the caring relation and to enhance the ideal of ourselves as one-caring.[56]

But what is this "caring"? It is "a state of mental suffering or of engrossment: to care is to be in a burdened state, one of anxiety, or fear, or solicitude about something or someone." Caring, like compassion, involves "feeling with." It is more than "empathy," which is defined as "the power of projecting one's personality into, and so fully understanding, the object of contemplation." More than just "understanding," caring and compassion involve receiving "the other into myself, I see and feel with the other." When we receive and share the viewpoint and feelings of another person we are moved to respond. "We must act to eliminate the intolerable, to reduce the pain, to fill the need, to actualize the dream." And our response will not be governed wholly by external rules or norms—nor "upon a prior determination of what is fair or equitable—but upon a constellation of conditions that is viewed through both the eyes of the one-caring and the eyes of the cared for."[57]

In feminist ethics our first ethical obligation is to meet the other person as one-caring. "We do not begin by formulating or solving a problem but by sharing a feeling."[58] We first respond to another person's pain, suffering, joy, or concern. Then we act to relieve their pain and to intensify their joy if we can.

Feminist ethics conceives "morality less in terms of rights and more in terms of responsibilities . . . [This form of] moral reasoning is more context-sensitive . . . more tuned to relationships . . . "[59] It focuses less upon abstract justice and more on "the good life." But in doing so it tends "to split caring from justice, failing to see that while justice requires abstraction, it is intended as the abstract form that caring takes when respect is maintained and responsibility assumed for people whom one does not know personally and may never come to know."[60] Feminist ethics, at least when broadened to its largest scope, is similar to theocentric ethics in rejecting rules and abstract goals. It focuses instead upon human relationships in the real world.

Compassionate Action

Expanding upon the premises of theocentric and feminist ethics, I maintain that the best ethical action is ultimately compassionate action. As Matthew Fox has said, "compassion means action, action that grows out of the truth of awareness of interconnections and interdependence. . . . Our work at undoing injustice and creating movements and alternative organizations of justice . . . is all compassionate action.[61] Compassionate action is an improvement upon mere deontological or teleological ethical systems because it allows us to move beyond rigid rules or laws, on the one hand, and abstractly formulated goals, on the other, while still honoring the essential impulse that led to the formulation of such rules and goals in the first place. Compassion catches up the impulse behind the Buddhist premise that all life is valuable; the Christian premise that all humans are brothers and sisters created by the same God; and the Augustinian formulation, "Love God and do as you please." Compassion moves beyond mere ethical premises, as it moves beyond mere rules, by being a process, a *path,* and a *way.* It is not because of our adoption of compassionate principles or assumptions but through our direct experience of compassion that we experience oneness with all life. Through compassion we bring ourselves into harmony with God's purposes. As feminist ethics affirms, when we feel the pain of other creatures directly, we are moved to act to eliminate their/our suffering.

Something like this is, of course, what Bonhoeffer meant when he said we must act so as to reveal the ultimate reality of God and show in our concrete situation "how Christ is formed in us." Compassion for our neighbor and our world allows us to be in touch with the "divine" as it manifests itself and as we manifest it in our world. It is a way of being one with God and, therefore, being able to know "What is God enabling and requiring us to do?"

Compassion is not mere feeling or sentiment; it is not even seeing God everywhere in the world; rather, the experience of others' suffering leads inevitably to compassionate action. It is compassionate action that is ethical, not feeling or discernment. This is the lesson of Bonhoeffer's life as well as his unfinished writing. Bonhoeffer's actions were not merely private charity or "good deeds" of pietism; they inevitably became public and political. This suggests that compassionate action, most certainly in our time, must include public political action as well as the ethical actions we take in private affairs and personal relationships. It is this public ethical stance that moves compassionate action beyond the feminist ethics of caring, although both share many of the same understandings about the nature of ethics.

Thus it is that compassion for the suffering of individuals leads to political action which has as its goal institutional transformation. Pain is eliminated by changing the conditions that cause pain. Thus, the best ethics is not to follow deontological rules or to adopt proper teleological goals. The best ethics, whether motivated by a religious concept of a compassionate God or by a passionate experience of caring, goes beyond personal good deeds. The best ethics requires political action leading to personal and societal transformation. Our actions may follow rules or may strive to achieve goals, but in deciding what to do we always seek to know what God wants done in the world, always act from caring and compassion, and always choose transformative actions. Compassionate action is the only ethics adequate for our times because it answers the question of what we are to do in the face of our world's crises. Our compassion causes us to act to alleviate as much of the current and future suffering as we can. Our heart and our head tell us how.

The broader realm of ethics as compassionate action can be illustrated by the premise proposed by Jose Miguez Bonino in *Toward a Christian Political Ethics:*

In carrying out needed structural changes we encounter an inevitable tension between the human cost of their realization and the human cost of their postponement. The basic ethical criterion is the maximizing of universal human possibilities and the minimizing of human costs.[62]

From such an ethical premise violent revolution necessary to overthrow the oligarchical and military elites in Central and South America can be justified on Christian principles, despite the fact that some people will be killed and others will suffer in the process. Political/ethical decisions on such basic questions demand more than merely having compassion as a sentiment or having sympathy for the poor and oppressed. Such decisions can not be based merely upon "caring" about the plight of the poor. Ultimately, compassion requires political decisions and political action.

Politics

Having explored a more adequate understanding of religion as compassion and ethics as compassionate action, we are ready to approach politics. My intent is to discover a religious, ethical politics more adequate to the crises of our time. Politics is often considered to be neutral at best (or irreligious and unethical at worst). "Realists" like Niccolo Machiavelli and Saul Alinsky argue that religion and morality are used only as rationalizations for pragmatic political actions.[63]

Realism

To divorce politics from religion is to render it either a "neutral" science without value commitments or merely Machiavellian advice on how to get ahead in practical political maneuvering. "Political behavioralism" or "positivist political science," which has dominated the field of political science since World War II, has attempted to provide a "neutral" science of politics. It has in the process focused on individual "behavior" and trivial questions. Because of this limited focus it has been inadequate to cope with the crises we face. As several political scientists declared at the American Political Science Association meeting of 1976:

> Modern political scientists can neither explain what is happening all around us nor tell us what to do to improve our society.
> Modern political science is irrelevant for public officials charged with government and for citizens who assume their rightful responsibilities in public life. What is relevant is often banned as "unscientific" and "unprofessional" by those who believe that the only "facts" worth having are generated by narrow hypotheses, attitude questionnaires, and quantitative techniques.[64]

If all questions of value and all answers to the question "What shall we do?" are ruled unscientific and outside the parameters of modern political science, then political science will necessarily be inadequate to guide us through the crises ahead. It inevitably will remain unconnected with the issues of religion and ethics.

Similarly, if political "realists" who scorn politics as a science also ignore religion and ethics, treat them as rationalizations for pragmatic action or as an "opiate of the people," then, naturally, they will be unable to propose actions that fulfill religious and ethical demands. Realists will continue to be limited to practical advice regarding particular political choices and narrow political maneuvers to gain or keep power. They will be unable to understand the broader sweep and purpose of politics.

Political Philosophy

One alternative both to behavioralism and realism is political philosophy. Philosophy seeks to discover fundamental principles whether it is applied to logic, ethics, aesthetics, or politics. According to Leo Strauss, philosophy seeks to replace opinions about beauty, truth, sense impressions, good behavior, and the best form of government with the truth about these matters.[65] According to Plato, such a philosophy treats its assumptions and principles as hypotheses, "things 'laid down' like a flight of steps" up which it progresses until it reaches that which is not hypothetical but certain.[66]

Jacques Maritain explains that "A philosopher is a [person] in search of wisdom. . . . Philosophy makes us grasp . . . what things are in the intrinsic reality of their being. . . . All notions worked out by philosophy are intelligible in terms of being, not of observation and measurement."[67] As John Plamenatz has written, philosophers "did not study the facts or did so only at random; they deduced their conclusions from axioms a priori and from definitions, or they relied on what they chose to consider the common sense of humankind. They were not scientific but speculative."[68]

Political philosophy identifies fundamental principles that define the appropriate goals for political action. Just as the study of religion identifies principles that define appropriate religious acts, and just as ethics identifies principles which define appropriate rules or goals for moral behavior, political philosophy is meant to guide our political acts.

There are, however, problems with relying solely on political philosophy as our guide to politics. Although philosophers agree that we should abide by principles, they do not agree what those principles should be. Among the many contenders for chief philosophical principles to guide our behavior are power, equality, justice, freedom, and democracy.

Moreover, even when philosophers seem to agree on the chief value to be maximized in society, they do not mean necessarily the same thing, and following their advice would lead to quite contradictory actions. Thus, Plato, John Locke, and Jean-Jacques Rousseau, as well as current philosophers John Rawls, Ronald Dworkin, and Robert Nozick, all assert that "justice" is the principle to be maximized. But they do not agree on what justice is. For instance, Rawls argues the modern liberal position that everyone should have equal rights and that any social or economic inequalities which still exist ought to be arranged so that they are reasonably expected to be nonhereditary and to everyone's advantage.[69] Nozick argues the modern conservative position that a person who acquires a holding is entitled to it as is any person to whom it is justly transferred, and no one else or any institution, such as a government, is entitled to take it from him or her.[70] Rawls argues for a nearly equal distribution of wealth and Nozick for nearly an absolute protection of private property. Both say that this is justice. The fault, as we have seen in similar instances in religion and ethics, lies in the abstract way in which these principles are formulated. Although they provide some guidance, they do not arise from actual circumstances. It seems clear that neither Plato's nor Rawl's nor Nozick's formulation of the justice principle can be directly applied to the approaching crises of our civilization. They are simply too abstract to tell us "What is to be done?"

Political Action

Given the narrowness of modern political science, the practical advice of political realists and the abstractness of political philosophy, another approach to the study of politics is needed. Politics should be approached in a way that is consonant with religion and ethics. Although religion and ethics are usually seen as antithetical to politics, it is important to ask how the three fields might be integrated. It may well be that the solution to the intellectual dilemmas of religion and ethics may provide the solution to the fundamental dilemma of politics in our time as well.

Religion, as the guardian of fundamental values, is always involved in the support of existing institutions. Some sort of religious values also support revolutionary attempts to replace existing institutions. The question is not whether religion and politics will be intermingled but which religion supports which politics. Religion and ethics are inevitably used to support competing claims of various political groups. Politics, which, broadly speaking, is the struggle to create, maintain, and destroy institutions, also includes struggles over substantive issues, basic values, and particular interests. So religion and ethics take up sides in "secular" political struggles. And, politics is equally involved in religious and ethical struggles. A religion or ethics which pretends to be devoid of politics is unconscious of its own role or is inhuman—fit for angels or devils but not for human beings who, as Aristotle said, are by their very nature "political animals."

Politics is the struggle for power, for values, and for institutions. The study of politics involves (1) political analysis, (2) political philosophy, and (3) political action. Thus, behavioralist political scientists were not wrong in focusing upon analysis, philosophers were not wrong in focusing upon political philosophy, and practical politicians were not wrong in focusing upon political action. It was only that their limited focus often led them to incomplete and, therefore, incorrect conclusions.

Political analysis describes actual political systems and the struggle for power that occurs within them. It should be able to answer such questions as "Who does have power?" Political philosophy inquires into what political outcomes are to be preferred and how political decisions should be made. In this it borrows from theology and ethics. Based on philosophical and ethical principles, it should be able to answer such questions as "Who should rule and what decisions should they make?" Finally, political action is composed of physical acts whose purpose is to affect political, institutional, or governmental outcomes. The study of political action leads to strategies of action and to actual deeds. Its question is "What can be done to gain or maintain power and to affect political decisions?"

Each aspect of the study of politics has its own methodology. The accepted behavioral methodology for political analysis uses hypotheses composed of concepts and statements of the relationship between concepts; in shorthand form, *If A, then B*. An example of such a hypothesis is "If citizens have a strong party identity, they will tend to vote for candidates of that political party in elections." Thus, elections can often be predicted merely by knowing the distribution of party identity in particular electoral districts. Deviating elections in which the party with the greatest popular support does not win can be explained by other measurable variables such as voter attitudes toward candidate personalities and toward particular issues.

In the same way that hypotheses serve political analysis, normative principles have been developed as the appropriate methodology for political philosophy. Normative principles specify goals and the characteristics of a society which maximize these goals. A shorthand form of such principles is: *The attainment of goal A requires society to be organized in manner B*. A statement of Platonic principles might be phrased: "If the *Good* is absolute and trained philosophers can know the *Good*, then society ought to be governed by philosophers so that the *Good* for the society can be achieved."

By themselves, neither simple hypotheses nor philosophical principles are adequate guides for a politics of compassion and transformation, although both have their uses. Instead, compassion must be a guide to political action—especially a guide to those acts necessary to meet looming crises. And such a politics must focus on political action rather than on analysis or philosophy alone.

The study of political action requires its own special methodology. Just as analysis uses hypotheses and philosophy develops normative principles, the methodology required for the study of political action utilizes *political action propositions.* Such propositions are composed of three different types of concepts and a statement of the relationship between these concepts. A shorthand way of stating such propositions is: *To achieve goal A under conditions B, C, and D requires actions E, F, and G.*

Political action propositions contain statements about goals, conditions, and actions. To develop these statements requires employing empirical political analysis, political philosophy, and political strategy. In order to define *goal A* we must formulate normative principles. To define *conditions B, C, and D* we must engage in hypothesis development and testing. To determine appropriate *actions E, F, and G* depends upon an accurate analysis of conditions, a decision as to the goals being sought, and, finally, a careful judgment of alternative possible actions based upon past experience.

The political action proposition is an important tool for the politics of compassion and transformation because making explicit the assumptions behind proposed actions will rule out many mistaken strategies that will not achieve our goals. Making our assumptions explicit may keep us from attempting actions that won't work in our situation, although they might be perfectly good strategies for other times and places. An example of such a proposition is the following proposition for political change:

To achieve the *goals* of more freedom and citizen participation

Under current *conditions* of a liberal-democratic government and post-industrial economy both of which are characterized by large bureaucracies dominated by a professional class,

Requires *actions* that create new political institutions for change (a) which are based on a correct but imaginative analysis of the situation; (b) are launched at the proper historical time; (c) attain early concrete victories; (d) possess able leaders, professional staff, and sufficient financing; (e) mobilize supporters with professional skills; (f) attract new participants; and (g) can sustain themselves over a relatively long period.[71]

This proposition suggests the types of strategies necessary to create new institutions to revitalize our civilization. It is a serious question whether conditions such as a liberal-democratic government still exist and whether essential new institutions for change can be created in time to cope with the crises we face. Nonetheless, making the philosophical goals, conditions, and proposed strategies explicit allows us to evaluate the potential of this liberal strategy for fundamental change.

The elaboration of political action propositions leads us to understand that there are three moments in the politics of compassion and transformation. First, there is the development of the goal. When our guts or wombs are wrenched by compassion for the pain of others, we choose to act to relieve this pain. With a deep feeling of compassion is born a determination that *I* will not let this evil continue. *I* will not let the poor go hungry; the homeless without shelter; the unemployed without a job, dignity, or meaning. *I* will fight to prevent nuclear annihilation of the planet, plunder of the planet's precious resources, and pollution of our air and water. When our passions become so powerful that we are forced to choose a political/religious/ethical goal, the first moment of the politics of compassion has occurred.

Second, a correct analysis of conditions must be made. This analysis may be intuitive or rational. But it must include identification of groups and institutions opposing the achievement of our goal. In this analysis we must consider human nature—the motivations and strengths of our opponents as well as those who support our cause. Until we are in tune with the situation, until, like the prophets of old, we really know "what time it is," any strategy will be flawed and will most likely fail.

Third, compassion demands action. Even if the political action proposition and our knowledge of the situation is incomplete, there comes a time to act. For we may learn from failures, revise strategies in defeat, and go on to win victories. As we act, we gain the experience to be better strategists in the future—able to predict what is likely to happen in response to any course of action we may choose. We act, reflect upon our action, and act again with more wisdom. But we begin by acting.

Thus, the three moments of the politics of compassion are (1) compassionate development of a goal, (2) compassionate understanding of the situation, and (3) compassionate action. Religion and ethics influence all three moments. It is easiest to understand how compassion shapes the development of a goal; however, compassion also allows us to understand situations from the position of those who suffer and spurs us to act to relieve their/our suffering.

Political action propositions are not simply formulated and then forgotten. They are improved and perfected in the midst of the actions themselves. We improve propositions by more accurately specifying the goals, conditions, and means to be used. Actions must be appropriate to changing circumstances. As we act, others react and conditions therefore change. Our actions must be consonant with our goals, and propositions must specify who should undertake these actions. As each step is undertaken, it will succeed or fail, and new information about conditions and alternatives for potential new actions will emerge. Thus, political action propositions constantly evolve as political strategists reevaluate the situation in which they find themselves.

The Politics of Compassion and Transformation

Having discussed the dilemmas in religion, ethics, and politics, and having asserted that they can be resolved by a religion, ethics, and politics of compassion and transformation, let me now turn to a more explicit discussion of politics in our society. Any civilization is built upon certain key social, economic, and political institutions and upon the values supporting these institutions. Religion, ethics, and politics provide both the values and some of the central institutions of the society. Individuals can affect their civilization only by affecting these values and institutions.

Ours is a civilization that claims to foster "individualism," and part of the mythology of our time is a "therapeutic" view that we can affect our civilization by getting ourselves psychologically "straightened out." In this view, personal transformation and growth is the key to societal transformation. Unfortunately, this is only a partial truth. Social change occurs ultimately by group action. Although individual religious, moral, and political leaders may have a profound impact, they do so only by persuading, organizing, and mobilizing others. Only by understanding corporate structures, group behavior, and collective action can we be effective. It may be that individuals who have achieved a higher level of consciousness are innately more capable of acting at the social, institutional, and societal levels, but self-awareness and psychological well-being do not guarantee societal success. Psychotics such as Hitler and Napoleon have been very powerful, and many psychologically well-integrated people have had no political impact.

We need concrete, practical political skills if we are to affect our civilization. We also need methods of effective analysis such as those provided by political action propositions. Finally, we must develop a corporate or communal understanding of our situation, a common vision of a better society, and a willingness to act on our understanding and vision.

Given a new religion, ethics, and politics of compassion and transformation, we can begin to make an explicit response to the crises we face. One way to do this is to formulate an explicit proposition of compassion and transformation: To achieve the goals of (1) peace; (2) food, clothing, and shelter for everyone; (3) a technology that allows us to live in harmony with the earth without unduly depleting our natural resources or polluting the environment; (4) good, meaningful work for all; and (5) democratic, responsive self-government; under conditions of an existing civilization dependent upon industrialization; the profit motive; human greed; the nation-state system; ever more autocratic, hierarchical governments; and a society characterized by overpopulation, war, resource depletion, pollution, inflation, and unemployment; the creation of new institutions based upon compassionate principles and values is required.

There is much to dispute in such a proposition. But assuming for the moment acceptance of the goals of peace and justice and the recognition that our world is characterized by overpopulation, industrialization, and an international system of nation-states leading to conflict and war, let us focus on the conclusion as to the required action.

Many people concede that we have problems internationally but believe that our current institutions are adequate to cope with them. They point with pride to the business firm now grown into the multinational corporation; to industrialization that has developed automation in manufacturing, mass media, and service industries; to a nation-state system that has created the greatest stockpile of weapons in the history of the world; and to churches and synagogues which bless these developments with a "modern theology" that has made its peace with science. In fact, it may be faith in science that now guides the modern world as scientists split the atom, undertake genetic engineering, and develop the computer as a mechanical superbrain to control forces of modernization.

The proposition of compassion and transformation denies that these institutions are adequate. Biblically, one might say that we have dared to be like God. Our civilization has stretched to its limits and has now gone too far. All civilizations reach the limits of their development. George Mendenhall, in *The Tenth Generation,* finds that in the ancient Near East that civilizations fell with rhythmic frequency about every 250 to 300 years. Often the destruction of these civilizations by about the tenth generation was so massive as to kill seventy-five percent of the human population within a generation or two. Yet, the tenth generation that lived before the destruction was characterized by wealth, not poverty; by a high density of population; by confidence in existing social and political organizations, despite their difficulties in meeting their social functions; by a loss of direction; by an increasing resort to illegitimate force and violence; and by a sense of foreboding and impending doom.[72]

Recognition of these historical cycles is echoed in Scripture. From a biblical perspective, if our civilization were to adopt compassion, to practice peace and justice by reorienting its institutions, then its collapse would not be necessary. As the prophet Jeremiah (7:5-7) declared to Israel: "For if you truly amend your ways and your doings, if you truly execute justice one with another, if you do not oppress the alien, the fatherless or the widow, or shed innocent blood in this place, and if you do not go after other gods to your own hurt, then I will let you dwell in this place in the land that I gave of old to your fathers forever." But the most likely course of events is that our civilization will not change its current course. We will continue to trust science and to support the industrial institutions of our civilization.

If the proposition of compassion and transformation were to be accepted, then we would still be left with the need to build new institutions based upon compassion. A new civilization would need to be built in the wake of planetary calamities. This organic process of reconstruction would require an explicit strategy for change and a recognized process of action.

From the discussion of political action propositions it should be clear that the strategies used to preserve and maintain institutions are different from the strategies necessary to replace institutions or civilizations with new structures and ideologies. Thus, to return to my earlier vision, my strategy for change involves developing a group or "network" across the globe based upon committed congregations or communities. The strategies available to this network are either to pressure existing institutions and individuals in power or to take over the reigns of power. The first type of strategy—pressure strategies—can be utilized to lessen the negative impact of the collapse of our civilization. Crises can be ameliorated by lobbying, political reforms, lawsuits, demonstrations, and protests. Existing institutions can be forced to provide minimum wages and better welfare benefits, to slow resource depletion and pollution, to develop international peace treaties and partial nuclear disarmament. These strategies are worth pursuing even though they can only partially postpone the collapse of civilization. They can alleviate some of the suffering that is already occurring.

The primary strategies in any overall effort to achieve fundamental change, however, must be takeover strategies. The mildest of these are electoral strategies in which a new president, prime minister, Congress, or Parliament would be elected in various nations of the world. Some powerful nations, of course, do not have democratic elections. Moreover, even in the United States we seem to have passed the time when merely different leaders could forestall collapse. As the just king of Judah, Josiah, could not by all his reforms and good intentions forestall the eventual collapse of that civilization, new U.S. rulers cannot forestall the collapse of the United States. The time for electoral change, as a fundamental pivot for salvaging the civilization is past, although electoral tactics may still be of use for those striving to make the future less bleak.

Other than elections, the standard takeover strategies are riot, revolt, or revolution. The intent of compassion politics is no less radical than revolution. However, there is a difference. With the breakdown of the old order, a violent overthrow of old institutions is unnecessary. They will fall of their own weight although they may be given a final push by a self-conscious movement erecting a new order. If crises like limited nuclear war and environmental disasters befall us before the turn of the century, there will be no need for any violent overthrow of existing governments. What is needed is a remnant to survive the holocaust in order to erect better institutions of a new civilization in the aftermath. This is the goal of the politics of compassion and transformation. Compassion politics involves a "takeover" strategy, but it is a strategy of communal survival and rebuilding after a series of crises undermine our civilization's major institutions.

Still more can be said. The proposition of compassion and transformation leads not only to a particular strategy with its own requirements, limits, and potentials but also to a particular organic process of growth by which particular communities of compassion are born, grow, flourish, and, eventually, take over. This process of action, which is true for all groups and strategies, follows the pattern of a good drama.[73]

The process of action has four inevitable steps based upon the process of human interaction in dramatic situations: Step 1 is introduction and preparation, step 2 is complication or introduction of a causal event, step 3 is crisis or kiros, and step 4 is resolution. Before any overt action takes place, a group of people must be brought together and must develop shared values. Networks must be formed of like-minded individuals who share feelings of compassion *and* who have the same analysis of their society. At the second stage something must happen. As we say of a novel or a play, the plot thickens. What happens will be beyond the control of the group. It may be a resource shortage, a famine, an environmental catastrophe, a war, or a change to a more autocratic form of government. We will be forced to act or react to this event. Then at the third stage a choice must be made: we must decide what we will do collectively to cause history to turn out in a positive way for those we love, for those we identify with through our compassion, and for all beings on the planet. The final action stage is resolution. Because of the causal event and the group response, things can not be the same as they were in the past. Not only institutions but also individual lives will be permanently transformed. Whether the network of compassion succeeds or fails in the short run, it will be bound together more closely by these crises and responses, it will draw to itself new members, and it will change existing social institutions. A new *status quo* will have been established until it is disturbed by the next crisis.

So what does the politics of compassion and transformation require? Peace is to be waged. Justice is to be achieved by producing and distributing enough food, clothing, and shelter for everyone. An alternative technology is to be created to displace current industrialization so that we may live lightly on the earth in harmony with nature. Good work is to be made available for all. All our institutions, especially our governments, are to be made more democratic, depending upon self-reliant, responsible individuals who are themselves the product of revitalized families, schools, and mass media in a more humane and sensible civilization. This depends not on a final gound plan but on a process that begins with actions to achieve peace and justice now and develops based upon responses by others to our initiatives.

All this sounds quite utopian. The politics of compassion and transformation is not simply the management of conflict as liberal and conservative politics tends to be. It utilizes empowerment, not force or violence. It embraces fundamental change as the only way to achieve its goals.

Realism raises three inevitable challenges to the politics of compassion and transformation based upon religion and ethics. Reinhold Neibuhr in *Moral Man and Immoral Society* asks: Can any political system, society, or civilization be moral, or is the best that a religious and compassionate person can do is act morally in what is inevitably an immoral society?[74] No civilization in the past has been totally moral, but some are clearly to be preferred over others. It is essential for us to envision a more "moral" civilization and to work conscientiously toward creating its institutions. It is not enough to lead a privately moral life in the face of global suffering. We must seek to transform our society and to make it better. Even if a perfectly moral civilization is not achieved, we can significantly improve global conditions.

The second challenge of the realists is: Are compassionate people hardheaded and realistic enough to do anything effective about their compassion and idealism? If compassion were only a private emotion and nothing more, then compassionate people would not be able to act effectively in the political arena. Their feelings would get in the way, and they would be rendered impotent. Scripture and personal experience provide resources for us. As Harvey Cox has written, we are not limited to "the individual 'religious experience' that William James describes in his famous book *The Varieties of Religious Experience.*" We can "experience the presence of God in the pain, anger, joy, and hope of disinherited peoples and in the effort to confront the causes of injustice wherever possible."[75] Our politics of compassion and transformation will be guided by political analysis as well as the anger we share with the disinherited. Compassionate action need not lead to individualism, sentimentality, or an ungrounded idealism that would interfere with a clear-headed understanding of how political systems and social institutions work. Compassion leads instead to conscious efforts of societal transformation based upon religion and ethics. Reinhold Niebuhr in *Moral Man and Immoral Society* asks: Can any political system, society, or

Finally, some realists believe that a politics of compassion is likely to be subject to perversion. Beliefs may blind us to reality. For instance, Professor Marvin Maurer in a paper delivered at the 1987 American Political Science Association meeting accused Quakers and the American Friends Service Committee of being biased in their foreign policy analyses.[76] According to Maurer, the Quakers were critical of the Soviet Union and communist nations up to the 1950s. With the Vietnam War, which they opposed on moral and religious grounds, they absolved North Vietnam of charges of wrongdoing, idealized Ho Chi Minh, compared Mao Tse-Tung to the Quaker founder George Fox, and have since failed to be outraged by Soviet aggression in

Afghanistan. Some American Friends Service Committee staff have gone so far as to argue that the USSR was waging a progressive war in Afghanistan. As Quakers became alienated from our society, Maurer charges that they have tended to idealize other societies despite the facts. While Professor Maurer may well have made a selective reading of statements by Quakers and the American Friends Service Committee, these dangers of perversion for those who would follow a politics of compassion must be taken seriously. We can easily become blinded by our beliefs and our ideologies. In fact, the more fervently we hold beliefs the more likely we are to mistake them for reality. The politics of compassion and transformation requires that we keep an open heart and an open mind, that we listen to a wide range of opinions, including those of our political opponents. We must not allow our original insights to rigidify into absolute and unbending ideologies. We can avoid perversion only by continual transformation.

Clearly, our politics of compassion and transformation will have to be fought for just like any other political goals. Institutions and the entrenched interest groups of our civilization naturally support the status quo. But power in history is more than brute force and a willingness to use violence. We will be joined in our struggle by many people because of the power of our analysis, because of the idealism of our goals, and because our sense of compassion is potentially widely shared. Religion, ethics, and politics can be united by a network of people transformed and connected by their compassion. By our actions, we can become co-creators with God, creating a better future for this planet. Thus it is that a religion which believes that God is compassion, an ethics which conceives proper actions as those which manifest God's will, and a politics based upon compassion and personal transformation pave the way for the birth of a new civilization which can overcome the contradictions and crises of our society.

Part II

COMPASSION

Chapter 3
TEACHERS OF COMPASSIONATE POLITICS

Once a heathen came before Shammai. He said to him:
I will be converted, if you can teach me all the Torah while I stand
on one leg.
Shammai pushed him away with the builder's measure he had in
his hand.
The man came before Hillel. He converted him.
He said to him:
What is hateful to you, do not do to your fellow.
That is all the Torah. The rest is commentary—go and study.

To achieve a deeper understanding of the politics of compassion and transformation, we must reflect upon religious men and women who have in their own special ways practiced and taught compassionate action. By deeper, I mean the depth that Paul Tillich spoke of in his sermon "The Depth of Existence" as a "spiritual quality." We need to understand the politics of compassion and transformation in a profound spiritual way. As Tillich wrote, "Both the light of truth and the darkness of suffering are deep. . . . Why have [people] always asked for truth? Is it because they have been disappointed with surfaces, and have known that the truth which does *not* disappoint dwells below the surfaces in the depth?" Despite its profundity, most people who have experienced depth seek "to return to the disrupted surface as though nothing had happened." Depth frightens most of us and we turn back. But Tillich urges us to go still deeper: "But we who know the depth of what has happened should not be content to rest upon the level that we have reached. We might become despairing and self-despising. Let us rather plunge more deeply into the ground of our historical life, into the ultimate depth of history. The name of this infinite and inexhaustible ground of history is God."[1]

Because God is compassion, we are inevitably led to God if we practice a politics of compassion and transformation. Yet the need to live in depth makes this the hardest politics to practice. Infinitely easier is the "realistic" politics of power and ambition. Because compassion and transformation requires depth, they cannot remain abstract theological concepts. They have to become concrete motivations and experiences of our lives. Meister Eckhart thus extolled compassion:

> And those who follow compassion
>   find life for themselves,
>   justice for their neighbor,
>   and glory for God.

Like Tillich, Eckhart finds a direct connection between compassion and God:

> The fullest work
> that God ever worked
> in any creature
> is compassion.
> The most secret and forbidden work
> that God ever worked on the angels
> was carrying them into compassion.
> This is the work of compassion
> as it is in itself
> and as it is in God.
> Whatever God does,
> the first outburst is always compassion.
> I do not mean that God forgives a person [their] sins
> or that a person takes pity on another.
> I mean much more.
> I mean that the highest work that God ever works is
> compassion.[2]

To find compassion requires depth and is related to finding God; but, as Matthew Fox warns us, this is not an easy process: "To develop compassion, then, means to develop an even keener awareness of the interdependence of all living things. But to develop such an awareness implies deep study, not only of books, of course, but of nature itself. It implies a spiritual discipline. . . . " Because finding compassion, realizing it, and giving it expression requires discipline and effort; because compassion requires our personal transformation, we seek to avoid it. But compassion is so profound that it is hard to ignore. Fox quotes Thomas Aquinas who wrote that "compassion is the fire which the Lord has come to send on the earth."[3] Compassion is an unquenchable, burning fire. Like fire, it has beauty and great power. As wood burned gives off light and heat, we manifest great energy when we are consumed by compassion.

To understand compassion and compassionate politics at depth, we need religious teachers. In this chapter, I will focus on Jewish prophets, Jesus of Nazareth, Meister Eckhart, Mahatma Gandhi, Martin Luther King, Jr., the current Hindu leader Sathya Sai Baba, and modern Catholic activist Dorothy Day. Many other religious leaders and gurus offer the lessons of compassion, but these suffice to lead us to the depths where transformation occurs.

The Jewish Prophets

The first prophet of Israel was Moses. What tradition of prophecy did Moses begin? He began prophecy as an "understanding of history which accepts meaning only in terms of divine concern, divine purpose, divine participation."[4] The God of the prophets is not a remote being who began the universe twenty billion years ago and then left with no concern for the result. No, the God of the prophets is involved in history as a God of justice and compassion.

Moses and later prophets were not only seers who communed with God; they were also deeply involved in history. With his God's help, Moses freed the Jews from Egyptian tyranny. Walter Brueggemann says that this break with the imperial reality of Egypt was "a break from both the religion of static triumphalism and the politics of oppression and exploitation." An oppressive religion and politics always go together, and prophets rise in opposition to them. By his miracles, Moses exposed Egyptian gods as false gods. By organizing the Jews, he countered the existing politics of exploitation with the politics of justice and compassion.[5]

Hundreds of years after Moses, the prophets of Israel continued to offer an alternative vision to slavery, to exile in Babylon, to worship of false idols, and to the tyranny of Israel's own kings. Whenever the people of Israel became self-satisfied, the prophets would call them back to their covenant with Yahweh and would warn them of pending destruction if they did not mend their ways. Finally, if necessary, they would deliver God's judgment upon the sins of "God's chosen people." But, whenever the people of Israel were broken and defeated, the same prophets would offer them the hope that Yahweh, the God of history, would save them. Thus, prophets had the two duties:

> I have set you this day . . . to pluck up and
> to break down, to destroy and to overthrow,
> to build and to plant.
> (Jeremiah 1:4–10)

To put it another way, a prophet is one who announces to us what time it is—that is, a prophet tells us what God is doing in history now.

Through their prophecy and preaching, the prophets always presented, although in different ways, the same message of justice. Thus, Jeremiah also declared:

> For if you truly amend your ways and your doings, if you truly execute
> justice one with another, if you do not oppress the alien, the fatherless
> or the widow, or shed innocent blood in this place, and if you do not go
> after other gods to your own hurt, then I will let you dwell in this place
> in the land that I gave of old to your fathers forever.
>   (Jeremiah 7:5-7)

Keeping the covenant with God required Jews to worship Yahweh, not the
false idol gods of other nations. But it also meant doing justice by avoiding
oppression of aliens, and by being generous to widows, orphans, the poor,
and the innocent. Because of injustices and the worship of false gods, God
had previously destroyed the Holy Temple at Shiloh. Jeremiah prophesied the
destruction of Jerusalem and the new temple if Jews did not return to the path
of justice and compassion. The Jews failed to listen to Jeremiah so the nation
and the temple were destroyed as prophesied.

Jeremiah was not the only prophet to cry out for justice. The quintessential
prophetic commandment was given by the prophet Micah who said "What
does the Lord require of you but to do justice, to love compassion, and to
walk humbly with your God?" This same theme was later picked up by Isaiah
and Isaiah's disciples. Much like Jeremiah who was called to break down and
to build up, the several prophets who took the name Isaiah were called to
bring good tidings to the poor, to bind up the brokenhearted, to declare liberty
and a year of Yahweh's favor, to comfort, to give joy, and to praise God. The
first Isaiah prophesied the complete destruction of Judah and the Babylonian
exile. The later Isaiahs were then to heal and bind up a broken people and to
be with them in the restoration of the nation. And why is all this to occur?

> Because I, Yahweh, love justice,
> I hate robbery and wrong,
> I will faithfully give the People of Israel their recompense,
> and I will make an everlasting covenant with them.
>   (Isaiah 61:8)

God restores Israel, which had been destroyed, because of God's compassion.
Yahweh forgives his/her people and sends prophets to give them hope but also
to command them to be just and compassionate with the poor.

What do the Jewish prophets teach us about God? They teach us that God is
like a strict parent who requires that we live in accordance with laws,
commandments, and restrictions. We constantly fail to live up to God's
standards for us. But God is also like a compassionate parent who forgives us,
who acts anew, who offers new covenants, and new beginnings for us.

The prophets teach us that ultimately there are only two commandments:
we are to worship only Yahweh, and we are to be just and compassionate with

our neighbor as God is just and compassionate with us. This justice and compassion which the prophets teach is not just a mechanical balancing of scales and keeping of laws. Rather, we are taught to stand in solidarity with the poor, to comfort the sick, to free those in prison as God comforts and frees God's chosen people from slavery in Egypt and exile in Babylon. For the Jewish prophets God is a divine warrior, a mighty force beyond our comprehension. In the prophetic view, God is stern but God is just and, most of all, God is compassionate. God is involved with history and with our lives just like good parents are concerned about the lives of their children.

Prophets like Moses, Jeremiah, and Isaiah have a personal lesson to teach us. They teach us to observe clearly what is going on in our historical situation. They call us to feel the pain, anguish, and despair as well as the hope and joy of our brothers and sisters. We, like the prophets, are called to heal and to help, to be faithful, and to eliminate pain and suffering.

Jesus of Nazareth

The supreme lesson that Jesus taught was compassion. He suffered with the poor and therefore ministered to them. He felt the pain of the sick and therefore cured them. He foresaw the horror of the coming fall of Israel and therefore prophesied the disaster that would befall if the Israelites did not change their ways.

Jesus was from the middle class. Yet he mixed with the lowest castes in Israel. He became an outcast and eventually was crucified. Because of his compassion, he sought to liberate his brothers and sisters from all forms of suffering and oppression. Jesus was concerned both for those who were poor in spirit and those who were materially poor. He did not distinguish between spiritual and material poverty but promised that both would be ended with the coming of the Kingdom of God.

The Gospel according to Luke provides us with Jesus' own definition of his ministry by recounting his first public appearance and teaching at his hometown of Nazareth.

> Jesus came to Nazareth, where he had been brought up, and went into the synagogue on the sabbath day as he usually did. He stood up to read, and they handed him the scroll of the prophet Isaiah. Unrolling the scroll he searched and found the place where it is written: "The spirit of the Lord is upon me, for God has anointed me. God has sent me to bring good news to the poor, to proclaim liberty to the captives, new sight for the blind, to set the oppressed free, to proclaim the year of the Lord's favor."
>
> (Luke 4:16-18)

Clearly, in this passage, Luke is telling us that Jesus is taking upon himself the prophetic mission first pronounced by Isaiah—to bring good news to the poor, to proclaim liberty to the captives, new sight for the blind, to set the oppressed free, and to proclaim the Jubilee Year of God's justice when land would be returned to the poor, debts would be forgiven, slaves would be freed, and just government would be reestablished.

Jesus did not pursue an apolitical or spiritualized ministry, as some later Christians have characterized it, but the disruptive path of a politics of compassion and transformation. John Yoder, in *The Politics of Jesus,* argues that:

> Jesus was not just a moralist whose teachings had some political implications; he was not primarily a teacher of spirituality whose public ministry unfortunately was seen in a political light; he was not just a sacrificial lamb preparing for his immolation, or a God-Man whose divine status calls us to disregard his humanity. Jesus was, in his divinely mandated (i.e., promised, anointed, messianic) prophethood, priesthood, and kingship, the bearer of a new possibility of human, social, and therefore political relationships. . . . [He was] a man who threatens society by creating a new kind of life.

Yoder concludes that Jesus is proclaiming the imminent arrival "of a new regime whose marks would be the rich would give to the poor, the captives would be freed, and [people] would have a new mentality *(metanoia)* if they believed this news."[6]

Compassion led Jesus to his most fundamentally political act which was to feel the suffering of the poor and, therefore, to identify with them. As the South African liberation theologian Albert Nolan has written:

> The remarkable thing about Jesus was that, although he came from the middle class and had no appreciable disadvantages himself, he mixed socially with the lowest of the low and identified himself with them. He became an outcast *by choice.*
>
> Why did Jesus do this? . . . The answer comes across very clearly in the gospels: compassion.[7]

This identification with the poor became a central theme in Jesus' more complete politics of transformation which seemed to have at least the following components: (1) solidarity with the poor; (2) forgiveness of sins; (3) healing of the sick; (4) calling for a Kingdom of God here on earth in which there would no longer be poor, oppressed, or sick; (5) using our surplus possessions to benefit the poor; (6) allowing the poor to participate fully in the ongoing life of the community; and (7) trusting in and praying to God that all this would be accomplished.[8] Because he identitied with those who suffered, Jesus forgave their sins and healed them. Because he felt the injustice of the society so strongly, his demand and promise of a just society was made. This transformation was to be accomplished by redistributing wealth and power so that all could share in this common community. Jesus trusted God to help make this possible.

His teaching and actions inevitably led Jesus into conflict with the authorities. He concluded "that there is nothing sancrosanct about the Roman social order [or the Jewish religious establishment]."

> Jesus himself does not show deference to the officials who oversee this order. Whether they are officials of the stature of Herod Antipas or the Jerusalem chief priests, and even if they have the more exalted title of Benefactor, Jesus criticizes them freely. Moreover, Jesus does not submit to the social patterns and practices to which the Romans and their allies are commited. He rejects the violence and exploitation that they accept as a normal part of living, and his teachings and conduct run counter to many of the other patterns that they accept and endorse. . . .

> Jesus is no particular friend of the Roman order. On the contrary, the social practices he espouses were profoundly at variance with those of the Roman order.[9]

Much of Jesus' teaching is to be found in his parables. In three parables in the fifteenth Chapter of Luke, Jesus offers us a special vision of God. The God of Abraham, Isaac, Jacob, Moses, Jeremiah, and Isaiah has been moved by compassion both for Israel and for all the peoples of the world. The fierce warrior God has become the God of compassion. This is the inner meaning of these parables of the lost sheep, the lost coin, and the lost son.

In the parable of the lost sheep, a shepherd leaves ninety-nine sheep who are safely in the flock to find the one lost sheep before it is attacked by wolves, starves to death, or dies of thirst. Jesus tells us that the moral of this story is that "there will be more joy in heaven over one sinner who repents than over ninety-nine righteous persons who need no repentance." This is contrary to the ways of the world and, especially, our modern culture in which quantity is what counts—how big is it? how many are there? what is their dollar value? Yet the God revealed by this parable must be a God of compassion. We are told that our divine parent does not deal in numbers but suffers with and is concerned for each of us.

Similarly, in the second parable of the lost coin of the widow the moral is that there is great joy "over the one sinner who repents." And this leads to the final parable of the lost son. The lost son is a sinner who has wronged his father. He squandered in loose living all the wealth his father had given him as his inheritance. Rather than perish from hunger, he returns home. But the father of the parable does not disown, reject, or lecture his son as we might. He does not demand restitution of the squandered wealth, nor does he punish as our notions of justice require. Rather, the son is given a hero's welcome with rejoicing and a grand feast.

Attend to the reasonable complaint by the elder son in Jesus' parable. The dutiful son says to the father, "I have served you, never disobeyed you, and yet you never even gave me a kid goat so that I might have a party for my friends while for my brother who has lived with whores and squandered your money, you have ordered a celebration." By such parables Jesus teaches that God does not act with measured justice but with compassion, giving us gifts beyond our merit. In this parable the father is concerned for his son and glad to have him home. He had believed him dead and is overjoyed to find him alive. The son had been lost but now is found. Thus, the celebration.

If the God of the parables can best be understood as the divine and forgiving parent, embodying both aspects of father and mother, Jesus can be considered our older brother. He gives us wise counsel and guidance. He seeks to show us the path to God and to bring about the Kingdom of God on earth. In his life he practiced compassion, healed the sick, and comforted the poor. He provided solace for the brokenhearted and where there was fear, he brought hope.

Meister Eckhart

Meister Eckhart was a fourteenth-century Dominican who had the audacity to preach in vernacular German rather than Latin, to support the Beguins (a women's liberation movement of the day), and to announce to peasants that they were royal people. This, of course, brought great consternation to the nobility, and his preaching earned his censure by the pope. Matthew Fox has summed up his status as "a spiritual genius and a declared heretic."[10] As a mystic, Meister Eckhart teaches a path of compassion by which we can discover ourselves, relate to God, and become connected to our neighbor.

Eckhart's fourfold path to God was sketched in the last chapter so it can be summarized here briefly. The first path is the positive path of creation, the second is the negative path of letting go and letting be in which we empty our life in order to be refilled, the third is the personally creative path of breakthrough and birthing, and the fourth is the path of social transformation and social justice.[11] Eckhart's path of compassion "does not demand a lot of baggage for the journey, it demands no gurus, no fanciful methods other than the discipline that all art requires, no excessive exercises or retreats. . . . [It] is available to all . . . 'she who has found this way needs no other.' "[12]

In his teaching, Eckhart shows that the path of compassion is a spiral journey of personal and social transformation rather than a static condition we can achieve and possess like property. The positive, creative life of the first path is living life like "the rose which lives without a why." It is to take joy in the created world and our life within the greater web of existence. And the appropriate response to this positive experience of our life is also simple. Eckhart says,

> If the only prayer
> you say in your entire life
> is 'Thank you,'
> that would suffice.[13]

The second path to God involves emptying ourselves. We humans are often so full of ourselves that there is no room for God to get in. But by loneliness and suffering, we are forced to let go of what we have. We lose loved ones to death. We lose the innocence of youth. We have painful physical accidents. We become divorced, or our children grow up and our family is no longer there to protect us from discovering ourselves. We sit in silence and we discover a part of ourselves in the silence and emptiness that we have not known before. Mystics, including Eckhart, teach us that when we have removed and gotten rid of all that is not-God we find God.

> This spirit seeks to be
> broken through by God.
>
> God leads this spirit
> into a desert
> into the wilderness and solitude of the divinity
> where God is pure unity
> and where God gushes up within himself.[14]

Having passed through the joy of the positive path and the suffering of the negative path, we are led almost inevitably to the creative path in which we discover that both we and God are meant to give birth. In this birthing we find goodness, consolation, delight, being, and truth.

> It is good for a person
> to receive God into himself or herself
> and I call this receptivity the work of a virgin.
> But it is better
> when God becomes fruitful within a person.
> For becoming fruitful as a result of a gift
> is the only gratitude for the gift.

> I call such a person a wife
> and in this sense the term wife is the noblest term
> we can give the soul,
> it is far nobler than virgin.
> Every day
> such a person
> bears fruit a hundred times
> or a thousand times
> or countless times,
> giving birth and becoming fruitful
> out of the most noble foundation of all.[15]

The positive, negative, and creative paths might seem entirely private and "mystical" in the sense of a subjective, personal experience. But the path of compassion is not exclusively private. Its public side is seen most clearly in the fourth path of social transformation.

If the essence of God is compassion and we recognize God within ourselves (and our oneness with God), then our nature must also become compassionate and loving. Then we can no longer luxuriate in contemplation. Because we feel genuine compassion for the suffering of every living creature; we groan with the extinction of plants and animals on the planet; we cry out with the pain of war; and we suffer with the homeless, hungry, and helpless. Thus, on the fourth path we can not rest in metaphysical bliss but must rush to help, to save, and to serve.

When we have acted with compassion to seek social transformation, we may well find ourselves returned to the path of joy or to the path of negativity or to the path of creativity. Our journey continues down all the paths of compassion to God. The path to compassion does not end with a single breakthrough but circles to ever deeper experiences, to ever greater awareness, and to ever greater power to act more effectively in the world.

If the prophets teach us justice, and if Jesus teaches us that God is a forgiving parent and urges us to heal and comfort the poor and brokenhearted, Meister Eckhart provides a guide to the path to compassion by which we may find strength, comfort, forgiveness, and justice. This path through joy and sadness, through birthing and transformation, leads to God. This path does not require the rites of a church, belief in a particular creed, acceptance of special doctrines, degrees of formal education, nor high social status. Following Eckhart we can all be men and women on the path of compassion and transformation. The Christian mystics along with mystics of other faiths such as the Sufis provide a map to guide us on this journey.

Mahatma Gandhi

Gandhi, the political saint of modern India, advocated and lived a life of karma yoga—of meditation in service and action. Another modern Hindu religious leader, Swami Sivananda, has said of karma yoga:

> Work is worship. Work is meditation. Serve all with intense love without any idea of agency and without expectation of . . . reward. You will realize God. Service of humanity is service of God.
> Work elevates when done in the right spirit without attachment or egoism. . . . All work is sacred. . . . Real spiritual progress starts with selfless service.[16]

Gandhi took the philosophical and contemplative religious principles of India and applied them to the practical problems of the world. While his teaching derived from Hindu thought as set forth in the Vedas and the Bhagavad Gita, he gave them a special new emphasis by applying them to social and political issues.

Gandhi's first principle and chief goal was *satya* which can be translated as "Absolute Truth" or "Being." Gandhi said that "nothing exists in reality except Truth, everything else is illusion." Following earlier sages of India, he believed that "behind the illusory flux of fleeting phenomena there is an eternal substratum of noumenal reality, a single bedrock of supreme Truth."[17] Gandhi wrote in 1933: "What I am concerned with is my readiness to obey the call of Truth, my God, from moment to moment. . . . " Earlier in 1931 he wrote that "the pursuit of Truth is true *bhakthi* [devotion]. It is the path that leads to God and there is no place in it for cowardice, no place for defeat."[18]

This is the lesson that the god Krishna attempted to teach Arjuna in the Bhagavad Gita. Krishna is believed by the Hindus to be an incarnation of God just as Christians believe Jesus Christ to be. In the Gita, Arjuna was a great warrior who, upon arriving at a battlefield and seeing his kinsman in the opposing army, didn't want to fight them. As he discussed the terrible consequences of war with his friend and charioteer, Krishna, he was taught the true nature of our life. Krishna counseled Arjuna that most of what we see in life is really illusion: "He who is regarded as a slayer and he who thinks he is slain are both ignorant. He slays not, nor is he slain. He is not born nor does he die; nor having been, he does not cease to be; unborn perpetual, eternal, and ancient, he is not slain when the body is slaughtered."[19] Thus, Krishna explained reincarnation in which dying is like casting off worn-out clothes. Hindus, including Gandhi, believe that each person has an eternal element of Being or God which is permanent and immortal.

Many Indian spiritual teachers adopted a privatistic and fatalistic approach to life based upon these doctrines. But in the Gita, Krishna teaches that our task is not to abstain from action but to perform right actions in the right spirit. By proper actions from correct motives and with a correct expectation we move ever closer to an understanding of God and Truth. In the Gita, Krishna counsels Arjuna regarding right action thusly:

> Man does not win freedom from action by abstaining from activity, nor by mere renunciation does he rise to perfection. Nor can any one, even for an instant, remain really actionless; for helplessly is every one driven to action by the qualities born of nature. He who sits controlling the organs of action, but dwells in his mind on the objects of the senses, that bewildered man is called a hypocrite. But he who, controlling the senses by the mind, oh Arjuna, with the organs of action without action, performs yoga by action, he is worthy. Perform right action, for action is superior to inaction, and inactive even the maintenance of your body would not be possible.[20]

From such Hindu teachings Gandhi adopted as his supreme principle the worship and obedience to Truth.

He titled his autobiography, *The Story of My Experiments with Truth,* and wrote in it the following explanation:

> What I want to achieve . . . is self-realization, to see God face to face, to attain *Moksha* [freedom from birth and death, that is to say, salvation]. . . .
>
> Truth is the sovereign principle . . . This truth is not only truthfulness in word, but truthfulness in thought also, and not only the relative truth of our conception but the Absolute Truth, the Eternal Principle that is God. . . .
>
> I worship God as Truth only. I have not yet found God, but I am seeking after God . . . as long as I have not realized this Absolute Truth, so long must I hold by the relative truth as I conceive it. That relative truth must, meanwhile, be my beacon, my shield and buckler.[21]

Gandhi understood that pure Being or Truth could not be comprehended merely by contemplation. Karma yoga or meditation in action was required. Because it is Truth that we seek, we need another principle or method to guide our actions so that we come ever closer to Truth. For Gandhi this other principle was *ahimsa*. He linked *ahimsa*, which means nonviolence to any living thing, to the idea of nonattachment which brings freedom from hatred, pride, anger, and other emotions. *Ahimsa* in its negative means not injuring any living being or *non*-violence. Positively, it means love and charity in the sense that Jesus of Nazareth taught that we should love our neighbors and even our enemies. Gandhi accepted the demands of *ahimsa* because he believed that we are all fellow seekers after Truth.[22]

In the *Yoga Sutras* [or teachings] that Gandhi studied, we are told to follow certain rules called Yamas and Niyamas. Like *ahimsa* these involve both negative and positive regulations. The Yamas require the avoidance of violence, stealing, covetousness, and lying. The Niyamas require purity, austerity, contentment, repetition of sacred words, and devotion to God.[23]

It is possible, following either Western or Eastern religions, to take religious vows, to become a recluse or monk, and to live a spiritual life away from the temptations of the world in which Yamas and Niyamas are followed. But Gandhi, because of his compassion for the suffering of those living under apartheid in South Africa and Indians living under British colonial rule in their homeland, applied these Hindu spiritual principles to practical struggles for freedom and justice on two continents.

From the principles of *satya* and *ahimsa* he created the doctrine of Satyagraha [truth force or "soul force" as Martin Luther King later translated it]. Satyagraha led to active but nonviolent resistance to authority. Gandhi came to see nonviolent protest demonstrations as "the deliberate suffering of a [person] of outraged conscience" in such a dramatic form that it becomes "a moral sanction that compels respect and secures results."[24]

Satyagraha differs from methods of rational persuasion and violence chiefly in its unique reliance upon self-suffering. Because of the suffering involved, it demands prior purification, devotion, the taking of religious vows, and deliberate, unswerving action. It depends upon an absolute faith that God will take the dedicated actions of the person of faith and turn them to good results. As Krishna says in the Gita, our actions must be "free from the moulding of desires . . . [and we must abandon] attachment to the fruit of the action."[25]

What then does Gandhi add to our understanding of compassion in addition to the teachings of Jewish prophets, Jesus, and Eckhart? First, he affirms that we need not withdraw from the practical world of politics in order to be religious. Indeed, both Gandhi and Krishna teach that it is precisely through practical actions in the world that we are religious. We may, of course, withdraw to meditate, pray, or study, but we withdraw only to better prepare for our work, our karma yoga, in the world. Second, Gandhi demonstrates that we must select a few basic religious principles which we will not compromise. To these will be added our political analysis of the situation, and our acts of transformation. For Gandhi, compassion led to the principle of *satya* or God as Being and Truth, and to *ahimsa,* based on his love of all fellow creatures. From these two religious principles, most of the rest of his teachings and actions can be derived. Although Gandhi was willing to compromise on tactical questions and willing to negotiate political settlements with opponents, he would not compromise his belief in *satya* and *ahimsa*.

Gandhi is important as a teacher of compassion because he was able to take private religious principles such as *satya* and *ahimsa* and translate them into the practice of satyagraha in the political arena. As Susanne Rudolph and Lloyd Rudolph put it in *Gandhi: The Traditional Roots of Charisma,*

> Gandhi realized in his daily life and his public actions cultural ideals that many Indians honored in their own lives but could not themselves enact. He and his followers shared, for example, the traditional Hindu belief that a person's capacity for self-control enhanced [their] capacity to control [their] environment. This was the key to Gandhi's political potency. In a self-fulfilling prophecy of mutual expectations and recognitions, Gandhi and those to whom he spoke believed that the more he could realize the cultural ideal of ascetic self-control over enslaving or destructive passions, the more qualified he became as their leader.[26]

It was from Gandhi's practice of spiritual disciplines and by his self-sacrifice and self-control that he gained his political following, his charisma. His personal virtue as well as his advocacy of Hindu beliefs made him a popular political figure whom thousands of Indians would assemble to hear and whom thousands would follow in political action campaigns. But Gandhi did not just adopt private religious practices for public effect. As the great Indian poet Rabindranath Tagore wrote of Gandhi:

> The secret of Gandhi's success lies in his dynamic spiritual strength and incessant self-sacrifice. Many public men make sacrifices for selfish reasons. It is a sort of investment that yields handsome dividends. Gandhi is altogether different. He is unique in the nobility. His very life is another name for sacrifice. He is sacrifice itself. He covets no power, no position, no wealth, no name and no fame. . . . His power of sacrifice becomes all the more irresistible because it is wedded with his paramount fearlessness. Emperors and Maharajas, guns and bayonets, imprisonments and tortures, insults and injuries, even death itself, can never daunt the spirit of Gandhi. He is a liberated soul.[27]

Gandhi with his political program of satyagraha "'solved' psychological problems of Indian self-esteem arising from acceptance of the negative judgments of Englishmen."[28] Indians could not lack "components of moral worth—like courage" if they pursued such a courageous course as self-sacrifice and civil disobedience. Thus, through satyagraha they liberated themselves from the psychological effects of colonialism even as they dismantled its objective institutions.

Finally, Gandhi, like the Jewish prophets and Jesus, teaches us the effect of compassion upon our own life. Because he felt so deeply the suffering in South Africa and India, he was motivated to act radically and fearlessly to end that suffering. Because he was a man of deep religious principles, he was able to lead successfully a movement of nonviolent direct action which, through righteous suffering, transformed society. He made and kept his vows to God. And because he was able to give up the fruits of his actions, because he left the outcome to God, his actions were both powerful and effective.

Martin Luther King, Jr.

Martin Luther King, Jr., held two visions. The first was to extend the American Dream to blacks. He understood the phrase in the Declaration of Independence that "all men are created equal" to mean that *all* Americans, black and white, men and women, were created equal. Therefore, they should be accorded equal rights, equal opportunities, and equality before the law. Now this was a great vision—the same vision that had fueled the Civil War and brought the emancipation proclamation. Two hundred years after the Declaration of Independence and one hundred years after our bloody Civil War, these promises were finally to be kept.

But King's other vision was still deeper, broader, and more powerful. It was indigenous to the black church and grew from King's study of religion. He believed in the promised Kingdom of God which most Christians seem to think is promised only after Christ's Second Coming or, as the song has it, "there will be pie in the sky by and by." Yet, Jesus' Sermon on the Mount says that the poor and those who are persecuted will enter into the Kingdom of God. The Gospel of Luke has the wonderful image of people coming from east and west, from north and south to sit at the common table in this kingdom. As a Christian minister, Martin Luther King, Jr., believed in the brotherhood and sisterhood of all people and in the Beloved Community promised in the Christian Scriptures. He struggled to bring this community into existence.

King believed in the power of love to transform people so that they could be brothers and sisters to one another. He didn't believe that we had to wait for the beloved community. He believed that by our actions we could bring it into existence now. Thus, his ultimate goal was not just equal rights and equal opportunities but that we human beings should indeed become members of a single family through the transforming power of love. Hate would be overcome and suffering ended.

For an American and a Christian to believe that all people are created equal and that we are brothers and sisters is no more unusual than for a Hindu to believe in *satya* and *ahimsa*. Most Americans, and most religious people of any faith, would say they believe in these goals. But like most Hindus, they don't translate their religious beliefs into political actions. Like Gandhi, King pushed his "private" religious beliefs to their limit in the public arena. By doing so, both leaders eliminated the oppression of millions of people. King and Gandhi took religious "sentiments" and transformed them into powerful actions.

Thus, King sought to create a "beloved community" by achieving social and economic justice. This beloved community would be integrated. All races and classes would live in justice and harmony. Most strikingly, King concluded that this struggle for justice and equality could be achieved only if white American society were redeemed by Christlike suffering and love by its black outcasts.[29] This paralleled Gandhi's conclusion that Indian independence could only be won by converting British opinion through self-discipline and suffering by Indians.

These are very significant conclusions. Despite the fact that King and other blacks were discriminated against in all aspects of their lives by a racist white society, King still saw clearly that blacks would have to redeem whites in order to achieve the beloved community for themselves.

> King not only accepted the [existing] black mythology of a saving Christ, he made it the cornerstone of his political philosophy. [In King's view] it was the mission of the black . . . to teach the white . . . the capacity to love. The white man's sickness, as King perceived it, stemmed from his need for ego-gratification, which led to the pursuit of material things and status; which in turn caused man's alienation from his fellowman and dehumanization.[30]

The final goal of the civil rights movement was not just freedom and equality for blacks. It was the transformation of our entire society so that it more closely approximated the beloved community, the Kingdom of God promised by Jesus of Nazareth.

Martin Luther King, Jr., sought explicitly to merge the practical and the idealistic, politics and religion. He put it this way:

> Whereas science and politics give [people] knowledge which is power; religion gives [people] wisdom which is control. Politics and science deal mainly with facts; religion deals mainly with values. Whereas science and politics merely investigates; religion interprets. The two are not rivals. They are complementary. Politics and science keep religion from sinking into the valley of crippling irrationalism and paralyzing obscurantism. Religion prevents science and politics from falling into the marsh of obsolete materialism and moral nihilism.[31]

Like his hero, Gandhi, King was determined to bring religion into the practical realms of politics, economy, and society. So he, like Gandhi, adopted the practical methods of nonviolent direct action which he coupled with pragmatic economic boycotts to force the end of segregation in America. In his last book, written before his assassination, King concluded:

> It is not overlooking the limitations of nonviolence and the distance we have yet to go to point out the remarkable record of achievements that have already come through nonviolent action. The 1960 sit-ins desegregated lunch counters in more than 150 cities within a year. The 1961 Freedom Rides put an end to segregation in interstate travel. The 1956 bus boycott in Montgomery, Alabama, ended segregation on the buses not only of that city but in practically every city of the South. The 1963 Birmingham movement and the climactic March on Washington won passage of the most powerful civil rights law in a century. The 1965 Selma movement brought enactment of the Voting Rights Law.[32]

If the list were continued today, local and state civil rights legislation would be added, along with prominent black elected officials such as the mayors and former mayors of cities like Atlanta, Chicago, Philadelphia, and Los Angeles; affirmative action programs in job hiring; and more blacks in key professional positions than ever before in U.S. history. But even more impressive than the effectiveness of King's political tactics was his philosophy of love which guided his entire program. It is only because King first felt deeply and compassionately the effects of segregation upon himself and upon other blacks that he was motivated to act to end segregation. And it was only because he held firmly to the philosophy of love that he was able to act nonviolently. A testimony to how deeply he felt the impact of segregation is contained in the letter he wrote from his jail cell in Birmingham to white clergy who had questioned the Birmingham demonstrations. In his letter he explained at the gut level why blacks and all people of goodwill had to protest segregation.

> We have waited for more than 340 years for our constitutional and God-given rights. The nations of Asia and Africa are moving with jetlike speed toward gaining political independence, but we still creep at horse-and-buggy pace toward gaining a cup of coffee at a lunch counter. Perhaps it is easy for those who have never felt the stinging darts of segregation to say, "Wait." But when you have seen vicious mobs lynch your mothers and fathers at will and drown your sisters and brothers at whim; when you have seen hate-filled policemen curse, kick and even kill your black brothers and sisters; when you see the vast majority of twenty million Negro brothers smothering in an airtight cage

of poverty in the midst of an affluent society; when you suddenly find your tongue twisted and your speech stammering as you seek to explain to your six-year-old daughter why she can't go to the public amusement park that has just been advertised on television, and see tears welling up in her eyes when she is told that Funtown is closed to colored children, and see ominous clouds of inferiority beginning to form in her little mental sky, and see her beginning to distort her personality by developing an unconscious bitterness toward white people; when you have to concoct an answer for a five-year-old son who is asking "Daddy, why do white people treat colored people so mean?"; when you take a cross-country drive and find it necessary to sleep night after night in the uncomfortable corners of your automobile because no motel will accept you; when you are humiliated day in and day out by nagging signs reading "white" and "colored"; when your first name becomes "nigger," your middle name becomes "boy" (however old you are) and your last name becomes "John," and your wife and mother are never given the respected title "Mrs."; when you are harried by day and haunted by night by the fact that you are a Negro, living constantly at tiptoe stance, never quite knowing what to expect, and are plagued with inner fears and outer resentments; when you are forever fighting a degenerating sense of "nobodiness"—then you will understand why we find it difficult to wait. There comes a time when the cup of endurance runs over, and [people] are no longer willing to be plunged into the abyss of despair.[33]

To lead the civil rights movement, King had to feel the pain and pangs of all who suffered; otherwise he would not be willing to make the sacrifices required, which he well knew might include giving up his life. Only because he felt compassion for those who suffered could he provide heroic and wise leadership. Given the suffering, King and every black had a perfect right to hate whites for the evil they perpetuated. But instead, King sought to channel the pain and frustration into love, including love of whites and even the love of segregationists. He sought to transform love from the sticky sentiment we see on television soap operas into the powerful force that it can be. He renamed Gandhi's satyagraha, "soulforce," and because the blacks of America had the most soul and the most love, he was convinced that this would give them the power they needed to end segregation. They would transform themselves from second-class citizens and they would transform whites from the hatemongers of segregation by compassionate action.

King believed that a successful civil rights movement must be based upon a philosophy and ethic of love, because only love is able to transform such a situation. Love is able to overcome the hate and fear in each heart, but violence only perpetuates hate. With violence, the victor of one battle simply oppresses the losers until one day the losers are able to collect enough weapons to overcome the winners and then oppress them in turn in a never-ending cycle of violence. Love allows the participant to obtain his or her full dignity from the beginning, to prove that he or she is somebody. Equally important, love allows for the permanent transformation of both the oppressor and the oppressed. But a strategy based on an ethic of love requires great sacrifices on the part of the people in the movement.

Just as King was not sentimental about love, he was not sentimental about human nature either. He saw humans as a mixture of good and evil, and he saw clearly that in our collective, social life, evil tends to prevail. Yet within each human he believed that there is an amazing potential for goodness. Human beings, no matter how degraded, have in themselves the divine spark. Because of this, they have a limitless potential for growth, for transformation, and for responding to generous treatment. Human nature is susceptible to change; evil can be converted into good because people have in their souls an impulse to realize the inherent divinity of their self. What a powerful vision of human nature. How seldomly we believe that our brothers and sisters can be changed, that they too are children of the same God.

King's views were not left abstract because he always remembered the suffering of his people. He began his leadership of the civil rights movement in Montgomery in 1956 with a firm vision of the Beloved Community, with a knowledge of the nonviolent, direct-action tactics already developed by Gandhi, and with a commitment to use Christian suffering to overcome the entrenched system of segregation. By the end of his life a decade later, King had added to these the vision of the Exodus experience central to Judaism. King saw that blacks were in a situation comparable to the Jewish slaves in Egypt. Now that they had been freed, they were wandering in the wilderness. King, like Moses, had been up to the mountaintop and had personally seen the promised land. He knew he would not live to enter this land of freedom, justice, and equality with his people. But he promised that we would make it, that the children of former slaves and of former slaveholders would learn at last to live like brothers and sisters.

What makes King an even greater hero is that he was not parochial and narrow in his vision. He struggled not only for civil rights in America, but he also spoke against the Vietnam War long before Americans generally recognized the mistakes of that war. If he were alive today, there is no doubt he would be against U.S. policies in Central America and South Africa because his vision was that we would all eventually live together in peace in a single-world household.

Martin Luther King, Jr., has many lessons of compassion to teach us. He teaches that it is not enough to worry about our own plight or about members of our immediate family or our friends. We must come to see the suffering of all our brothers and sisters. Giving a few dollars to churches, charities, or good causes is not enough to save our conscience. Brother Martin teaches us that if we believe in the Kingdom of God, in the Beloved Community, then we are called to active struggle against injustice. We are called actively to oppose oppression without hating the oppressor. We are called to put our bodies on the line in the struggle for freedom from injustice. We are called to witness, to take risks, and to act. Sentiment is not enough. Only action is a sufficient response to injustice.

Martin Luther King, Jr., was not just an effective political leader. His leadership of the civil rights movement was possible only because of a profound religious experience that transformed his "inherited religion" into "an experience with God in the way that you must . . . if you are going to walk the lonely paths of life." His most profound conversion or transformative experience occurred late Friday night, January 27, 1956, during the Montgomery bus boycott. He had been jailed that day and that evening received yet another phone call in which the caller threatened, "Nigger, we are tired of you and your mess now. And if you aren't out of town in three days, we're going to blow your brains out and blow up your house."

> I sat there and thought about a beautiful little daughter who had just been born. . . . She was the darling of my life. I'd come in night after night and see that little gentle smile. And I sat at that table thinking about that little girl and thinking about the fact that she could be taken away from me any minute.
>
> And I started thinking about a dedicated, devoted, and loyal wife, who was over there asleep. And she could be taken from me, or I could be taken from her. And I got to the point that I couldn't take it any longer. I was weak. Something said to me, you can't call on Daddy now, he's up in Atlanta a hundred and seventy-five miles away. You can't even call on Mama now. You've got to call on that something in that person that your Daddy used to tell you about, that power that can make a way out of no way.
>
> And I discovered then that religion had to become real to me, and I had to know God for myself. And I bowed down over that cup of coffee. I never will forget it . . . I prayed a prayer, and I prayed out loud that night. I said, 'Lord, I'm down here trying to do what's right. I think I'm right. I think the cause that we represent is right. But Lord, I must confess that I'm weak now. I'm faltering. I'm losing my courage. And I can't let the people see me like this because if they see me weak and losing my courage, they will begin to get weak."
>
> Then it happened:
>
> And it seemed that at that moment that I could hear an inner voice saying to me, 'Martin Luther, stand up for righteousness. Stand up for

justice. Stand up for truth. And lo I will be with you, even until the end of the world.' . . . I heard the voice of Jesus saying still to fight on. He promised never to leave me, never to leave me alone. No never alone. . . .

That experience gave King a new strength and courage. "Almost at once my fears began to go. My uncertainty disappeared." He went back to bed no longer worried about the threats of bombings.[34]

King knew the pain of segregation in his life, but he also felt the love of God. When others became bitter and discouraged or turned to violence, he held fast to nonviolence. He taught that "your highest loyalty is to God . . . If any earthly institution conflicts with God's will, it is your Christian duty to oppose it." He believed, at a minimum, that a righteous person must refuse to cooperate with an evil system. Loyalty to God also gave him the faith that "we shall overcome." And to overcome meant, as the Gospel of Luke foretold, that from east and west and north and south we would all come. We would all gather around a common table and share food, fellowship, and love. For King, who had been to the mountaintop, promised us that we would enter the promised land.

Sathya Sai Baba

Sathya Sai Baba is a spiritual leader currently living in India. Like Jesus Christ, he claims to be an avatar, an incarnation of God. His teachings are based upon Hindu principles as reflected in sacred Hindu Scriptures, although he quotes from other sacred texts such as the Hebrew and Christian scriptures. In this he is much like his countryman, Gandhi.

The path Sai Baba offers to his devotees is one of bhakthi yoga, the path of dedication and devotion to God. This compassionate worship has two aspects—love of God and service to our brothers and sisters.

Sai Baba teaches that "the only method by which the delusion of desire can be destroyed is to dedicate all activities to God and engage in them in a spirit of worship, leaving the consequences to [God] and ceasing to attach yourself to them. Look upon everyone as an embodiment of the Divine and worship each as such, by offering Love, Understanding, and Service." Thus, Sai Baba expands the traditional Hindu teaching of Krishna in the Bhagavad Gita. Krishna taught that we should act and leave the fruit of the action to God. Sai Baba teaches that we should have as our motive for action the worship of the God aspect we see in other people. Our action is thus guided by compassion which lets us see God in others. Sai Baba proclaims: "The joy one gets while promoting another's joy is incomparable. Your heart must melt in compassion when the eye sees another person suffering."[35]

The religious path Sai Baba offers is based upon two fundamental principles: *bhakthi,* or devotion to God, and *prema* or selfless love, compassion, *agape.* As Sai Baba puts it, "The fulfillment of [a person's] life on earth consists in filling [themselves] with love of God and transmuting that love into acts of service, service [to others] who [are] the embodiment of God."[36]

Thus, devotion to God brings *prema* which leads inevitably to acts of compassion which are known in sanskrit as *seva* [service]. Service is not simply a byproduct of religious belief but the spiritual discipline known as karma yoga. It is said by many gurus to be the most direct path to God:

> More than austerities, more than meditation, service to others is the means by which [we] transform [ourselves]. . . .
>
> You should believe that service is a path to God realization. These activities are to be undertaken not for Sathya Sai or even for society. They are purely and essentially for your own sake. It is to transform your life that you undertake service. Through the medium of service you can reap the fruits of recitation of [God's] name and meditation. By making your fellow beings happy you are making God . . . happy. You should not do service out of a sense of compulsion or to please others. It should be wholehearted and spontaneous.[37]

Prema allows us to overcome six stumbling blocks to self-realization or our merging with God. According to Sai Baba, they are lust, anger, greed, attachment, conceit, and hatred. Thus, *prema* as love is not lust, not anger, not greed, not attachment, not conceit, and not hatred. *Prema* is connected to the love of God or *bhakthi,* but we have to worship God in human form. God appears before us as a blind beggar, an idiot, a leper, a child, a decrepit old man, a criminal, or a madman. We must see behind those veils the Divine Embodiment of Love, Power, and Wisdom, the Sai, and worship God through *seva* to our fellow human.[38] This is very similar to Mother Teresa's description of the lepers she cares for as "Christ in all his distressing disguises." In *How Can I Help?* Ram Das and Paul Gorman quote a woman who comes to see the common identity with her cancerous father the same way: "But what came through to me was a feeling for my father's identity as . . . a child of God. That was who [God] really was behind the 'distressing disguise.' And it was my real identity too, I felt a great bond with him which wasn't anything like I'd felt as father and daughter."[39]

When we give to our fellow beings, we are giving to God, and we receive God's blessing in return. As Sai Baba says: "When you offer milk to a hungry child or a blanket to a shivering brother on the street, you are only placing a gift of God into the hands of another gift of God! You are placing the gift of God in a repository of the Divine Principle."[40]

Sai Baba, like Jesus, teaches compassion as simultaneous love of God and love of our fellow children of God. As Gandhi developed his teaching from the Hindu principles of *satya* and *ahimsa,* Sai Baba grounds his in a *bakthi yoga* of *prema* and *seva.* Service given from right motives provides the most direct path to self-realization and oneness with God:

> Do not think of the fame or praise you win; think of the good that people derive. Do not crave for publicity; crave for the joy that shines in the face of the people whom you help. *Seva* brings you nearer to me. . . .
> Through *seva,* you realize that all beings are waves of the Ocean of Divinity. No other *sadhana* [spiritual discipline] can bring you into the incessant contemplation of the One-ness of all living beings. You feel another's pain as your own; you share another's success as your own. To see every one else as yourself and yourself in everyone, this is the core of the *sadhana* of *seva.* Again, *seva* makes the ego languish for the want of food. It makes you humble before the suffering of others, and when you rush to render help, you do not calculate how high or low [their] social or economic status is. . . .
> Whatever you do as service, to whomsoever, you offer the act, believe that it reaches the God in that person . . .[41]

Sai Baba is by no means alone among modern leaders of Eastern religions in his teachings. For instance, Bapak Mhd. Sumohadiwijojo, an Indonesian religious leader, teaches the path of Subud, which is an abbreviation of three Sanskrit words—*Susila, Budhi,* and *Dharma.*

> Susila means to be able to live according to the Will of God as really true human beings.
> Budhi indicates that in every creation, in every creature of God, including [humans], there is divine power which works within [them] as well as outside [them].
> Dharma means the possibility for every creature, including [humans], to surrender completely to the Will of God, of whom [each of us] is only a creation and has therefore, inevitably, to submit to the Will of [our] Creator.[42]

The teachings of Bapak include a particular method, similar to meditation, of achieving direct contact with God. Like Sai Baba's *bakthi yoga,* "the only way to attain contact with the Great Life or with the Power of God can never be other than by [a person's] complete and sincere surrender."[43] The spiritual exercises in Subud lead directly and naturally to service not only to other Subud adherents but to the poor. Thus, the Subud organization, like many religious groups, has opened a host of clinics and service projects, particularly in the developing nations, to help the sick, orphans, and the very poor. This service results not only from directions given by Bapak himself but from the teachings received directly by devotees in the spiritual exercises of Subud.

Chogyam Trungpa, a Tibetan spiritual teacher now living in the United States, provides yet another slant on many of the same lessons as Sai Baba. Trungpa teaches of *shambhala*, or the sacred path of the warrior, that has evolved out of Tibetan Buddhism. In a secular form of this philosophy Trungpa teaches that "the key to warriorship and the first principle of *shambhala* vision is not being afraid of who you are. Ultimately that is the definition of bravery: not being afraid of yourself."[44] In this understanding, every person has a basic nature of goodness. As with many Eastern religious paths, we confirm this through meditation. Meditation allows us to recognize our own value, to develop gentleness toward ourselves, and fully to appreciate the goodness of our world.

Having made the discovery of basic goodness, the warrior is able to generate warmth and compassion for others. For *shambhala* bravery "is the courage to be—to live in the world without any deception and with tremendous kindness and caring for others." The *shambhala* path is one of both inner development and outer action. Trungpa writes that "if we try to solve society's problems without overcoming the confusion and aggression in our own state of mind, then our efforts will only contribute to the basic problems, instead of solving them. That is why the individual journey of warriorship must be undertaken before we can address the larger issue of how to help this world."[45]

Thus Eastern religious teachers like Bapak and Trungpa—but most especially, Sathya Sai Baba—enlarge our understanding of compassion. Their message in its simplest form is that God is available to us either through meditation or through direct contact with avatars. In response, we are called upon to surrender ourselves to God and to discover the God within us. Upon discovering God within us, we are moved by compassion to undertake direct service to others. When we properly discover ourselves, eliminate the confusion and aggression in our own state of mind, we are able more effectively to achieve self-realization by our actions in the world. Devotion to God and discovery of oneself lead not to a retreat from the world, but, through love, to effective service. As we rid ourselves of lust, anger, greed, attachment, conceit, and hatred, we gain the understanding, strength, and clarity to act effectively in the world although always leaving the results of our actions to God.

Dorothy Day

The final teacher of compassion to be considered is Dorothy Day. Her path is particularly instructive because she began as a political radical and as a thoroughly secular person. Only later did she turn to a religious path and in the process create the unique Catholic worker movement in the United States. Like King and Gandhi, she made a synthesis of religion and politics—beginning, however, with politics and adding to it a deep piety rather than beginning with religion and later discovering politics. Daniel Berrigan has called her an "exemplar, mystic, lover of life, fighter of the good fight." He concludes that "in Catholicism she came not so much to her own place . . . as to her true self. . . . what she had lost (her lover and friend) she measured against all she had gained: a terrible beauty was born." She wrote of herself after her religious experiences: "I have not always felt the richness of life, its sacredness. I do not see how people can, without a religious faith."[46] So Dorothy Day's life was a long journey from secular joys, concerns, and experiences to a discovery of the richness of life and its sacredness. In her journey she did not discard her secular experiences; rather, she enriched them as she reordered her life.

In her youth, Dorothy Day was disillusioned by the church. If God meant everyone to be happy, she could not understand the misery and poverty of the world. Out of her disillusion she joined the Socialist party and turned her back on religion. As she wrote in her autobiography:

> Children look at things very directly and simply. I did not see anyone taking off his coat and giving it to the poor. I didn't see anyone having a banquet and calling in the lame, the halt and the blind. And those who were doing it, like the Salvation Army did not appeal to me. I wanted, though I did not know it then, a synthesis. I wanted life and I wanted the abundant life. I wanted it for others too. I did not want just the few, the missionary-minded people like the Salvation Army, to be kind to the poor, as poor. I wanted everyone to be kind. I wanted every home to be open to the lame, the halt and the blind . . . [47]

After two years of college in Illinois, Dorothy Day moved to New York and began her career as a journalist with a Socialist newspaper. There she lived with the poor in tenements. She wrote of the poor, of the struggling labor movement, and of injustice. She was soon jailed for participating in a suffragist protest. In general, she lived fully the life of a secular, political radical.

After several years of happiness in a common-law marriage, she gave birth to a child, Tamar Teresa. Her decision to baptize the child and to be baptized as a Catholic herself brought drastic changes in her life. As she wrote: "I knew that I was going to have my child baptized, cost what it may. I knew that I was not going to have her floundering through many years as I had done, doubting and hesitating, undisciplined and amoral. I felt it was the greatest thing I could do for my child. For myself, I prayed for the gift of faith."

So Dorothy Day came to the point of decision:

> It was all very well to love God in [God's] works, in the beauty of [God's] creation which was crowned for me by the birth of my child. Forster [her lover] had made the physical world come alive for me and had awakened in my heart a flood of gratitude. The final object of this love and gratitude was God. . . .
>
> It was not because I was tired of sex, satiated, disillusioned, that I turned to God. . . . It was because through a whole love, both physical and spiritual, I came to know God.[48]

Dorothy's decision also meant leaving her other love, the radical political movement. Joining the church seemed to be going over to the opposition "because of course the Church was lined up with property, with the wealthy, with the state, with capitalism, with all the forces of reaction." But Dorothy met a former French peasant Catholic leader, Peter Maurin, who helped her merge her political radicalism with her fervent Catholicism. Together they created a new movement with a four-point program including roundtable discussions, houses of hospitality for the poor in the cities, the *Catholic Worker* newspaper, and agronomic universities or communal farms in the countryside. They adopted a dual approach of charity and direct service on the one hand and education and protest on the other. They concluded that "the spiritual works of mercy include enlightening the ignorant, rebuking the sinner, consoling the afflicted, as well as bearing wrongs patiently, and we have always classed picket lines and the distribution of literature among these works."[49] Thus, political action was merged with piety.

The Catholic worker movement was not a separate movement for justice which knew of the poor only in theory. It was with the poor in their struggles. Day put it this way:

> Going around and seeing . . . [the poor]is not enough. To help organizers, to give what you have for relief, to pledge yourself to voluntary poverty for life so that you can share with your brothers [and sisters] is not enough. One must live with them, share with them their suffering too. Give up one's privacy, and mental and spiritual comforts as well as physical. . . .
>
> Yes, we have lived with the poor, with the workers and we know them not just from the streets, or in mass meetings, but from years of living in the slums, in tenements, in our hospices . . . [50]

Obviously, these are heavy demands. But they are not meant to be the demands for acts by individual saints and martyrs. Day's call is for a community of people. "The only answer in this life, to the loneliness we are all bound to feel, is community. The living together, working together, sharing together, loving God and loving our brother, and living close to him in community so we can show our love for [God]."[51] Once again the message of compassion and transformation is confirmed. We can only discover and be one with God when we find God in the suffering and the joys of our brothers and sisters.

Beginning as a political radical who later became an ardent Christian, Day reinforces many of the lessons from the other teachers of compassion. Worship God, build community, serve the poor and those who suffer most—this is the path of the good life and the only escape from the long loneliness of our individual existence. Religiously and politically, compassion provides the only path to true community with our brothers and sisters, with ourselves, and with God.

Dorothy Day summed up the results of the politics of compassion and transformation as community and love.

> I found myself, a barren woman, the joyful mother of children. It is not easy always to be joyful, to keep in mind the duty of delight.
>
> The most significant thing about *The Catholic Worker* is poverty, some say.
>
> The most significant thing is community, others say. We are not alone any more.
>
> But the final word is love. At times it has been, in the words of Father Zossima, a harsh and dreadful thing, and our very faith in love has been tried through fire.
>
> We cannot love God unless we love each other, and to love each we must know each other. We know [God] in the breaking of bread, and we know each other in the breaking of bread, and we are not alone any more. Heaven is a banquet and life is a banquet, too, even with a crust, where there is companionship.
>
> We have all known the long loneliness and we have learned that the only solution is love and that love comes with community.[52]

Conclusion

What ultimately do we learn from these teachers of compassion? How do they deepen our understanding of a politics of transformation? They do not share a single, monolithic view of God; they do not define a single form of compassion that can be identified by clear, superficial characteristics; and they do not even advocate, in all circumstances, a single course of political action which we can unthinkingly adopt. Rather, these teachers of compassion provide us a richer understanding of compassion because they come from different cultures, from different historical periods, and each possesses unique personalities. Instead of defining compassion for us in rational terms, they point to what it would mean for *us* to practice a politics of compassion and transformation as they did. They cause us to ask what it would mean to feel so deeply absolute religious principles, to know ourselves so completely, and to feel such sympathy with our fellow humans that we would have no choice but to act, to proclaim, to protest, and to strive unceasingly to alleviate suffering. These teachers of compassion call us to act despite our personal inadequacies, our unheroic natures, and possible risks or dangers. They demonstrate that the aware person has no choice but to act compassionately.

Although these teachers, by their lives, as well as by their formal teachings, provide role models for us, they offer explicit lessons as well. And their lessons amplify each other's messages. Despite their differences in circumstance, experience, and temperament, these teachers share a politics of compassion and transformation that they exemplified in their lives.

The Jewish prophets teach us to oppose "the religion of static triumphalism and the politics of oppression." By showing that idol gods are false, by offering an alternative politics of justice and compassion, they both destroy and build, pluck up and plant as the times demand. These prophets enjoin us to do justice, to love compassion, and, thereby, to walk humbly with our God.

Jesus extends the lessons of the prophets and teaches love as the supreme lesson. The fierce warrior god is transformed into the God of compassion. As a consequence Jesus himself healed the sick, comforted the poor, provided solace to the brokenhearted, and brought hope to the hopeless. The church which he founded, for all its faults, has continued to offer comfort and guidance for two thousand years. Nor was Jesus apolitical as many Christians have suggested. He was executed as a political prisoner. He drove the merchants out of the temple in Jerusalem. He frightened both the Jewish and Roman establishment of his day. Through the ages Jesus and his followers have continued to preach the necessity for justice, equality, and mercy, and, frequently, Christians have struggled for political transformations.

Meister Eckhart elaborated the compassion of the prophets and Jesus into a multifaceted, fourfold path of creativity, emptying, birthing, and transformation. He invites us to change ourselves, to discover the depth within us, so ultimately to transform the world. Eckhart teaches us that the positive, negative, creative, and transformative paths all lead to God.

Mahatma Gandhi was able to draw upon the religious principles of Hinduism as well as Christianity. He created a unique merger of contemplative religious principles and practical political action. This is his special contribution. Gandhi demonstrated how seemingly private, abstract Hindu principles of *satya* and *ahimsa* can become springboards and guides to action. From them he developed his doctrine of satyagraha and nonviolent direct action. He teaches us that we need not withdraw from the practical world of action in order to be religious; rather, we should act religiously in the world. Additionally, Gandhi teaches the importance of individual commitment, of religious vows, and of trusting the outcome of our actions to God.

Martin Luther King, Jr., extends Gandhian lessons of compassion to our own time and experience. He translated Jesus' Kingdom of God into his own Beloved Community which echoed the American dream of equality, justice, brotherhood, and peace. King transformed the pain of segregation, through compassion, for both oppressor and oppressed. He saw the need for blacks to redeem whites, as well as to free themselves, by self-sacrifice. Finally, he also proved that compassion need not be sentimental; that practical principles of nonviolent direct action, economic boycott, and political bargaining could flow from compassion. Indeed, with compassion to guide political action, the never-ending cycle of hate and violence could be broken, and the social transformation envisioned by Eckhart and demonstrated by Gandhi could become a reality even in our modern world.

Gandhi's fellow countryman, Sathya Sai Baba, along with many of the Eastern gurus and teachers, deepens our understanding of how religious devotion leads to love and love leads to positive action and service in the world. Once again, Hindu principles of *bhakthi*, *prema*, and *seva* are applied to the practical realities of developing India and to the broader world. Reinforcing the same message as Jews and Christians, Sai Baba teaches that we find God in others so that when we act to create justice we give the gift of God to God. The dualism of the inward journey of self-development and the outward concern for problems of the world is overcome as we act to discover ourselves while acting to resolve worldly problems. The path to peace and justice involves ridding ourselves of lust, anger, greed, attachment, conceit, and hatred. It also involves filling ourselves with God's love whether we achieve that through self-discovery or through worship of incarnations of God like Jesus and Sai Baba.

Dorothy Day demonstrates that there are many ways to create lives of compassion and transformation. She began as a secular, political radical. She bore a child out of an unsanctioned common-law marriage. But she turned to the church for the baptism of her child and became a devout Catholic. She was a lay leader—not an ordained priest or nun. Yet, she founded the Catholic worker movement in which members lived with the poor; served them directly with food, shelter, and hope; and which constantly agitated for social progress, justice, and peace. Like Jesus and Gandhi, Dorothy gave up the comforts of higher classes to live and to serve the poor. And she joined together the teachings of religion with direct political action in an unceasing struggle guided by compassion.

Each of these teachers of compassion moved in their lives toward depth and toward God. They had direct contact with God in differing ways—through visions, meditation, and prayer. They came to be motivated not by mere ambition but by religious principles. Yet their religion called them not only to pray, to study, and to teach but also to act. It was through their actions that they best demonstrated their compassion. Their actions displayed both a quality of self-sacrifice and an obedience to the will of God.

Theirs was not the sort of politics taught in civic texts, advocated by television news commentators, or proposed by politicians in Rotary Club speeches. Nor is their religion usually recommended in sermons from the pulpit, in Sunday School lessons, or in most seminary courses.

No, compassionate politics is deeper, more profound, and more demanding than traditional politics or religion will admit. These teachers can open our hearts and our minds to this path. Even so, there comes a point when studying their words and deeds will no longer suffice. We must find our own way to God. Ultimately, there comes a time when we must act as our conscience demands.

Can these teachers help us to find a path, a way to combat the great crises facing our world today? Are their teachings, their example, and their faith a sufficient support in our struggle? They point the way to finding ourselves and to finding God. As they had the strength to face the terrible crises of their times—the destruction of earlier nations, colonialism, racial discrimination, and war—they provide an example of hope. Through a politics of compassion and transformation, our individual efforts can be made effective—light can yet shine in the darkness of our time and guide us to overcome the worst aspects of the crises we face. These teachers of compassion do not promise us easy victories, nor do they guarantee that the entire human race will be easily transformed. But they demonstrate how to be cocreators with God in the continuation of life on the planet. They show us how to combat injustice.

Chapter 4
THE CALL TO JUSTICE AND COMPASSION

The eighth and most meritorious degree of charity is to anticipate charity by preventing poverty.
                                        Mishnah Torah,
                                        Matnot Aniyim 10:17

[People] today tend to waste their time in selfish pursuits instead of devoting it to selfless service. They are eager to receive help from others, but have no desire to render help.
   There are two types of human beings: the degraded and the sublime. The degraded are those who seek or receive things from others and not only forget to repay the obligation, but even try to harm those who have helped them. The sublime are those whose natural trait is to go to the help of others.
                                        Sathya Sai Baba, Christmas 1985

Compassionate and transformative politics is based upon a theology of compassion. Components of that theology are formed from teachings of different religious groups, but a theology of compassion achieves its most comprehensive expression by integrating diverse theologies.

The original teachers of compassion demonstrated how the compassionate life is to be lived. They also founded religions and religious movements that developed formal theologies. These theologies in their own way also lead to compassion, but they have been diverted to many other purposes as well. Although each religious sect has something special to teach us about compassion, an explicit theology of compassion is a more adequate expression of their religious thought. Collectively their lessons are great.

In one sense compassion is a spontaneous movement of the heart and, therefore, requires no careful thought to be understood. But a theology of compassion is a deeper reflection upon that direct experience. Knowing what is to be done and understanding how to do it requires reflection. Let us begin by considering the important contributions various religions can make collectively to our understanding of compassion, justice, and social transformation.

93

Judaism

Judaism teaches us that the ultimate goal of compassion, both ours and God's, is justice. The prophets of the Hebrew Scriptures are unequivocal. Israel and Judah were constantly rebuked for their unjust treatment of the poor. Consider the preaching of the prophet Amos:

> Thus says the Lord: For the three and for the four crimes of Israel I have made my decree and will not relent; because they have sold the virtuous for silver and the poor for a pair of shoes, because they trample on the heads of ordinary people and push the poor out of their path. . . .
> Listen to this, you who trample on the needy and try to suppress the poor people of the country, you who say, "When will New Moon be over so that we can sell our corn, and sabbath, so that we can market our wheat?" Then, by lowering the bushel, raising the shekel, by swindling and tampering with the scales, we can buy up the poor for money, and the needy for a pair of sandals and get a price even for the sweeping of the wheat. . . .
> Let me have no more of the din of your chanting, no more of your strumming on harps. But let justice flow like water and integrity like an unfailing stream.
> (Amos 2:6-7; 8:4-5; and 5:23-24)

Amos condemns Israel when land is stolen from the poor, when peasants suffer at the hands of the rich and are cheated by landowners and merchants. God demands, according to Amos, not just worship in the temple or synagogue using certain prayers, hymns, and rituals, not merely formal observation of the sabbath, but justice, integrity, and charity.

An important continuing theme in the Hebrew Scriptures is the relationship to the land. "The earth is the Lord's," and the corollary to this principle is that "you are all strangers and sojourners with me." (Leviticus 25:23) Additional provisions of Jewish religious law are:

● Land could never be sold in perpetuity.

● Fields were not to be mowed twice nor harvested to the edge.

● Third year tithes were to go not to the temple but to alien newcomers, single parents and the parentless.

● Bread was to be dealt to the hungry and the homeless brought into the home, but the needy were also to be received in ways that made for stability "that they may dwell with you and you with them."

● Interest was not to be charged on loans since this was an instrument of dispossession.

● During a sabbath year land was to lie fallow serving as a commons affording an opportunity for indentured people to work themselves free.

• During a seventh sabbath or jubilee year land acquisitions were to return to original family lines.[1]

The intent of these provisions was to prevent absolute poverty and oppression. However, in our time these laws need to be translated to appropriate actions that guarantee work and substance for everyone. The bounty of the earth belongs to all God's creatures, not just to the rich. Our task is to restore the just balance in society as the religious laws required in ancient Israel. Obviously, an America which has nearly forty million poor people, at least twelve million hungry, and three million homeless has failed to follow Hebrew teachings.

As to the Hebrew prophets, B. D. Napier has written that "prophetism may legitimately be defined as that understanding of history which accepts meaning only in terms of divine concern, divine purpose, divine participation." The prophet receives and reports by prophetic oracle the Word of God:

> The prophet receives, possibly and even probably in ecstatic concentration, the actual *dabhar*, the real Word of Yahweh; and here we are confronted by a significant aspect of the phenomenon of revelation. But the Word thus received is not always precisely intelligible in a process of recall which requires its appropriation and integration in the rational mode; and the prophet in consequence, feels himself [or herself] called upon by means of the speech of invective to interpret and direct, to point and apply, the word of judgment, the revealed Word of Yahweh.

Thus, a prophet is "an announcer" or "the one who 'announces' the purpose and activity of God."[2] And this Word of God is powerful. Psalm 33: 6-9 declares:

> By his word the heavens were made,
> and all their host by the breath of his mouth.
> For he spoke, and it came to pass;
> he commanded, and it stood forth.

Rabbi Abraham Heschel has given perhaps the definitive modern Jewish interpretation of prophets and their task: "The prophet is a [person] who feels fiercely. . . . Prophecy is the voice that God has lent to the silent agony, a voice to the plundered poor, to the profaned riches of the world. It is a form of living, a crossing point of God and [human]. God is raging in the prophet's words." It is thus the task of the prophet "to declare the Word of God to the here and now; to disclose the future in order to illuminate what is involved in the present." So prophecy tells a people what God is doing and, therefore, what humans should do. As Rabbi Heschel declares, "the phenomenon of prophecy is predicated upon the assumption that [we are] both in need of, and entitled to, divine guidance. For God to reveal [God's] word through the prophet to [God's] people is an act of justice or an act seeking justice. The purpose of prophecy is to maintain the covenant, to establish the right relationship between God and [humans]."[3]

I previously quoted Walter Brueggemann's *Prophetic Imagination* to show that Moses and the later prophets were involved in a break from the "religion of static triumphalism and the politics of oppression and exploitation." Brueggemann goes on to suggest that the prophet has three basic tasks:

(a) To *offer symbols* that are adequate to the horror and massiveness of the experience which evokes numbness. . . .

(b) To *bring to public expression those very fears and terrors* that have been denied so long and suppressed so deeply. . . .

(c) To *speak metaphorically but concretely about the real deathliness that hovers over us and gnaws within us* . . . with the candor born of anguish and passion.[4]

At first it may appear that the role of the prophet is not particularly political: "Moses did not engage in anything like what we identify as social action. His concern was with the consciousness that undergirded and made the [Egyptian] regime possible. . . . The prophetic purpose is much more radical than social change . . . because the issues that concern the Mosaic tradition are much more profound than the matters we usually regard as social action." Yet the prophet's opposition to the regime provides a vision of newness: "It is the vocation of the prophet to keep alive the ministry of imagination, to keep on conjuring and proposing alternative futures to the single one the king wants to urge as the only thinkable one."[5] Thus, prophets, in criticizing the religious underpinnings, in decrying the social injustices of their time, in calling a people back to their covenant with God, and in upholding a vision of alternative positive futures, are engaged in religious acts intended to bring fundamental social transformation.

It is important to realize that Jewish prophets, or at least followers of Jewish prophetic demands for justice, did not die out two thousand years ago. Rabbi Abraham Joshua Heschel is only one example of modern Jews who carry the mantel of the prophets. Speaking of God Heschel said, "God wants justice and compassion." Speaking of the ancient Jewish prophets he said, "The message of the prophets was that love is alive." Working on his book about the prophets changed his own life so that by the time he marched with Dr. King on civil rights marches he concluded that "my legs were praying." He worked ecumenically to found Clergy and Laity Concerned, which led the anti-Vietnam War Movement. In summing up Heschel's life and his contributions to practical Jewish theology Rabbi Byron Sherwin concludes:

> Heschel's life was a "passion for truth," a struggle for sincerity. His harsh critique of contemporary Jewish life drew few Jewish partisans to his banner during his lifetime. [He died in 1972.] An institution in Jewish life himself, he posed too great of a threat to Jewish institutional life. He was rebuked by some Jewish leaders for his activities in civil rights, denounced by others for his repudiation of the war in Vietnam, and condemned by many for his opposition to Richard Nixon [and his support of George McGovern in the 1972 election]. But Heschel's quest was for integrity not popularity. He aspired to be an heir of the prophets rather than to become a modern celebrity. He preferred radical authenticity to institutionalized mediocrity.[6]

It must be understood that the teachings of Judaism do not depend only upon the prophetic tradition. Jewish theology is embedded in the Scriptures themselves. For there is not a single author of the Torah; rather, it was rewritten by different writers during different historical circumstances. The ancient oral history was written first by authors from the Northern kingdom whose country had been destroyed and by authors in the Southern kingdom which was threatened. Additional passages were added by priestly editors living after the Babylonian captivity. To the Torah and historical books of the Hebrew Scripture were added wisdom literature, the prophets, and the psalms.

A continuing theme throughout all these Scriptures is the call to justice and compassion. For instance, the Mosaic laws, from the Ten Commandments to the more than six hundred Deuteronomic rules, are meant, fundamentally, to create a just society, a community governed by "Shalom" [peace and justice]. Interpretations of these laws in the Talmud and the Mishnah Torah, are meant to provide the same kind of guidance—to show how the covenant with God and the just community is to be achieved in activities of everyday life. For example, there is the teaching in the Mishnah Torah that the "most meritorious degree of charity" is to prevent poverty.

Jewish theology may focus on the "chosen people" but the stranger is to be treated as a member of the family, the poor are to be provided for, and justice is to prevail. The "chosen people" are to be an example to the rest of the world so that all people may come to worship God and build just societies. All this is the work of compassion. The Jewish teachings of compassion from the ancient prophets up to Rabbi Heschel today remain unbroken.

Evangelical Christianity

Evangelical Christians take the Gospel according to Matthew as the biblical starting point for developing their theology of compassion:

> When the Son of Man comes in his glory and all his angels with him, he will sit in state on his throne with all the nations gathered before him. He will separate the people into two groups, as a shepherd separates the sheep from the goats. And he will place the sheep on his right hand and the goats on his left . . . Then he will say to those on his left hand, "The curse is upon you; go from my sight to the eternal fire that is ready for the devil and his angels. For when I was hungry you gave me nothing to eat, when thirsty nothing to drink; when I was a stranger you gave me no home, when naked you did not clothe me; when I was ill and in prison you did not come to my help." And they too will reply, "Lord, when was it that we saw you hungry or thirsty or a stranger or naked or ill or in prison and did nothing for you?" And he will answer, "I tell you this: anything you did not do for one of these, however humble, you did not do for me."
>
> (Matthew 25:31-33, 41-45)

The commandment is clear enough. Christians are to feed the hungry, provide shelter for the homeless, and comfort the poor. Providing direct assistance to those in need is the heart of the evangelical movement, and it is based upon direct scriptural authority. This can, of course, promote a personal and individualistic response to fundamental problems when social and economic systems are the real cause of poverty. But such a limiting interpretation need not be taken.

Evangelical Christianity has gone from being apolitical and divorced from politics to active involvement. As Rev. Richard Neuhaus asserts in his 1985 article, "What the Fundamentalists Want," America has not become the totally secular society predicted by social scientists during the 1960s and 1970s.[7] In the 1970s social scientists were concluding that "a normative order based on religious beliefs and values is no longer possible."[8] Today, "94 percent of the American people profess belief in God, 88 percent say the Bible is the inspired Word of God, 90 percent identify themselves religiously with a specific Christian denomination or as Jews, [and] 89 percent of us say we pray regularly. . . ."[9] Religions, including Evangelical Christianity, have remained important in our lives.

In Judeo-Christian America, "fundamentalists" are united around certain critical beliefs or fundamentals: "the inerrancy of Scripture (the Bible contains no errors in any subject on which it speaks); the virgin birth of Jesus (the Spirit of God conceived Jesus in Mary without human intervention); the substitutionary atonement of Jesus Christ (on the cross he bore the just punishment for the sins of the entire world); his bodily resurrection; the authenticity of the biblical miracles; and pre-millennialism [the belief that Jesus will return to establish a thousand-year reign of peace before the end of the world]." Fundamentalists have become more politically active recently because "they are responding to an assault upon their religious freedom." They are responding to the outlawing of prayer in the public schools, to aggressive "interference" by the IRS in taxing their religious activities such as their private schools, to attempts by states to regulate their Christian day schools, and to the legalizing of abortion. Moreover, through the American Coalition for Traditional Values, fundamentalists have agreed to ten political proposals to "restore traditional moral and spiritual values" to American life. "The list includes prayer and Bible reading in public schools, a 'pro-life' amendment (or some other instrument for overruling *Roe v. Wade*), legal restrictions on pornography, an end to state 'harassment' of Christian schools, resistance to feminist and gay-rights legislation, increased defense spending, and terminating social programs that, it is believed, only increase the dependency of the poor."[10] Put succinctly by Rev. Jerry Falwell, the Moral Majority which he founded in 1979, is "prolife, protraditional family . . . opposed to the illegal drug traffic and pornography . . . [and] pro-American which means strong national defense and [support for] the State of Israel."[11]

Evangelical Christians need not be politically conservative. Strong biblical faith can also be combined with radical leftist politics. Jim Wallis and the members of his Sojourners Community in Washington, D.C., are no more friendly to mainstream liberal religion than Jerry Falwell. Wallis has written that

> liberal religion has often produced a secular theology which also has become a conformist religion. The lack of biblical foundations, the eroding of transcendence in theology, the depreciation of personal conversion and commitment, and the uncritical conformity to contemporary social and political options and trends have led to a secularization in liberal religion and conformity as real as that of the cultural theology of conservative religion. . . . Without a firm basis in revelation, the theological agenda can only be derived from the changing assumptions, thought forms, and social movements of secular culture.[12]

According to Wallis, our religious duty is to oppose those institutions in our society that oppress people. We experience these "powers and principalities," as they are called by Saint Paul, "in their dominion over us."

Biblical faith brings a word of judgment and correction to any culture or political system and suggests that the state is never to be made an object of religious loyalty. . . .

Our obedience [to Christ] must necessarily consist in public and visible nonconformity which embraces specific attitudes and acts, demonstrating opposition to these powers and idols and thereby witnessing to Christ's victory over them.[13]

From Wallis's point of view, religious people are to oppose the evil in society and to create "structures and relationships which are more serving of human life, justice, and freedom. . . . As a demonstration in history of God's love and purposes for human life in the world."[14] His Sojourner community attempts to be an example of King's "beloved community" and Jesus' Kingdom of God. It also acts politically in the broader community. It initiated the Pledge of Resistance campaign in which more than 50,000 people have pledged to engage in acts of civil disobedience if the U.S. government launches a military attack on Nicaragua. Already the Pledge of Resistance has coordinated regular demonstrations against U.S. policies in Central America and has been among the most visible opponents of Contra-Aid funding proposals by President Reagan.

Both conservative and radical evangelical Christians conclude that Christianity requires compassion in the form of service to the hungry, the poor, and the wretched. They also believe that political action is required to protect and advance moral principles. For fundamentalists this means participation in the electoral process, lobbying, and public demonstration against abortion clinics and pornography stores. For groups like Sojourners it means civil disobedience and the creation of alternative institutions closer to biblical mandates. Both engage in political action and are motivated by deeply held religious beliefs. The weakness of evangelical Christianity for most believers is its tendency to remain privatized, more concerned with personal salvation than with social transformation. When most fundamentalists enter politics it is in reaction to government rather than in response to broader social consciousness and concern. But both conservative fundamentalists and radical leftist evangelicals demonstrate that compassion can also lead to social transformation.

Liberal Christianity

Liberal Christians are concerned with social problems like hunger, homelessness, and joblessness. Because they tend to identify the church with the larger culture, they desire to "make the system work." They generally believe that educational programs, such as job training, will raise individuals from joblessness and therefore eliminate hunger and homelessness. Charitable organizations have emerged from this liberal perspective as responsible religious people attempt to reform the existing system to make it more just.

Liberal Christian theologians, from at least the publication in the 1920s of Friedrich Schleiermacher's *The Christian Faith*,[15] have attempted to answer modern science's skepticism about traditional Christian beliefs. They have tried "to show how a proper reinterpretation of modernity's most basic value commitments and a proper reinterpretation of Christianity's historic claims to truth and value can be—indeed must be—reconciled."[16]

David Tracy maintains that theologians address three audiences or publics: the wider society, the academic community, and the church.[17] This gives rise to practical, systematic, and fundamental theologies. Liberal theologians have attempted to convince the general public that Christianity was "modern," to convince their academic audience that Christian beliefs could be defended by reasoned arguments, and to convince the faithful in the church that Christianity was compatible with the modern work-a-day world in which they lived.

To do so, liberal Christians gave up believing (as fundamentalists do) in the absolute inerrancy of the Bible, the Virgin Birth, and biblical miracles as literal descriptions. They accommodated the general spread of scientific skepticism and modern cultural beliefs. The Calvinist principle of two kingdoms—the world and the Kingdom of God represented by the church—prevailed. In the worst cases this meant support for any government and an absolute "separation of church and state."

An example of liberal Christianity is to be seen in a 1981 letter from Elmer Johnson, a lay leader in the Presbyterian church, to officials of the American Enterprise Institute.

> We would like a society in which each individual is enabled and encouraged to develop his or her full potential as a rational and moral being; and we would like a society of intermediate communities (including enterprise units) in which these members interact with one another in mutually enriching and supportive ways.
>
> Though I start with some such ideals in mind, I am not a utopian. Rather my approach is to ask how we can best try *to modify the organization of economic life* so as to come closer to these ideals. . . .
>
> I think the "aggregative common good" is well served by a system that provides big incentives to entrepreneurs and managers and that encourages savings for investment. I also envision a system that would oblige successful entrepreneurs, managers and investors to become stewards of their wealth and their power. . . .
>
> If, as I believe, the market has this inherent weakness [unlimited faith in the capacity of the unguided masses to determine by their

individual decisions in the market place what goods and services shall be produced], then the real remedy lies in nature and in limited paternalistic restraints: restraints on credit extension, on advertising, maybe even on the hours and days that retail shops may open for business, and so on.[18]

Liberal Christianity need not lead to blind support of the status quo and the existing social, economic, and political system. Liberal Christians advocate, for example, an improved social welfare system, restraints upon economic elites, affirmative action in employment, and an enlarged sphere of civil rights.

However, many recent statements of faith by major denominations are silent on the duty of the religious individual, congregations, or the denomination in the civil arena. Thus, the statement of faith of the United Church of Christ adopted in 1959 says only that God calls us into [God's] Church to accept the cost and joy of discipleship, to be [God's] servants in the service of [humanity], to proclaim the gospel to all the world and resist the powers of evil, to share in Christ's baptism and eat at his table, to join him in his passion victory. [God] promises . . . courage in the struggle for justice and peace.[19]

Later denomination statements, such as the Presbyterian Confession of 1967, address some of the social and political crises of our times.

> This community, the church universal, is entrusted with God's message of reconciliation and shares [God's] labor of healing the enmities which separate [people] from God and from each other. . . .
>
> Wherever the church exists, its members are both gathered in corporate life and dispersed in society for the sake of mission in the world. . . .
>
> The church disperses to serve God wherever its members are, at work or play, in private or in the life of society. . . .
>
> In each time and place there are particular problems and crises through which God calls the church to act. . . . The following are particularly urgent at the present time. . . .
>
> The church labors for the abolition of all racial discrimination and ministers to those injured by it. . . .
>
> The church, in its own life, is called to practice the forgiveness of enemies and to commend to the nations as practical politics the search for cooperation and peace. . . .
>
> The reconciliation of [people] through Jesus Christ makes it plain that enslaving poverty in a world of abundance is an intolerable violation of God's good creation. . . .
>
> The relationship between man and woman exemplifies in a basic way

God's ordering of the interpersonal life for which [God] created [humankind]. Anarchy in sexual relationships is a symptom of [our] alienation from God, [our] neighbor, and [ourselves].[20]

Despite its social concerns, the overwhelming danger of liberal Christianity is that either in its acceptance of the status quo or in its attempt at reform, it will degenerate into merely a "civil religion" that supports "my country right or wrong." As Robert Bellah points out in *The Broken Covenant*: "In the beginning and to some extent ever since Americans have interpreted their history as having religious meaning, they saw themselves as being a 'people' in the classical and biblical sense of the word. They hoped they were a people of God."[21]

Thus, religion was used to bless expansionist aims of government. As Lewis Mudge argues in *Why Is the Church in the World?* "some of the most serious instances of idolatry occur in the absolutization of political and economic systems—social structures often so close to [people] that they fail to see how much they are enslaved by them." He argues that the Christian predisposition in politics, if it is to be true to the gospels must be "particularly concerned about the interests of the poor." He goes further to argue that

> The role of the church . . . is . . . *to see that the message of the contemporary revolution of dispossessed peoples gets through.* For just as God used the power of foreign nations against Israel, so we believe God is working today to tell us something, to confront us with our misunderstandings, our shortcomings, our lack of faith. . . . [This] *means that we must be involved in these events in such a way that our involvement becomes a parable of the message.*[22]

If liberal Christianity is not to be merely the servant of modern society and the particular government in power, if it is not to worship the culture rather than God, it must confront the crises of society and, at a minimum, insure that the voice of the poor and the dispossessed is heard.

The tendency of liberal Christians to become identified with the dominant culture rather than with those harmed and exploited is not a new trend but a recurring tension in Christianity. H. Richard Niebuhr, in his classic *Christ and Culture* labels this approach "Christ of Culture." He found it prominent among the Gnostics, for instance. "In the Gnostic version, knowledge of Jesus Christ was an individual and spiritual matter, which had its place in the life of the culture as the very pinnacle of human achievement. It was something that advanced souls could attain . . . [but] when what is called religion is separated from ethics it becomes something very different from what it is in the church: it is now a metaphysics, a 'Gnosis,' a mystery cult rather than a faith governing all life."[23]

In the Middle Ages, this reconciling of Christianity and culture was carried forward by church leaders like Peter Abelard. Others picked up this work in later centuries so that it has become in modern times the dominant Christian theological strand. In each era, theologians advocating the "Christ of Culture" seek to "reconcile the gospel with the science/and philosophy of their time." They also reconcile themselves to their government and the society in which they live comfortably. But this theological project is ultimately unsuccessful. Niebuhr writes:

> In so far as part of its purpose is always that of recommending the gospel to an unbelieving society, or to some special group, such as the intelligentsia, or political liberals or conservatives, or workingmen, it often fails to achieve its end because it does not go far enough, or because it is suspected of introducing an element that will weaken the cultural movement. It seems impossible to remove the offense of Christ and his cross even by means of these accommodations. . . .
>
> The cultural Christians encounter and partly recognize the presence of a revelation that cannot be completely absorbed into the life of reason.[24]

When liberal Christianity goes beyond mere idolatry and accommodation, it makes a major contribution to society. Because liberal Christians accept and understand modern science, culture, and institutions, they are able to bring the message of faith and the cry of the poor to secular society in a language in which it will be understood. Because of their own involvement in the world, they are able to advocate changes which, although they fall short of the Reign of God, improve society. Moreover, liberal Christians go beyond merely caring for individual victims to propose institutional reforms that can alleviate the misery of many.

In desperate situations, the spirit of liberal Christianity can stretch further than mere cultural accommodation and support for the regime. Compassion forces it to do so. Thus, Dietrich Bonhoeffer, who is sometimes characterized as theologically conservative but socially radical, could write from jail in Germany at the height of Hitler's reign that

> . . . it is precisely to the depths of downfall, of guilt and of misery that God stoops down in Jesus Christ; that precisely the dispossessed, the humiliated and the exploited, are especially near to the justice and mercy of God. . . .
>
> The hungry man needs bread and the homeless man needs a roof; the dispossessed need justice and the lonely need fellowship; the undisciplined need order and the slave needs freedom. To allow the hungry man to remain hungry would be blasphemy against God and

one's neighbor, for what is nearest to God is precisely the need of one's neighbor. It is for the love of Christ, which belongs as much to the hungry man as to myself, that I share my bread with him and that I share my dwelling with the homeless. If the hungry man does not attain to faith, then the guilt falls on those who refused him bread. To provide the hungry man with bread is to prepare the way for the coming of grace. . . .

The coming of grace is the ultimate. But we must speak of the preparing of the way, of the penultimate . . . [25]

Liberal Christians can, in times of crises, be moved to confront "penultimate" social and political problems and to propose solutions. Generally, however, their compassion is limited to the amelioration of problems and to comforting society's victims.

Liberation Theology

Unlike liberal Christianity, liberation theology is written from the perspective of the poor, not from the perspective of dominant elites. Liberation theologians assert that the message of liberation is at the heart of the Gospels. In Exodus 3:7-8, God says, "I have indeed seen the misery of my people in Egypt. I have heard their outcry against their slave-masters. I have taken heed of their sufferings and have come down to rescue them from the power of Egypt." Similarly, Mary, Mother of Jesus, says:

God has shown strength with God's arm
God has scattered the proud in the imagination of their hearts,
God has put down the mighty from their thrones,
And exalted those of low degree;
God has filled the hungry with good things,
And the rich God has sent empty away.
(Luke 1:51-53)

In these passages, God takes the side of the poor, frees them from bondage, and exalts them above the rich. In liberation theology, the oppressed are recognized as knowledgeable about their own situation; the hungry know most about hunger, the homeless know most about not having a home, the jobless know what it means not to have a job. And God is believed to be on the side of the poor, working for their liberation. According to Robert M. Brown in *Theology in a New Key: Responding to Liberation Themes,* liberation theology differs from liberal Christianity (and from evangelical Christianity) in the following ways: (1) a different starting point: the poor; (2)

a different interlocutor: the nonperson; (3) a different set of tools: the social sciences; (4) a different analysis: the reality of conflict; (5) a different mode of engagement: praxis; and (6) a different theology: the "second act" [reflection upon action].[26] Liberation Theology sees the world from the point of view of the poor, the "nonperson." To understand the reason for the suffering of the poor analytical tools of social science are employed. To change the situation requires action, conflict, and, perhaps, violence. Theology becomes a reflection upon the existing situation, the biblical promise of liberation, and those actions needed to bring liberation. Gustavo Gutierrez speaks for many liberation theologians when he writes: "I discovered that *poverty* was a destructive thing, something to be fought against and destroyed . . . I discovered that *poverty* was not accidental . . . but the result of a structure. I discovered that poor people were a social class. . . . In order to serve the poor one had to move into political action."[27] Liberation theologians, realizing the situation of the poor, apply religious teachings to support the oppressed. Liberal Christianity, on the other hand, uses religion to support dominant elites and institutions. Liberation theologians marry religious goals with political analysis to create a theology that demands political action in the world.

In liberation theology the nature of theology is changed from questions of how we can know God by special mental faculties (Kant), by a universal religious affection (Schleiermacher), by revelation (Barth), or by our own mental constructions (Kaufman). Instead, we discover God in human action. "Theology, as here conceived, is not an effort to give a correct understanding of God's attributes or actions but an effort to articulate the action of faith, the shape of praxis conceived and realized in obedience. . . . Theology has to stop explaining the world and start transforming it." A central task of this theology is "to unmask and expose the ideological misuse of Christianity as a tool of oppression."[28]

However, liberation theology is neither abstract speculation nor solely personal engagement in revolutionary struggles. It is developed by "base communities" in which the poor directly participate in the study of the Bible, in religious services, and in political actions. Harvey Cox writes that these "base communities" have three common characteristics.

1. Although they may have been initiated by clergy, and priests or nuns may continue to share in the leadership, they have a significant degree of lay control and direction, an ethos which is more egalitarian than the one found in most congregations and parishes.
2. There is an internal liturgical life of singing, prayer, the sharing of bread and wine, sometimes informally but often in a eucharistic [communion] fashion. The base communities are places of festivity where the historic images of biblical faith are celebrated.

3. Study and critical analysis of the real life "secular" situation in which the participants live in the light of the Bible's message becomes a basis for political engagement by the community and related groups as well as individuals.[29]

Political and religious aspects of the "base communities" are intertwined. Their methodology has political as well as religious significance.

> By starting at the lowest level and drawing people into genuine decision making, the base communities are actually rebuilding the nuclei of a *polis* in places where it had never developed or where it had been destroyed by political repression. . . .
> The attitude toward political participation in the base communities is premised on the belief that every human being is both *homo religiosus* and *homo politicus*. To sever the two is unnatural and produces a kind of schizophrenia in the individual, as well as the trivialization of faith and the abandonment of society to the toughest powermongers, untrammeled by spiritual restraints. . . . The secret is that the base communities do not work from the top down, through the institutionalized power of the state and the ruling classes, but from the bottom up, as those without power gather and try to effect change.[30]

The only way to understand the real nature of the base communities is to consider their discussions and actions. Ernesto Cardenal, currently Minister of Culture in Nicaragua, recounts the method of Bible study used in the small island community of Solentiname as follows:

> Each Sunday we first would distribute copies of the Gospels to those who could read. There were some who couldn't, especially among the elderly and those who lived on islands far away from the school. One of those who could read best (generally a boy or a girl) would read aloud the entire passage on which we were going to comment. Then we discussed it verse by verse. . . .
> The authors of this book are these people and all the others who talk frequently and say important things, and those who talk infrequently but also say something important . . .
> I am wrong. The true author is the Spirit that has inspired these commentaries (the Solentiname *campesinos* know very well that it is the Spirit who makes them speak) and that it was the Spirit who inspired the Gospels.[31]

This is the discussion of these peasants with Father Cardenal of Luke 1:46-55, the Song of Mary, Mother of Jesus:

Now young ESPERANZA read this poem, and the women began to comment on it.

My soul praises the Lord,
my heart rejoices in God my Savior,
because he has noticed his slave.

"She praises God because the Messiah is going to be born, and that's a great event for the people."

"She calls God 'Savior' because she knows that the Son that he has given her is going to bring liberation."

"She's full of joy. Us women must also be that way, because in our community the Messiah is born too, the liberator."

"She recognizes liberation. . . . We have to do the same thing. Liberation is from sin, that is, from selfishness, from injustice, from misery, from ignorance—from everything that's oppressive. That liberation is in our wombs too, it seems to me. . . . "

The last speaker was ANDREA, a young married woman, and now OSCAR, her young husband, breaks in: "God is selfish because he wants us to be his slaves. He wants our submission. Just him. I don't see why Mary has to call herself a slave. We should be free! Why just him? That's selfishness."

ALEJANDRO, who is a bachelor: "We have to be slaves of God, not of men."

Another young man: "God is love. To be a slave of love is to be free because God doesn't make slaves. He's the only thing we should be slaves of, love. And then we don't make slaves of others."

ALEJANDRO'S MOTHER says: "To be a slave of God is to serve others. That slavery is liberation."

I said that it's true that this selfish God Oscar spoke about does exist. And it's a God invented by people. People have often invented a god in their own image and likeness—not the true God, but idols, and those religions are alienating, an opium of the people. But the God of the Bible does not teach religion, but rather he urges Moses to take Israel out of Egypt, where the Jews were working as slaves. He led them from colonialism to liberty. And later God ordered that among those people no one could hold another as a slave. Because they had been freed by him and they belonged only to him, which means they were free.

And TERESITA, William's wife: "We have to keep in mind that at the time when Mary said she was a slave, slavery existed. It exists today too, but with a different name. Now the slaves are the proletariat or the *campesinos*. When she called herself a slave, Mary brought herself closer to the oppressed, I think. Today she could have called herself a proletarian or a *campesina* of Solentiname."

And WILLIAM: "But she says she's a slave of the Lord (who is the Liberator, who is the one who brought freedom from the Egyptian slavery). It's as if she said she was a slave of the liberation. Or as if she said that she was a proletarian or a revolutionary *campesina*."

Another of the girls: "She says she's poor, and she says that God took into account the 'poverty of his slave,' that is, that God chose her because she was poor. He didn't choose a queen or a lady of high society but a woman from the people. Yes, because God has preferred us poor people. Those are the 'great things' that God has done, as Mary says."[32]

The essence of this method and its net effect is to apply the religious principles of justice to the political questions of the day. In so doing, existing institutions often stand condemned as inadequate. By comparing their concrete life experiences to the liberation and justice promised in Scripture, the poor are enabled to develop for themselves a commitment to a better society, a different life, and to the actions necessary to transform their situation. They discuss and debate the meaning of particular scriptural passages until they are convinced of its message *for them.*

A similar approach is used in Europe as part of political theology and in the United States as part of feminist theology and black theology. For instance, the feminist theologian, Rosemary Ruether, argues that the critical principle of feminist theology is "the promotion of the full humanity of women . . . whatever diminishes or denies the full humanity of women must be presumed not to reflect the divine or an authentic relation to the divine . . . "[33] Black theology denies that God is white, and feminist theology denies that God is a man. Both critiques expand religion and they go on to denounce any society that is racist or patriarchal. This use of religious principles to criticize modern society inevitably leads to political action. This is true of liberation, feminist, black, and political theologies. Each of these theologies and the religious groups for which they speak are motivated by compassion as they struggle with and for the oppressed.

Liberation theology is explicitly a theology of compassion for the poor. In this respect it is an improvement over mainstream evangelical and liberal theologies. Its political analysis of repression and its engagement in revolutionary struggles are also to be admired. Its development of base communities and participatory Bible study are of great significance. However, liberation theology is too narrow in three respects. The principle of liberation is narrower than compassion—compassion can encompass liberation, but liberation cannot encompass compassion. Liberation theology does not allow for compassion for the rich or even the middle class. Therefore, it has no program to transform or liberate them. Finally, liberation theology is confined to human political struggles. It offers no protection for other species or the planet as a whole. It does not provide solutions to such global problems as nuclear war, environmental disasters, and resource depletion.

Planetary Theology

It can be argued that evangelical, liberal, and liberation theologies are contextual theologies arising from a particular class, sex, or culture. Tissa Balasuriya, in *Planetary Theology,* writes that:

> Contextual theologies by their very nature tend to be partial, being rooted in local situations and experience. . . .
>
> The action-orientation of contextual theologies may lead to liberation struggles that are necessary but only partial. . . . What is needed, therefore, is a dialectical interchange between local struggles and the world situation, between local theologies and a theology that tries to read the significance of global realities. . . .
>
> By extension, the whole planet earth, as an entirety, must also be seen as a context for theology. The human search for meaning and fullness of life takes place on this planet, with all its potentialities and limitations. Today the destinies of all people are closely interrelated and linked to the future of the earth: the land, the seas, the atmosphere, and outer space.

In this theology we are inevitably led to focus upon creation and cosmos.

> The Bible clearly teaches that God created the universe, the earth and human life. God entrusted the earth to the human family. God cares for all human beings and draws them toward their fulfillment in relationships of love and justice. . . .
>
> God as revealed in the Old Testament is the Creator of the world and of the human race . . . God cares for the whole of creation and "saw that it was good. . . . " The earth is given to humanity for its sustenance; the human race in turn is to develop the earth, to bring out its potential through human activity.
>
> The doctrine of creation can be the basis of a theology of planet earth itself and of human relationships to it. We have to respect its norms and inner dynamic if we wish to preserve and develop it. The earth will sustain human life if human beings do not destroy the earth. If we ruin the earth, human life is ruined.[34]

And where can such a planetary theology lead but "toward a spirituality of justice"? Again, in Balasuriya's words,

> True human fulfillment cannot come from a conscious participation in exploitation, from destroying the livelihood of others, from possessively grabbing the little that others have, from competitiveness that brings the law of the animal kingdom into the human sphere, from deceiving and miseducating ignorant peoples, from suppressing discontent and legitimate expressions of selfhood and freedom, from alienating persons from their true well-being by consumerism, advertising and ostentation. Yet all these are daily features of the capitalist world system.
>
> True human happiness can be found only in unselfishness, in an effort to live for others—according to one's possibilities and situations. . . .
>
> A universal approach is needed that can motivate all human beings to give of their best toward building a sound and just world order.[35]

Planetary theology, rethinking creation, and developing a new cosmology can lead to a radical new understanding. Such a cosmology is not primarily a critique of existing "powers and principalities," nor primarily solidarity with oppressed peoples of the world. It does not depend upon particular Scriptures, religious traditions, or the teachings of any one spiritual leader. Instead, the planet and cosmos become the Scriptures to teach us how humans should behave. As Matthew Fox and Brian Swimme say in *Manifesto for a Global Civilization*,

> Our understanding of the cosmogenesis will begin with the conviction that the desire for compassion and justice and the intelligence and creativity that are so deeply interwoven in the human, are themselves revelatory of the cosmogenetic dance itself. . . . Indeed, in the emerging era we will understand that the human being is far from being the only being capable of compassion. The human is that modality of the cosmogenesis where the compassion inherent in the full cosmos finds its incarnation in the works of the world. The human being is that space where the cosmogenesis is able to exhibit the heart of creation, is able to gather all the compassion implicit throughout creation and bring it forth into actual works of creativity.[36]

Thomas Berry argues that human beings are not just the caretakers or spokespeople for the earth but that "the human is that being in whom the universe attains reflexive consciousness of itself."[37] Berry sees the earth as an organic reality, not a mechanism. Like any viable biological community the earth is self-emergent, self-nourishing, self-educating, self-governing, self-healing, and self-fulfilling. For humans, then, the earth should be the primary educator, healer, and economy. Instead, companies, individuals, groups, and nations become alienated from the natural world and exploit the planet. They believe they can bankrupt the planet and still survive and profit themselves.

As Berry would have it, we are of the earth and the cosmos: "We are earthlings. The earth is our origin, our nourishment, our support, our guide. Our spirituality itself is earth-derived. If there is no spirituality in the earth then there is no spirituality in the [human. Humans are] a dimension of Earth." Four hundred years ago, scientific developments began to bring about human technological dominance which Berry interprets as "the earth awakening to consciousness of itself in [humans]."[38] But our limited spiritual development caused us to attack and exploit the earth savagely. This has changed our relationship with the earth.

> What is happening has been unthinkable in ages gone by. [We are] now in control of forces that once controlled [us], or more precisely, the earth process that formerly administered the earth and guided its affairs directly is now accomplishing this task in and through [us] as its conscious agent. Once a creature of earthly providence [we are] now the expression of this earthly providence. [We have] the power of life and death not only over human life but over the earth itself in its higher forms of life.[39]

Berry concludes his cosmological view of humans and their place in the creative process with a series of principles. He writes that the universe, the solar system, and the planet earth, in themselves and in their evolutionary emergence, constitute for the human community the primary revelation of that ultimate mystery whence all things emerge into being. The universe is a unity, an interacting and genetically related community of beings bound together in an inseparable relationship in space and time; the human is that being in whom the universe attains reflexive consciousness of itself; the earth, within the solar system, is a self-emergent, self-nourishing, self-governing, self-healing, self-educating community; and the main human task of the immediate future is to assist in activating the intercommunion of all the living and nonliving components of the earth community in what can be considered the emerging ecological period of earth development.[40]

Brian Swimme in *The Universe Is a Green Dragon* reaffirms the basic conclusion that Berry reaches.

The human provides the space in which the universe feels its stupendous beauty. Think of it this way: before the human arrived, the Earth and universe were magnificent realities. However, some of the depths of this magnificence were yet to be felt, yet to be appreciated. We enabled some of the depths of the universe to be tasted, and we have only just begun our venture; much waits on our maturity.

Our human society has evolved on earth a new awareness and a new global community that changes our relationship to the earth.

At present, the human species moves into its fourth era, what we might call the age of the Earth . . . a form of human life that envisions itself within the interconnected dynamics of the unfolding reality. The tribe will not be the center of the human world, nor will the civilization, the culture, nor the nation-state. It will be the Earth community as a whole that will be understood as our home, our womb of creativity and life. . . . From the planet's point of view, we can say that the Earth is awakening to its own beauty, power, and future possibilities. The Earth awakens to the unfolding vision of a self-aware entity.[41]

On the one hand, we humans help the planet complete its "work." We help bring creation to its next stage.

We are the self-reflexion of the universe. We allow the universe to know and feel itself. We were brought forth so that these experiences of beauty could enter awareness. The primeval fireball existed for twenty billion years without self-awareness. . . . That star could not, by itself, become aware of its own beauty or sacrifice. But the star can, through us, reflect back on itself. In a sense, you are the star, brought into a form of life that enables life to reflect on itself.

Unfortunately, our collective actions are not so benign. Only compassion can motivate us to change our current pattern of exploitation and domination so that we may fulfill our cosmological and planetary function.

The Earth suffers under the weight of accumulated misery and pathology, all of which has its ultimate source in acts of egocentric craving. . . . Each individual person has the power of participating in the transformation of the whole Earth. The evil that reaches you after so many millions of years of existence can be absorbed and transformed. You have the power to accept the suffering, to refuse to pass it on to another, to forgive, to end the needless torment, and, most of all, to transmute evil into energy for the vitality of the whole.[42]

Compassion or love has the power to transform the pattern of suffering upon the earth. The planet itself becomes our teacher as we become aware of the beginnings of creation and its current unfolding through our scientific investigations and our sympathetic participation in life. Whatever the dangers, we humans ultimately shall decide the fate of the entire planet. Swimme boldly declares "we are the creative, scintillating, searing, healing flame of the awesome and enchanting universe."[43] We will either use our potential awareness to further the evolution of the planet or, we will misuse our awesome power to end life.

This new understanding of cosmology, creation, and the interconnection of all life stretches all previous theologies. In planetary theology our religious task is to understand our human place in the order of life and to enhance the life processes upon the planet. Justice in such a theology is extended not only to all oppressed peoples but also to all forms of life and to the planet itself.

Although planetary theology and cosmology has a great intellectual sweep and comprehensiveness, it has faults common to the ecological movement. It is primarily based on middle-class sensibilities, can become sentimentalized, and seldom leads directly to the radical political action necessary to overcome the dominant elites and institutions of our civilization. Because it is not organized around local congregations as are evangelical and liberal Christianity, or around new groups like the base communities of liberation theology, it has not yet developed a genuine constituency other than individual members of ecological interest groups. To reach its full potential, planetary theology must become both more practical and grounded in local congregations as well as in political and religious networks.

Practical Theology

In direct contrast to the grand sweep of planetary theology stands practical theology. David Tracy defines practical theologies as those that guide action and reflections upon action.[44] He offers the following as its hallmarks:

Practical theologies are related primarily . . . to the concerns of some particular social, political, cultural or pastoral movement or problematic which is argued or assumed to possess major religious import. . . .

[Practical theologies] assume praxis [practice] as the proper criterion for the meaning and truth of theology. . . .

Practical theologies will be concerned principally with the ethical stance of responsible commitment to and sometimes even involvement in a situation of praxis. . . .

Practical theologians will ordinarily assume personal involvement in and commitment to either a particular religious tradition or a particular praxis movement bearing religious significance.

Practical theologies will ordinarily analyze some radical situation of ethical-religious import (sexism, racism, classism, elitism, anti-Semitism, economic exploitation, environmental crises, etc.) in some philosophical, social-scientific, culturally analytic or religiously prophetic manner. . . . The notion of truth involved will prove a praxis-determined, transformative one.[45]

Statements by Catholic and Protestant churches in the United States on major political problems are current examples of practical theology. These pronouncements have guided practical actions in lawsuits, lawmaking, and protest movements. These pronouncements and the actions that have followed fit the criteria of practical theology. They are addressed to society and particular social groups, they concern social problems, they require commitment and involve praxis, they are based upon particular religious traditions, they analyze a radical ethical-religious situation, and they affirm praxis-determined, transformative truths.

Consider the Pastoral Letter on War and Peace, issued by the National Conference of Catholic Bishops on 3 May 1983. It began with a defense of the right and necessity of religious leaders speaking on political issues.

Our contribution will not be primarily technical or political, but we are convinced that there is no satisfactory answer to the human problems of the nuclear age which fails to consider the moral and religious dimensions of the questions we face. Order in human society must be shaped on the basis of respect for the transcendence of God and the unique dignity of each person, understood in terms of freedom, justice, truth and love.

Having begun with an affirmation of basic theological principles, the bishops then apply Catholic social teaching to the problems of nuclear war, "limited" nuclear war, the policy of deterrence, and the task of peacemaking.

Catholic teaching begins in every case with a presumption against war and for peaceful settlement of disputes. . . . It is never permitted to direct nuclear or conventional weapons to "the indiscriminate destruction of whole cities or of extensive areas along with their population." The intentional killing of innocent civilians is always wrong. Even defensive response to unjust attack can cause destruction which violates the principle of proportionality, going far beyond the limits of legitimate defense. No defensive strategy which exceeds the limits of proportionality is morally permissible.

The bishops then proceed to declare that deterrence is permissible as a short-term policy but that progressive disarmament is the proper long-term goal. Moreover, they conclude that there are no circumstances in which a "first strike" or a "limited" nuclear war could be justified.[46]

The Catholic bishops also answer the argument that some forms of nuclear war may be justified by the historic "just war" doctrine of the church.

> Just-war teaching has evolved . . . as an effort to prevent war; only if war cannot be rationally avoided, does the teaching then seek to restrict and reduce its horrors. It does this by establishing a set of rigorous conditions which must be met if the decision to go to war is to be morally justifiable. War is permissible only to confront "a real and certain danger. . . ."
>
> Just response to aggression must be discriminate; it must be directed against unjust aggressors, not against innocent people caught up in a war not of their own making. "Any act of war aimed indiscriminately at the destruction of entire cities or of extensive areas along with their population is a crime against God and [humans]."[47]

So the "just war" doctrine, which has a fifteen-hundred-year history in the Catholic church, is given a limited and restricted definition. If the "just war" doctrine were followed it would severely restrict many "conventional" wars, revolutions, and all forms of nuclear war.

The Catholic bishops end their pastoral letter with a plea to reject both nuclear war and the arms race. Instead, they declare that the agenda of religious people must be peacemaking.

> In the words of our Holy Father, we need a "moral about-face." The whole world must summon the moral courage and the technical means to say "no" to nuclear conflict; "no" to weapons of mass destruction; "no" to an arms race which robs the poor and the vulnerable; and "no" to the moral danger of a nuclear age which places before human kind indefensible choices of constant terror or surrender. Peacemaking is not an optional commitment. It is a requirement of our faith. We are called to be peacemakers, not by some movement of the moment, but by our Lord Jesus. The content and context of our peacemaking is set, not by some political agenda or ideological program, but by the teaching of the church.[48]

Similar documents opposing U.S. policies on nuclear war and the arms race have been issued by many Protestant denominations. The United Methodist Council of Bishops goes further than the Catholic bishops in their repudiation of deterrence strategy, their disavow of the US Strategic Defense

Initiative (SDI or "Star Wars"), their belief that the nuclear arms race is "a matter of social justice as well as world peace," and their call for a new world order to replace the nation-state system. In their pastoral letter *In Defense of Creation* they declare:

> *Nuclear deterrence* has too long been reverenced as the idol of national security. In its most idolatrous forms it has blinded its proponents to the many-sided requirements of genuine security. There can be no unilateral security in the nuclear age. . . .
>
> Nuclear deterrence has become a dogmatic license for perpetual hostility between the superpowers and for their rigid resistance to significant measures of disarmament. A still more fundamental flaw is at the very core of nuclear deterrence: a contradiction between inordinate confidence in the rationality of decision makers and the absolute terror of annihilation. . . .
>
> The ideology of deterrence must not receive the churches' blessing, even as a temporary warrant for holding on to nuclear weapons.

The Methodist bishops, in addition to rejecting deterrence as a legitimate national policy, make several other contributions to the practical discussion by Christians and the secular public of the nuclear arms race. They begin the discussion not only from a concern for human life but from a concern for the entire creation as advocated by planetary theology.

> We write in defense of creation. We do so because the creation itself is under attack. Air and water, trees and fruits and flowers, birds and fish and cattle, all children and youth, women and men live under the darkening shadows of a threatening nuclear winter. We call the United Methodist Church to more faithful witness and action in the face of this worsening nuclear crisis. It is a crisis that threatens to assault not only the whole human family, but the planet Earth itself, even while the arms race itself cruelly destroys millions of lives in conventional wars, repressive violence and massive poverty.

They concur with the Catholic bishops that "No just cause can warrant the waging of nuclear war or any use of nuclear weapons." But they conclude that the final political solution must involve "the transformation of our conflict-ridden nation-state system into a new world order of common security and interdependent institutions. . . . " In their pastoral letter the Methodist bishops write, "Therefore, we say a clear and unconditional *No* to nuclear war and to any use of nuclear weapons. We conclude that nuclear deterrence is a position that cannot receive the Church's blessing. We state our complete lack of confidence in proposed 'defense' against nuclear attack and are convinced that the enormous cost of developing such defenses is one more witness to the obvious fact that the arms race is a social justice issue, not only a war and peace issue."[49]

A similar document directed at the church itself as well as at national politicians and government officials was adopted by the United Church of Christ at its national gathering in the summer of 1985 when it voted to become a "Just Peace" church. The United Church of Christ thus took the Catholic theme of "Just War" and stood it on its head.

> A Just Peace is an alternative to Just War, and it identifies the church's vocation today as actively witnessing to the good news of God's presence and promise of justice and peace on earth. At the same time, it is a reaffirmation of a powerful tradition—biblical and post-biblical: the prophetic linking of justice and peace and the gospel emphasis on the present and coming Realm [of God]. The theme of Just Peace brings together into a single reality the imperatives and promises of both justice and peace, and it addresses the whole of life—personal and social dimensions, spiritual and political dimensions, attitudinal and structural dimensions.[50]

In calling for a "Just Peace," the United Church of Christ was not naive. Although affirming that "peace is possible," it recognized that major structural and historic changes would be required.

> Sin is deeply structural. It is deeply historical. And what is historical and structural can be changed. The Spirit gives everyone the power to change themselves and structures. The specific responsibilities for changing these structures may and will differ, depending on the extent of power and insight possessed by individuals and groups. And much, indeed most, of the responsibility for ending violence, destruction, and death belongs to those in relatively more powerful positions than those in less. Specifically, most of the responsibility for ending poverty, militarism, and imperialism belong to those in the United States who are affluent and privileged.[51]

The United Church of Christ joined the Catholic and Methodist bishops in rejecting any form of nuclear war. But the United Church of Christ also rejected "unilateral full-scale disarmament as a currently acceptable path out of the present international dilemma," and instead, advocated a freeze on testing and deployment of nuclear weapons.

> We affirm the mutual and verifiable freeze on the testing, production, and deployment of nuclear weapons as the most important

step in breaking the escalating dynamics of the arms race, and call upon the U.S. and the U.S.S.R. and other nations to take unilateral initiatives toward implementing such a freeze contingent upon the other side responding, until such time as a comprehensive freeze can be negotiated.[52]

The pronouncement goes further than the Catholic and Methodist bishops' statements in its intent to reorganize the entire denomination from local congregations to national church structures. It calls for the entire United Church of Christ *to become a "Just Peace" church.*

The Fifteenth General Synod calls for the development of four key components within local churches: spiritual development, Just Peace education, political advocacy and community witness.

1. We call all local churches to the inward journey of spiritual nurture: prayer for a Just Peace, study of the Scriptures, theological reflection upon the work of the Holy Spirit, celebration and worship which center the life of the community in the power and reality of the God who creates a Just Peace. . . .

2. We call all local churches to the inward journey of education. . . . We call for a steady program of Just Peace education, a steady flow of information on Just Peace issues into the life of the congregation.

3. We call all local churches to the outward journey of political witness, enabling all members to join the search for the politics of a Just Peace. Just Peace is both a religious concept and a political concept, and participation in the political arena is essential. . . .

4. We call all local churches to the outward journey of community witness. We call for local churches to make their convictions known in their communities through public forums, media, and presence in the public arena. We call for local churches to help shape public opinion and the climate in which the issues of a Just Peace are shaped. . . .

Because the times are so critical, we call for extraordinary witness as well as ordinary political involvement to break the power of the structural evils which prevent a Just Peace. We call upon local churches to be understanding and even supportive of persons who out of individual conscience take the responsibility for such non-violent extraordinary witness. Examples of such witness might include: becoming a conscientious objector to war; refusing acceptance of employment with any project related to nuclear and biochemical weapons and warfare; refusing any and all assignments to use weapons of mass destruction as a member of the military; withholding tax money in protest of the excessively militaristic policies of our government; and engaging in acts of non-violent civil disobedience, willingly going to jail to call attention to specific outrages.[53]

The proclamation calls upon state conferences "to develop regional centers able to link local churches into effective regional and national strategies." The conferences are also urged to fund Just Peace staff to coordinate these activities. Finally, the proclamation calls for changes in national church structures as well.

> 1. We call for the strengthening of our advocacy work in Washington, D.C., with more funding to develop the capacity of the UCC to make its witness known in the national political arena, to expand its capacity for policy analysis, to increase its presence on Capitol Hill in shaping legislation, to develop stronger communication links with churches around the country, to share political developments and urge action, and to build coalitions.
> 2. We call upon the United Church of Christ Board for World Ministries to explore and develop new models of peace and justice ministries globally to address particular situations of injustice, oppression and real or potential violence, and to develop communication links between Christians in these critical situations and Christians in the U.S., developing global partnership and global awareness in the search for a Just Peace. . . .
> 3. We call for more resources to develop national strategies of advocacy and action to increase the witness of the UCC for a Just Peace.[54]

The Just Peace church proclamation by the United Church of Christ is beginning to redirect church resources toward creating conditions for justice and peace. A number of the individual congregations are beginning to initiate changes at the local level. One example of local churches beginning to translate general church peace pronouncements into action campaigns is the Nuclear Weapon Free Zone campaign in Chicago. In Chapter 6 this campaign will be discussed more fully. It is sufficient for the moment to point out that it began when local churches and synagogues, motivated by the same sentiments as Catholic and Protestant bishops, first adopted declarations for their own sanctuaries which said:

> We, the people in this place, declare the following:
> We choose a life for ourselves that will also allow and ensure life for all others.
> We demand that we not be "defended" by dropping nuclear bombs on other people and other living things. . . .
> We commit ourselves and our possessions to dismantling nuclear

weapons and nuclear weapons systems, and to replacing them with human sharing, work, friendship, and understanding. . . .

   We name this community of faith and this place where we stand as a nuclear weapon free zone forever.

   In the name of God, nuclear hell shall not be built, stored, or launched from at least this place.[55]

The declarations by twenty-two schools, churches, and synagogues of their own property as nuclear weapon free zones created a political movement which led to the adoption of a Chicago ordinance banning "the design, production, deployment, launching, maintaining or storing of nuclear weapons or their components within the city limits."[56] Thus, the general rhetoric of church leaders about the nuclear arms race was translated into a binding law in Chicago, which is now the largest nuclear weapon free zone in North America and which has expanded to include the unincorporated areas of Cook County and six suburban towns.

The practical theology of the Catholic bishops' pastoral letter on the economy was even more controversial than their letter on war and peace. The bishops begin with the theological premise that an economy must be judged by its effect upon the poor.

> The poor have a special claim on our concern because they are vulnerable and needy. We believe that all—Christians, Jews, those of other faiths or no faith at all—must measure their actions and choices by what they do for and to the poor. As pastors and as citizens, we are convinced of one fundamental criterion for economic decisions, policies and institutions: They must all be at the service of human beings. The economy was made for people, all people, and not the other way around.[57]

Given this premise and the rising rate of poverty, which in 1984 was at its highest level since 1965, the bishops called for major changes in the U.S. economy. "We want to call all persons, no matter what their income or status, to a new commitment to economic justice. Such a commitment is an inescapable implication of the belief in Jesus Christ. From a perspective shaped by the Gospel, no one can turn a deaf ear to the voice of the poor. No one can claim the name Christian and at the same time acquiesce in the hunger and homelessness that exists around the world and in our own country." According to the bishops, the test of an economy is that there be full employment, that work allow for self-realization, that it be properly remunerated, and that it create solidarity within the nation and the world community.[58]

What makes the pastoral letter controversial is that the bishops deny that private property is an absolute right. They say that "the support of private ownership does not mean that any individual, group, organization or nation has the right to unlimited accumulation of wealth. Especially when there are so many needy people in our world, the right to own must bow to the higher principles of stewardship and the common use of the goods of creation. There is a "social mortgage" on private property which implies that "private property does not constitute for anyone an absolute or unconditional right." The bishop's go on to support the right to organize unions, a program for full employment with the government as an employer of the last resort, and a greatly increased foreign aid program to help the poor in other countries.[59]

Archbishop Rembert G. Weakland of Milwaukee, the principal author of the pastoral letter on the economy, outlined its four major programmatic thrusts as follows:

> We have chosen [to organize the pastoral letter around] four areas. The first is employment generation. There is a case to be made from Catholic social teaching for making job creation a real national priority. We also want to discuss the question of adequate income for the poor and disadvantaged. Church teaching about human dignity demands that we address this both in terms of policy and implementation. . . .
>
> We also wanted one area outside the United States, something that could be read in the Third World, like that of U.S. trade with developing countries. Pope John XXIII began to shift our reference point from the common good of individual nations to the common good of the universe. . . .
>
> Our last area is economic planning and policy. Not so much *what* but *who* is involved in economic planning. . . . One of the most challenging statements in John Paul II's *Laborem Exercens* (1981) is that the dignity of the workers demands that they have a part in the decisions that affect their lives.[60]

Once again the Protestants followed the Catholic bishops with statements of their own on the economy. The most important of these was a document entitled "Doing Theology in the Economic Crises" adopted by the Ecumenical Great Lakes/Appalachian Project on the Economic Crisis (GLAP) meeting in Cleveland in December 1984. Like the Catholic bishops, the authors begin with God's preferential option for the poor. "Historically, the Biblical revelation has indicated God's preferential commitment to the oppressed, a vision of a society that would include the people of Israel and all humanity as full participants in a covenant community. God's special commitment to the poor and the oppressed judges this society on the basis of whether or not it treats all people justly."[61]

But the GLAP document goes further in identifying the causes of the current economic problems:

God calls us to say clearly that:

—It is a sin to take away a person's work and their means of production so that they cannot participate in community or share in God's creativity.

—It is a sin to exploit employees by paying wages too low to allow them a decent, secure place in the community.

—It is a sin to hide away from the dispossessed, to "harden your heart against your brother or sister" and not "lend them sufficient for their need" (Deuteronomy 15:7-8).

—It is a sin for anyone, the unemployed or the securely employed, to be apathetic about the exclusion of persons from meaningful work.

—It is a sin to destroy communities for the sake of greater profits or even higher productivity.

These theological principles lead to political principles that then guide economic decision making. According to the church leaders and community activists at the Cleveland meeting, among the principles that can help churches and synagogues move toward the biblical vision are the following:

1. Community is primary, profits are secondary.

2. The primary goal of an economic policy should be to afford a basis for meaningful and sustaining work for all in stable communities.

3. Communities and workers have a right and an obligation to participate meaningfully in economic decisions that shape the character of productive work and the quality of life in their community.

4. The quality of life for workers, their families, and communities must have priority over the interests of investments and corporate management as implied in Pope John Paul II's concept of the "priority of labor over capital."

5. The churches and synagogues, because of the transnational character of their traditions and institutions, should facilitate international solidarity among workers and communities that can begin to match the power of the transnational corporations.

6. Governments, churches and synagogues, unions and corporations, should enable, through laws and capital investment, new forms of economic development that build stable, participatory communities, including forms of worker and community ownership.[62]

In 1987 the United Church of Christ began discussing another fundamental document entitled *Christian Faith and Economic Life,* which affirmed the call by the Catholic bishops and the Third World churches to "give priority to the poor." Like the GLAP document they recognized that "Social sin embodied in the systems and structures, can harm whole sectors of society: the poor, racial and economic minorities, women. And unlike personal sin which is susceptible to identification, conversion and rectification, social sin, interwoven into institutions, is more difficult to reform and change." In their pronouncement on the economy they derived six Christian principles of economic justice: (1) fulfilling basic material needs of all members of the human community; (2) economic democracy and participation in economic decisions; (3) enhancing human community; (4) enhancing human rights; (5) a viable economic system based on responsible and equitable use of the earth's limited resources; and (6) promoting international peace. These six principles lead to specific proposals, the two most important of which are an "Economic Bill of Rights" to be amended to the U.S. Constitution and new international institutions leading to a new international economic order to be funded by a global tax based on a percent of each country's gross national production.[63]

The idea of a new "Economic Bill of Rights" was further elaborated by the national interfaith organization, Clergy and Laity Concerned. This "Economic Bill of Rights," which is based upon articles 22 through 28 of the Universal Declaration of Human Rights adopted by the General Assembly of the United Nations on 10 December 1948, is to be accomplished by passing new federal legislation. It includes the following nine articles:

Article 1. Everyone, as a member of society, has the right to social security, and is entitled to realization of the economic, social and cultural rights indispensable for his/her dignity and the free development of his/her personality based upon national effort and international cooperation and in accordance with the resources of the United States.

Article 2. (1) Everyone has the right to work, to free choice of employment, to just and favorable conditions of work and to protection against unemployment.

(2) Everyone, without discrimination, has the right to equal pay for equal work.

(3) Everyone who works has the right to just and favorable remuneration ensuring the worker and his/her family an existence worthy of human dignity, supplemented if necessary, by other means of social protections.

(4) Everyone has the right to form and to join trade unions for the protection of his/her rights.

Article 3. Everyone who works has the right to rest and leisure, including reasonable limitation of working hours and periodic holidays with pay.

Article 4. (1) Everyone has the right to a standard of living adequate for the health and well being of each person and his/her family, including food, clothing, housing and medical care and necessary social services, and the right to security in the event of unemployment, sickness, disability, death of the breadwinner, old age or other lack of livelihood in circumstances beyond his/her control.

(2) Motherhood and childhood are entitled to special care and assistance. All children, whether born in or out of wedlock, shall enjoy the same social protection.

Article 5. (1) Everyone has the right to education. Education shall be free. Elementary education shall be compulsory. Technical and professional education shall be made generally available and higher education shall be equally accessible to all on the basis of merit.

(2) Education shall be directed to the full development of the human personality and to the strengthening of respect for human rights and fundamental freedoms. It shall promote understanding, tolerance and friendship among all nations, racial or religious groups, and shall further the activities of the United Nations for the maintenance of peace.

Article 6. (1) Everyone has the right to participate freely in the cultural life of the community, to enjoy the arts and to share in scientific advancement and its benefits.

(2) Everyone has the right to the protection of moral and material interests resulting from any scientific, literary or artistic production of which he/she is the author.

Article 7. Everyone is entitled to a social, national, and international order in which the rights and freedoms set forth in this document can be fully realized.

Article 8. Efforts to achieve economic justice, such as the adoption of the right to just and fair remuneration, will remain inadequate if they do not address and seek to correct the fundamental underlying inequality of wealth and resources between the rich and the poor.

Article 9. Everyone has the right not to be discriminated against on the basis of their race, class, sex, sexual orientation, or religious beliefs. Economic justice cannot be obtained through the exploitation of one group or its resources by another group either within or outside a single nation-state. The role of racism especially in establishing and maintaining an inequitable distribution of wealth must be recognized and rejected.[64]

In 1985, a dozen Chicago religious leaders and religious groups applied the principles of the Catholic bishops' pastoral letter on the economy and the GLAP statement on the economy to the problem of a plant closing. In many ways they anticipated the principles propounded by the U.C.C and by Clergy and Laity Concerned. They intervened in an important court case on moral grounds in order to have a very practical effect. In their motion to intervene as *amici curiae* in the *Playskool* case in District Court they declared that

> the *amici* are interested in this litigation for three reasons. The entire urban community is negatively affected by decisions such as Playskool's relocation, religious groups included. The loss of 700 jobs in a poor neighborhood will cause dislocation and suffering. Further, the *amici* are united by a belief that religious leaders must play a role in seeking solutions to society's economic and social problems. Each of the organizations has a long history of involvement in serving the community in this way. Finally, the *amici* present the views and interests of many church-goers and community residents directly affected by the Playskool plant shut-down, including former and prospective employees.
>
> The brief of *amici curiae* will present a moral and religious perspective on the instant litigation which has not been touched on by the parties. Their arguments are a reflection of a positive vision of the law—a vision in which justice and the public interest are held paramount. The *amici* do not ask or expect the Court to espouse any particular religious view. Read in conjunction with Plaintiffs brief in opposition, it will be clear that this is a matter of both legal substance and great public interest.[65]

The facts behind the case are straightforward. In 1979, Playskool obtained a $1,000,000 Industrial Revenue Bond issued by the city. In doing so it pledged to increase employment. The terms of the agreement for repayment of the bond at low interest was twenty years. Employment actually dropped, Playskool was taken over by Hasbro Industries in a corporate merger, and the company began to close its Chicago plant. In intervening, the *amici* specifically cited the GLAP statement as to the effect of unemployment on the seven hundred Playskool workers.

> The human impact of the Playskool plant closing will be serious and profound. The Playskool plant, with nearly 700 workers was one of the largest employers in the predominantly minority West Side neighborhood where it was located. A majority of those were black and Hispanic, and a substantial number were female. For many of these employees, the unemployment and then welfare lines will be the only option if Playskool leaves. There simply are no new opportunities

available even for skilled inner city workers, and those that now exist are shrinking by the day.

Unemployment means more than being bored at home. "The effects of sustained unemployment are well-documented. Workers lose their sense of personal worth. Child and spouse abuse, suicides, separation, family disorganization, ill health and mortality rates all increase. . . . Businesses, schools and local governments lose their economic base. Churches and social agencies no longer have the resources to meet the escalating family and personal problems. Unemployed youth become a threat, not a resource. And as people lose their sense of worth and retreat into themselves or television, the social networks—including both taverns and churches—fall apart. People grow cynical about all forms of organization and all leaders." (*Doing Theology in the Economic Crisis*, The Ecumenical Great Lakes/Appalachian Project, December 4, 1984, Cleveland Ohio, pp. 2-3.)

The GLAP document was also cited to bolster the *amici's* argument that human costs of economic decisions must be considered by government and the courts.

The *amici* believe that the legal system and our governments should attack head-on one aspect of the problems of urban and industrial decay by taking contracts such as the one here seriously, and enforcing them. Too often our economic system encourages business and individuals to ignore the human side of economic decisions.

"Our economic structure often fails to take into account human values. The assumption legitimating the structure is that economic activity is the core of society's life and only economic reasoning free from all other value commitments is rational. Whatever increases productivity and profits sets the rules, controls the decisions and shapes the future. Families and communities are left to pick up the pieces after the primary decision is made according to economic rationality, intensified by short-range interests." (*Doing Theology in the Economic Crisis*, supra p. 4.)[66]

Not only did the religious leaders intervene directly in the court case but they also mediated between the city government and Hasbro Industries to effect an out-of-court settlement. In the final settlement, which was one of the most generous of any plant closing in the United States, the company agreed to keep the plant open through November, 1985 and to continue to employ 100 of its original 683 workers; Hasbro-Bradley set up a $300,000 advertising and job-search program for fired workers, including payments to other companies who hired its former workers; and the company guaranteed to find a purchaser for the factory or, failing that, to give it to a charitable group.[67] As of this writing, the factory is about to be given to a community economic development corporation, and the new owners expect to develop an industrial park with new jobs for the area.

Encouraged by their success in the Playskool case, religious leaders joined with the American Civil Liberties Union to intervene in *United States of America v. City of Chicago*, a lawsuit in which the federal government attempted to eliminate affirmative action hiring in the Chicago police department. The *amici* brief summarized the religious position in the suit this way:

> Several churches, religious organizations, and organizations of clergy of many faiths who have joined in this brief also believe very strongly that the concept of affirmative action is rooted in the Judeo-Christian tradition of justice for the poor and oppressed. A number of religious groups represented here have, in fact, translated that belief into policy by making or joining in public policy statements.
>
> Recent statements of that policy include, for example, a statement prepared in December, 1984, by the Ecumenical Great Lakes/ Appalachian Project on the Economic Crisis, signed by leaders of virtually every major Christian denomination. The statement, titled "Doing Theology in the Economic Crisis," makes clear the signers' belief that they are obligated by God to seek justice and fairness in every aspect of human society:

> > "God's covenant supersedes all the political and economic structures we may devise. It calls us to relationships of justice and mercy with neighbors and strangers in their concrete circumstances. Governments and economies are to be ordered according to this demand for covenantal faithfulness."[68]

The city of Chicago, with the support of the civic and religious groups, prevailed and maintained affirmative action in its employment.

Urban ministry is another area in which practical theologies are emerging. Nearly all national religious groups have recognized the biblical basis, the theological necessity, and the practical demand to focus on urban problems. The Episcopal church's Standing Commission on the Church in Metropolitan Areas in 1982 called upon the Episcopal church "to make a major new commitment to a ministry of joint discipleship with poor and oppressed people, in the United States and abroad, to meet basic human needs and to build a just and peaceful global society." A series of practical projects and programs were to be organized around the biblical theme of the Jubilee Year:

"The Year of Jubilee decreed by God (Leviticus 25) demands a time of new beginnings, when the relationships of power and servitude come to an end and all members of the society are restored to equality and freedom. . . . " The sixty-seventh General Convention of the Episcopal church went on to declare that

> the Old Testament concept of Jubilee, and its subsequent revitalizing through the life and work of Jesus, has been chosen as the symbol of a renewed effort by the Episcopal Church to minister to the poor and oppressed. Biblically, the 50th year was to be recognized as one of celebration, in which slaves were liberated and lands were returned to their original owners. In the Gospel of St. Luke, Jesus identifies himself with Isaiah's prophecy and the jubilee year . . .
>
> In choosing jubilee as descriptive of its goal, the convention resolution calls the meeting of human needs and the building of a just society the heart of the church's mission. Commitment to the Jubilee Ministry involves the following aspects: "A primary focus is to increase the awareness among church members of the problems of poverty and injustice and to encourage efforts to meet the needs of their victims."[69]

The call to create a Jubilee Ministry is grounded in a biblical view of poverty. "Even a casual reading of the scriptures indicates how seriously the biblical writers take poverty. More than 300 references in the Bible refer to oppression; nearly half of those clearly identify poverty as related to oppression. Indeed, in some of the Hebrew texts the meaning overlaps so that the best translation would be "oppressed-poor." Episcopals believe that the required biblical response to poverty and suffering, based upon the teaching of both Hebrew and Christian Scriptures, is *shalom* and Jubilee.

> We believe that this proclamation of *shalom* and Jubilee—of peace with justice for poor and forgotten people—calls the Episcopal church to be agents of that *shalom*. Certainly we are called to minister to the immediate suffering which afflicts the victims of society whom we see all around us: distribution of food, medical care, shelter, and other immediate and primary needs.
>
> But we also know that such ministries are not enough, because they do not address the *injustice* which causes the pain in the first place. The People of God share a mission to *change whatever causes the oppression*. We do so because we know that God cares not only about the suffering but about that which causes the suffering. Of course we take on the role of the Good Samaritan, because we cannot ignore human need. But to stop at that point leaves untouched the institutions and values and structures which cause the misery, and places us in the

positions of leaving them in control, unless our gestures of generosity are accompanied by actions to end the oppression. To do so will, of course, place the Church in conflict with the principalities and powers of our time, and with many of our own members who do not share our understanding of God's demand for justice.[70]

The Presbyterian church reaches a very similar conclusion in its theological documents on urban ministry. Presbyterians also believe that we are called by God to work with the poor and oppressed in the city and that we must "redeem" structures and institutions rather than merely provide social services.

> The Lord's agenda compels us to work for the deliverance of those presently held captive by the "principalities and powers" of this world, to "bind up the broken-hearted," to "raise up the former devastations," "to give garlands instead of ashes." (Isaiah 61:1-4) We believe that God's agenda compels us to work on behalf of a just community wherein the needs of the poor, the alienated, and the dispossessed are the first priority. . . .
> We believe God's agenda compels us to work as agents of [God's] reconciling love, to establish communities responsive to the claims of justice and the principles responsive to the claims of justice and the principles of peace, and the renewal of the resurrection hope. "All this is from God, who through Christ reconciled us to [God] and gave us the ministry of reconciliation."(II Corinthians 5:18)
> We believe that God's agenda compels us to work for the salvation not only of individuals, but for the redemption of the structures and institutions that can make human community possible. It is in the context of community and institution . . . the "New Jerusa-lem" . . . that the great declaration occurs, "Behold, the dwelling of God is with [humans]. [God] will dwell with them, and they shall be [God's] people, and . . . will be with them; [God] will wipe away every tear from their eyes, and death shall be no more. . . . " (Revelation 21:3-4)[71]

In a later denominational statement on urban ministry the Unitarians at an Urban Ministers Convocation in October 1985 confronted explicitly the structural and systemic aspect of our urban crisis.

> We are called to respond to our city life—
>   its brokenness, tensions, and exclusions;
>   its beauty, wholeness, and joy.
> The fullness of our ministry begins when we confront

> The issues of race, class, and sex in the cities
> and in ourselves.[72]

Thus, Protestant denominations have begun to be clear on the need to be engaged in an urban ministry rooted in justice. Equally, ecumenical groups and conferences have been critical of both liberal denominations and evangelical churches for not making urban ministry a significant priority in practice. A Congress on Urban Ministry, with more than seven hundred participants from all denominations, adopted a resolution in April 1986 which read in part:

> NOW THEREFORE BE IT RESOLVED that the members of the many faiths meeting at the Congress on Urban Ministry on April 11, 1986 call upon all denominations to make Urban Ministry a high priority and to dedicate a higher percentage of their national staff and financial resources in support of congregations and religious agencies in urban/metropolitan areas;
> BE IT AFFIRMED BY THE MEMBERS OF THIS CONGRESS ON URBAN MINISTRY that genuine Urban Ministry must have an equal emphasis on spirituality, spiritual development, and social justice. . . .
> BE IT FINALLY AFFIRMED that the goal of Urban Ministry must be to preach the good news to the poor; to heal the brokenness of the people of the urban and metropolitan areas; to eliminate racism, sexism and classism; and to bring the Realm of God to further realization in our day. To this end we rededicate our lives and our work.[73]

Through contact with the poor and oppressed in America and through the unavoidable involvement with the issues of foreign policy and war, religious leaders are turning away from personal pietism to institutional commitment. Practical theology is transforming the church in the United States. As Archbishop Rembert Weakland has said:

> We are living at a time in which we must re-imagine the Catholic Church. It isn't easy but it is necessary for every Catholic. We must examine our own moral convictions, work them through in the light of the Gospel so that we hold them deeply for ourselves. In these pastoral letters, the bishops are not writing for political reasons, but to begin serious discussions on the major issues of our times.[74]

Practical theology is causing Christians to reimagine the nature and role of religion in our society. The religious denominations, which were once silent on controversial public issues and which once automatically supported government and business corporations, have begun to find their prophetic public voice. As national religious officials speak out on political and social issues, local congregations and ecumenical groups translate their pronouncements into deeds. Theology is leaving the seminaries and the church corridors and moving into legislative chambers, courtrooms, and onto the picket lines.

Advantages of an Explicit Theology of Compassion

Given this variety of theologies, several conclusions are warranted. First, Jewish and Christian theologies are all based upon and contribute to an enriched notion of justice and compassion. Each adds its own distinctive contribution to our understanding of "Shalom" and a "Just Peace." Just as the great teachers of compassion enlarge our understanding, so the thinking, debate, and reflection that produced these theologies enlarge our view of justice and compassion. That justice and compassion are central to such diverse religious groups suggests that they are fundamental to development of our spirituality. In the next chapter, I will consider disciplines, in addition to the study of Scripture, which further develop our compassion and which enable both personal and social transformation. It is enough for now to say that theology is one path to a politics of compassion and transformation.

Theology is a reflection upon action—it is the thought that guides praxis. In this sense, "theologies of compassion" leave the realm of mere emotion and join the realm of thought. Compassion is not only felt, but it is thought through. A theology of compassion is a touchstone to guide action so that "right" results are possible, remembering always that results are in God's hands, not ours. "Right action" can be wise and informed. It need not be limited to knee-jerk liberalism or conservative sentimentality. For these reasons I maintain that the separate theologies reviewed in this chapter are less adequate than an explicit theology of compassion. In fact, a theology of compassion is necessary to complete them.

How are we to assess the limitations and contributions of such diverse theologies? The Kairos Document recently issued by South African Christians helps. It distinguishes between "state theology," "church theology," and "prophetic theology." State theology includes those forms of theology that support the existing institutions. For instance, Judaism sometimes supported the kings of ancient Israel. Jewish priests sometimes became too powerful, and the religious laws they upheld became too narrow. But Jews also rallied to the cry of the prophets. The same pattern holds for various sects of Christianity. Evangelical Christians have traditionally withdrawn into private church experiences, liberal Christians have often accommodated unjust civil governments and decadent cultures, and liberation theologians have uncritically supported brutal revolutionary movements which would set up regimes as repressive as the ones they oppose. Each religious sect can easily fall prey to its own particular form of state theology.

The Kairos Document makes clear the flaws of "state theology," which "is simply the theological justification of the status quo with its racism, capitalism, and totalitarianism. It blesses injustice, canonizes the will of the powerful and reduces the poor to passivity, obedience and apathy. How does 'State Theology' do this? It does it by misusing theological concepts and biblical texts for its own political purposes."[75]

The flaws of church theology are less blatant. "It seeks moderation and reconciliation above all else. This leads to a neutrality that only serves to further entrench oppression."[76] The Kairos Document points out that church theology, like state theology, fails in its understanding of justice. "The justice that is envisioned is the *justice of reform* . . . a justice that is determined by the oppressor. . . . It does not appear to be the more radical justice that comes from below and is determined by the people. . . . "[77] Liberation theologians have pressed this point in their writings. "As Don Helder Camara once said, 'I fed the hungry and they called me a saint; I asked why they were hungry and they called me a "communist." ' "[78] Mainline Protestants, Catholics, and Jews, as well as evangelical Christians, easily fall into the trap of being involved in religion for its own sake rather than for the sake of the world. Practitioners of compassion are protected from this mistake because they are immersed in the pain of the world. In this way even a "passive religion" like Hinduism is transformed in the hands of Gandhi so that it stands not for withdrawal from the world but for engagement in the world—not for meditation away from worldly distractions but for "meditation in action."

Prophetic theology is closest to compassion theology. The authors of the Kairos Document argue:

> We are a divided church because not all of the members of our Churches have taken sides against oppression. In other words, not all Christians have united themselves with God "who is always on the side of the oppressed" (Psalm 103:6). As far as the present crisis is concerned, there is only one way forward to Church unity and that is for those Christians who find themselves on the side of the oppressor or sitting on the fence, to cross over to the other side to be united in faith and action with those who are oppressed. The church must avoid becoming a "Third Force," a force between the oppressor and the oppressed.[79]

The consequence of this position is made clear in *BASTA!* the magazine of the "Sanctuary Movement." "We cannot back away from admitting that a ministry of justice is inevitably political. Making love effective, defending life, bringing about a more just social order are all theological/political tasks."[80] But even the prophetic voice, unless inspired by God and enlarged by exposure to other issues and theologies, can narrow to support of only a particular political group and a particular political agenda. Jacques Ellul suggests that the proper theological and political stance is not merely to oppose the current social order or to support those currently oppressed but to be "involved in a state of permanent revolution."

> In consequence of the claims which God is always making on the world the Christian finds himself [or herself], by that very fact, involved in a state of permanent revolution. Even when the institutions, the laws, the reforms which [we] had advocated have been achieved, even if society be re-organized according to [our] suggestions, [we] still [have] to be in opposition, [we] still must exact more, for the claim of God is as infinite as [God's] forgiveness.[81]

There is no "cheap grace" in either religion or politics. We must struggle to achieve more than the aims of any particular social movement. The task of the prophet is sometimes to "tear down," but it can also be to "build up." At times it is to decry the current regime, but at other times it is to proclaim the new society that can be built. Prophetic theology must be enlarged to encompass liberation, planetary, and practical theologies.

A theology of compassion enlarges other theologies. It overcomes the weakness of state, church, and prophetic theologies. The Jewish concept of justice is greater when it is understood as "shalom," when the injunction of "an eye for an eye" is replaced by the "womb mercy" of God. Only justice understood as harmony with the earth, harmony with God, and harmony with all human beings is an adequate religious and political goal. Then the "Zealous Nationalism" so prevalent in both Israel's and America's history can be replaced with "Prophetic Realism."[82] Then any nation can be "a light unto the nations," showing the way to the peaceable kingdom proclaimed by Isaiah.

The evangelical Christian's commitment to do acts of humanitarian and social service can, in the broader understanding of compassion, include those social actions necessary to change the conditions that produce misery. The strong commitment they have to their religious beliefs and their unwillingness to give in to mainstream U.S. culture can be a base of broader political action. Simply refusing to make the state an object of religious loyalty is insufficient. Compassion directs that we transform the world in which we live. This is not merely a reaction against the secular world but is a positive yearning based upon our love for our fellow humans and for all life on the planet. Modern science and culture must be transcended rather than merely rejected if we are to give birth to a better civilization.

Compassion teaches liberal Christians not to be accomplices with "powers and principalities." Because of this, a theology of compassion is inevitably superior to church theology. Reform in some situations may be a legitimate response. But today's international crises and oppressions cannot be overcome by slow reform. Stronger actions of "liberation" which enlarge the scope of justice are required. Liberal Christians gain strength from their alliance with the modern culture, but they must not become absorbed within it. Compassion for those in pain, and for those who will suffer if new calamities are not averted, can prevent liberal Christians from falling into the trap of simply blessing the status quo.

Liberation and prophetic theologies directly heed the cries of the oppressed. They are based upon compassion, but they are not broad enough to confront potential nuclear war, environmental crisis, or more subtle situations of injustice in the "First World." Liberation theology fails to honor the teaching of Jesus, King, and Gandhi to "love your enemies" and to know that they can be transformed. Neither forgiveness nor conversion of oppressors are really expected in liberation theology. Compassion thus expands liberation theology. It does not blunt the call for action but provides a broader context in which actions to bring justice and transformation are taken.

Planetary theology has a broad scope, but often it does not lead to direct involvement in political action. The solution of both local and planetary problems will not be achieved by "cosmic forces" acting subtly over millennium. What is required is to oppose current political and social realities that have the potential for destroying all life on the planet and reversing creation. A theology of compassion combines the planetary and cosmic sensitivity with the earthy practicality of concrete political struggles.

Practical theologies reflect the efforts of religious leaders to come to grips with war and peace, the worldwide economic crisis, and pressing problems of our cities. Religious leaders are beginning to take the biblical mandate, theological principles, and practical structural problems more seriously. But religious statements— even when translated into lawsuits and lawmaking— do not resolve the underlying social problems that they address. Compassion demands stronger action and greater risks. In this respect, liberation and prophetic theologies are both superior to the practical theology practiced in the United States. A theology of compassion, however, not only describes the problems facing our civilization, but it also leads to the commitment necessary for their resolution.

A theology of compassion is informed by all these theologies and their understanding of the relationship between humans, the earth, and God. Compassion does not reduce these theologies to some simple formula but builds upon them, expands them, completes them, and puts them into practice.

Elaborating a theology of compassion requires study and reflection. But becoming a warrior of compassion requires developing other skills, abilities, and strengths as well. The path of compassion is difficult. It requires fortitude and resiliency. It also requires a sensitivity and openness that is not easily developed in our society. Study of other religions and theologies is not sufficient either. Eventually, we must seek the God within ourselves. We must undertake our own religious quest, following those religious disciplines that allow us to develop and practice our compassion. The path of compassion must lead to personal and social transformation.

Part III

ACTION

Chapter 5
BECOMING RELIGIOUS: THE INTERIOR WORK NECESSARY FOR EXTERIOR ACTION

The outward work
will never be puny
if the inward work
is great.
And the outward work
can never be great or even good
if the inward one is puny or of little worth.
The inward work invariably
includes in itself
all expansiveness,
all breadth,
all length,
all depth.
Such a work
receives and draws all its being
from nowhere else except
from and in the heart of God.
                                Meister Eckhart

There are many different paths to God even in our secular age when God is more often denied than sought. To say the same thing differently, there are many different ways to develop compassion—our ability to feel the pain and suffering of others. Although these paths may involve public political action and public participation in worship, all paths to God invariably involve inner work, away from our public persona and deeds. Meister Eckhart warns us that our outward work will not be great if our inward work is puny. We express our compassion in outer deeds, but we must develop that compassion by inner work.

Thought and reflection are inner mental activities that help to guide our religious and political life. Although study, thought, and reflection are important, a different sort of interior work is also needed. To become more religious does not mean to become more "churched" or to obey the ethical laws and commandments of a particular religion; rather, it requires us to develop our own spirituality.

There is no one required path to develop spirituality. Neither prayers, meditation, fasting, yoga, nor any particular discipline is required to become a self-realized being, to become one with God. A simultaneous act of the heart, mind, and soul is required. Various disciplines only prepare us for this ultimate step. Although some people can take the final religious step quickly, most of us must come to this stage by dedicated practice of spiritual disciplines. The appropriate spiritual disciplines differ for each of us because we are unique. Each of us must overcome our own special barriers to the fulfillment of our life's purpose. Thus, Jesus, Dorothy Day, Sai Baba, King, and Gandhi did not follow the same path or undertake the same disciplines to develop compassion in their lives.

Because various religious disciplines have many teachers, and because there are many "how-to" manuals to guide religious seekers in their practice, there is no need to duplicate detailed instructions here. Rather, my intention is to discuss the purposes and general methods of some important disciplines used by practitioners of compassionate politics. I begin with the disciplines of the body: diet, fasting, hatha yoga, and aerobic exercises. Then I discuss the disciplines of the mind and emotions: meditation, psychoanalysis, dream interpretation, and journal keeping. Finally, I consider the spiritual disciplines of prayer and corporate worship. There are, of course, many other religious disciplines, but most of them share common characteristics with those I have named. For most of us a combination of physical, mental, emotional, and spiritual disciplines is necessary to prepare us to practice compassion at the deepest level. We develop our particular practice individually. But faithful practice of such disciplines helps to remove barriers standing between us and our fuller spiritual development.

The compassionate path to personal and political transfromation is a difficult path. The practice of compassion in service to others and in political action requires courage, strength, and sacrifice. It demands openness, tenderness, and deep feelings. It requires creativity, a deep faith, and imagination. All these dimensions of ourselves must be expanded gradually.

Even mastery and diligent practice of these disciplines is insufficient for achieving their higher purpose. As Richard Foster says in *Celebration of Discipline:* "To know the mechanics does not mean that we are practicing the Discipline. The Spiritual Disciplines are an inward and spiritual reality and the inner attitude of the heart is far more critical than the mechanics for coming into the reality of the spiritual life." Bhagwan Shree Rajneesh says in *Yoga: The Alpha and the Omega* "you should do the practice with reverent devotion. You can do a practice mechanically, with no love, with no devotion, no feeling of holiness about it. Then it will take a very long time, because only through love do things penetrate easily within you. Through devotion you are open—more open. Seeds fall deeper."[2] Although the mechanics and regular practice are essential, the devotion and spirit with which these disciplines are practiced are even more crucial to the effect that they have. There may be long lapses when we do not practice these disciplines, but again and again we find ourselves returning to them. We resume their practice out of devotion to God, love for ourselves, compassion for our brothers and sisters who suffer, and a deep commitment to life.

Disciplines of the Body

Many religions teach that our bodies are the temple of God. As Swami Vishnudevananda puts it, "The body, being the temple of the living spirit, should be carefully tended in order to make it a perfect instrument."[3] Most of us must achieve bodily health before we can successfully purify and develop our emotions, mind, and spirit. Our body is the vehicle we have been given in this life and we must give it sufficient care and attention so that it can function well. Just as a starving child can not be educated and just as we are unlikely to appreciate beautiful works of art while we are hungry, we are unlikely to have many spiritual achievements without physical health. Many physical handicaps, illnesses, and pain have been overcome by saints in their spiritual quests, but for most of us a healthy body is a prerequisite for spiritual development.

Our body is a direct window to the spiritual world. We learn about our world and ourselves through our senses, we meditate by controlling our breathing, we participate in public worship by speaking and singing. Our body is a more intimate part of our religious life than we realize.

Eastern religions teach that the body/mind/spirit, with its many aspects, sheaths, and layers, are united. What occurs on the physical plane affects the mental/emotional planes and spiritual/astral planes. Ultimately, the body, mind, and soul are one and we can affect our emotions, our mind, and our soul by what we eat, by exercise, and by direct control of our bodily functions. It is for this reason that Yogis maintain a vegetarian diet; do exercises; undertake rigorous cleansing and purification of their bodies; and learn to control their breathing, heartbeat, and other "involuntary" functions.

All bodily disciplines have as their goal the removal of physical impediments standing in the way of our leading healthy lives of compassion and service. Compassion includes not only sympathy with oppressed peoples halfway around the world or with threatened life forms—it also includes sympathy for ourselves beginning with our physical bodies. If we can not feel our own body, if we can not love it, if we can not bring it health, then it is unlikely that we will have the energy, strength, wisdom, or courage to help and heal others.

Diet

We are what we eat. Our health, our emotional outlook, and our ability to practice other disciplines depend upon our diet. Our diet also presents us with a moral choice that has planetary political consequences. Frances Moore Lappé in *Diet for a Small Planet* has written: "I feel . . . hopeful about focusing on food as a way to help us see our place in the world more accurately, as a way of relating to the world as world citizens with a sense of responsibility for how our actions and our government's policies affect all the world's peoples." One of the principal ethical and political aspects of our diet is that "the amount of humanly edible protein fed to American livestock and not returned for human consumption approaches the whole world's protein deficit!" Simply modifying U.S. diets to eliminate so much meat would solve much of the immediate problem of world hunger and starvation provided that our problems in economic distribution of food were also solved. "By relying more on non-meat protein sources we can eat in a way that both maximizes the earth's potential to meet our nutritional needs and, at the same time, minimizes the disruption of the earth necessary to sustain us."[4]

Our overconsumption of meat is wasteful and personally harmful. It is wasteful because it takes sixteen pounds of grain and soybeans to produce just one pound of beef. Our overdependence on meat poses a serious food problem for the rest of the world. Livestock now eat more grain than people do. By simply not eating beefsteak, Americans could provide sixteen times as much protein-bearing grains to feed people. American diets also depend too heavily on processed foods and include too much alcohol. Taken together, animal and processed foods, along with alcohol consumption, end up not only denying food to the starving but also harming our health. Lappé outlines eight major problems with the American diet: (1) eating animal protein rather than plants causes high cholesterol and arteriosclerosis; (2) both animal and processed foods contain too much fat, which causes heart disease and cancer; (3) Americans consume too much sugar; (4) there is too much salt; (5) there is too little fiber; (6) we consume too much alcohol, which leads to cirrhosis of the liver, birth defects, mouth cancer, and traffic accidents; (7) there are too many additives, antibiotic residues, and pesticides that contribute to various forms of cancer; and (8) there are too many calories that contribute to obesity, hypertension, and heart disease.[5] Thus our diets undermine our health, distort our emotions (including our feelings about ourselves), and shorten our lives. The addictions we have developed to tobacco, alcohol, and drugs may be the most harmful of all.

A further religious argument for vegetarianism is provided by Hindus in their practice of *ahimsa,* or nonviolence. Hindus believe that an animal that is slaughtered dies in agony. Its terror of death is passed on in the muscles of its body which become the "meat" we eat. Thus, eating animal flesh causes us to absorb their bad vibrations and to share their *karma*, or fate. American Indians, who hunted for part of their food, believed that, at the least, they had to ask the "permission" of animals before they were killed. Frank Waters, in his novel, *The Man Who Killed the Deer,* expressed the Indian sentiment this way: "How then can [humans] be lord of the universe? [We are] equal in importance to the mountain and the blade of grass, to the rabbit and the young corn plant. Therefore, if the life of one of these is to be used for [our] necessity, it must first be approached with reverence and permission obtained by ritual, and thus the balance of the whole maintained intact."[6] If we do not seek permission of beasts before we slay them, Indians believe that their spirits will be harmful to us in subtle ways.

Many vegetarians, who may not believe that the negative vibrations of killing are transmitted to us, still believe that it is immoral to kill animals with feelings and emotions so similar to human beings. Just as we would not agree to Jonathan Swift's "modest proposal" of eating human babies, we should not kill and eat the flesh of our fellow sentient beings. Their slaughter tends to perpetuate in us a willingness to kill and do violence.

Hindus go further in specifying a proper diet than merely abstaining from eating meat. Swami Vishnudevananda summarizes the Hindu understanding this way:

> According to the *Bhagavad Gita,* there are three types of food: namely *sattvic* food [pure food], *rajasic* food [stimulating food], and *tamasic* [impure and rotten food].
>
> Milk, butter, fruits, vegetables, and grains come under the category of good or *sattvic* foods. Spices, hot substances, meat, alcohol, fish, and eggs, which stimulate the nervous system, come under the heading of stimulating or *rajasic* foods, while food that is rotten, putrefied, and overripe comes under the *tamasic* or impure food category.
>
> [Our] preference for one of the above-mentioned types is in accordance with the evolution of [our] mind. Spiritually and mentally advanced people prefer the pure type of food. Average worldly people prefer the *rajasic* or stimulating food, and the *tamasic* or impure type of low, undeveloped [persons] prefers the last type of rotten and putrefied foodstuffs.
>
> Pure food brings purity and calmness to the mind and is soothing and nourishing to the body. *Rajasic* food arouses animal passions in [us] and brings a restless state of mind. It also causes nervous and circulatory disorders such as high blood pressure, hardening of the arteries, and uric acid diseases. . . .
>
> The third type, *tamasic* or impure food, makes a person dull and lazy. [Our] thinking capacity diminishes and [we] sink almost to the level of animals or bushmen. [We have] no high ideals or purpose in

life; on the physical side, [we] suffer from chronic ailments of the body. Thus, according to [our] degree of mental purity, [we] instinctively choose certain types of food.[7]

From this point of view, only *sattvic* food provides the right diet for spiritual advancement because it contributes to health, to a balanced mind, and to the quiet emotions necessary for spiritual progress. Cultivating a properly balanced diet requires considerable study and patience as a taste for a vegetarian diet is developed. Preparation of these meals takes time and planning, and they can not be purchased at most restaurants. Although the palate has to be introduced gradually to this new cuisine, in a short time our tastes do change and the foods we used to like will be rejected in favor of a more healthy diet.

Fasting

Closely related to food and diet is the religious practice of fasting. Many religious people, including Jews and Moslems, have explicit fast days on their religious calendars. Jesus fasted and expected his followers to do so. In religious tradition, "fasting always centers on spiritual purposes" even though it may have other healing and physical benefits. "Fasting must forever center on God. It must be God-initiated and God-ordained. Like the prophetess Anna, we need to be 'worshiping with fasting' (Luke 2:37). . . . John Wesley declared, 'First, let [fasting] be done unto the Lord with our eye singly fixed on [God]. Let our intention herein be this, and this alone, to glorify our [Parent] which is in heaven.' "[8] While accomplishing spiritual purposes, fasting also cleans the body of toxins, allows the internal organs to rest, and brings a weight loss of a pound or two per day of fast.

Most religious fasts mean abstaining from solid food but, normally, liquids are consumed. Frequently, fruit juice is taken in the morning in the place of breakfast and soup broth is consumed at one of the other daily meal times. Anyone who fasts must drink large amounts of water or juice, or the body will quickly become dehydrated.

Begin with a short twenty-four hour fast to gain experience. Such short fasts cure many common illnesses, particularly those associated with the stomach. Longer, more spiritually oriented fasts usually last from three to seven days. The physical effects of these longer fasts are described by Richard Foster.

The first three days are usually the most difficult in terms of physical discomfort and hunger pains. The body is beginning to rid itself of the toxic poisons that have built up over years of poor eating habits, and it is not a comfortable process. This is the reason for the coating on the tongue and bad breath. . . . You may experience headaches during this time, especially if you are an avid coffee or tea drinker. . . . By the fourth day the hunger pains are beginning to subside though you will have feelings of weakness and occasional dizziness. . . . By the sixth or seventh day you will begin to feel stronger and more alert. Hunger pains will continue to diminish. . . . The body will have eliminated the bulk of the toxic poisons and you will feel good. Your sense of concentration will be sharpened and you will feel as if you could continue fasting indefinitely. Physically this is the most enjoyable part of the fast.[9]

Fasting can be done in many circumstances, but I have found it easiest to fast with other religious seekers, away from my usual routines and in conjunction with exercise such as hatha yoga and swimming. For me, fasting contributes to more vivid dreams and to stronger visions during meditation. Its principal physical benefits are to cleanse the body of poisons and to reduce weight. Moreover, it serves as an aid to many spiritual disciplines and heightens their effects. Even if you are not fasting, you will quickly discover that you can't eat for several hours before doing effective yoga or meditation as the body will simply be too busy digesting food to be free to concentrate on these activities.

Hatha Yoga

In conjunction with proper diet and with fasting to purify the body, exercise is important for health and for spiritual growth. A set of powerful exercises have been developed into a system of hatha yoga.

Yoga, which means union with God as well as the disciplines to attain this union, has an ancient history reaching back thousands of years. Raja yoga, the royal eightfold path of yoga, was codified by Patanjali in about the second century B.C. in his *Yoga Sutras* or aphorisms. In that work he described the eight paths of raja, or royal, yoga:

1. *Yamas*—restraints
2. *Niyamas*—observances
3. *Asanas*—postures
4. *Pranayama*—control of breath
5. *Pratyahara*—control of senses
6. *Dharana*—concentration
7. *Dhyana*—meditation
8. *Samadhi*—self-realization.[10]

Bhagwan Rajneesh has said of the teachings of Patanjali:

> Yoga is pure science, and Patanjali is the greatest name as far as the
> world of yoga is concerned. This man is rare. There is no other name
> comparable to Patanjali. For the first time in the history of humanity,
> religion was brought to the state of a science: he made religion a science
> of bare laws. No belief is needed. . . .
>
> If you follow Patanjali, you will come to know that he is as exact as
> any mathematical formula. Simply do what he says and the result will
> happen. The result is bound to happen;. it is just like two plus two
> equals four. . . . No belief is needed: you simply do it and know.[11]

Following Patanjali, in A.D. 1500, Swatmarama systematized and
codified the science of hatha yoga in *Hathayogapradipika*. According to
Swatmarama, "ha" represents the sun and "tha" represents the moon so that
hatha yoga unites the energies of right and left, male and female, active and
passive. Hatha yoga consists of at least 108 *asanas* or exercises. These are
practiced for the sake of achieving higher states of consciousness and not
merely to perfect the postures themselves.[12]

In *The Complete Illustrated Book of Yoga* Swami Vishnudevananda says:
"The aim of all yoga practice is to achieve truth wherein the individual soul
identifies itself with the supreme soul of God." To achieve this identification,
no matter which religious path is taken, requires "morality, a spiritual
disposition, and regular Yogic exercises." Of its virtues he says, "Hatha Yoga
gives attention to the physical body, which is the vehicle of the spirit's
existence and activity. Purity of mind is not possible without purity of the
body in which it functions, and by which it is affected." *Asanas*, or exercises
of hatha yoga, are based on "stretching, relaxation, deep breathing, and
increased circulation and concentration."[13] Their purpose, as taught by
Swatmarama, is "to make one firm, free from maladies, and light of limb."[14]

In their introductory manual on hatha yoga, Samskrti and Veda expand this
explanation of its benefits and purposes:

> First, to prepare the body for meditation, making it calm, steady and
> firm; second, to free the body from disease . . . to develop superb
> health so the mind is not distracted by aches and pains after the body has
> been made steady for meditation; and third, to bring lightness to the
> body, not only literally, by reducing excess weight and increasing
> suppleness, but also figuratively, counteracting heaviness and
> depression by developing lightness of feeling and expression.[15]

Usharbudh Arya, in *Philosophy of Hatha Yoga,* argues that hatha yoga refines "the body to move a human being to a finer energy existence."

> A practitioner of Hatha Yoga should undertake his [or her] practice with the aspiration of making his [or her] body a fit temple of God—not merely figuratively but literally—to make it a proper vessel for the awakened divine ray called the *kundalini.* Otherwise, when the spiritual energy begins to build up the body will be unable to contain it because it has not been trained. Hatha Yoga is practiced to train the body to serve as a fit vessel for the Spirit of God within so that when the coils of Divine Energy are uncoiled, the body should not become a hinderance.[16]

The *asanas* or postures of hatha yoga are exercises in which the individual external muscles and internal organs of the body are stretched, strengthened, and developed as the spine and joints are made more flexible. The ultimate aim is to achieve harmony and balance, and the exercises work toward that end. Whenever one side of the body is stretched, the other side is also stretched before the exercise is completed. A yogic body is not muscle bound like the body of a weight lifter; rather, it is supple, flexible, tough, lean, and strong. Control is developed not only over the external muscles but over inner organs such as our lungs and heart so that breathing, heartbeat, and other "involuntary" functions can easily be controlled by the yogi. These postures teach the practitioner how to overcome fear and pain. They bring balance, sureness, and supreme confidence. All these exercises are done with an awareness both of the individual parts and of the body as a whole. The development of full bodily awareness contributes to the focusing of attention required in meditation.

A single yoga posture may be taken as an example of all the *asanas.* In the shoulderstand or *sarvangasana* (all members' posture), the individual lies on his or her back, with the arms along the side of the body and the legs together. Inhaling, he or she slowly raises their legs until they are perpendicular. The hips are then raised off the floor, and the hands are placed on either side of the spine with the palms as close to the shoulders as possible. This upside-down pose is held at first for twenty or thirty seconds. Later, with practice, it is held for more than three minutes, so that the blood may drain in the opposite direction from the way it normally flows when one stands or sits.

This posture benefits the shoulders, arms, legs, head, neck, back and internal organs; strengthens arms, chest, and shoulder; slims legs and hips; strengthens back and abdominal muscles; and places gentle traction on the cervical vertebrae, keeping this important area healthy and flexible. In addition, venous drainage of the legs occurs quickly and completely, especially benefiting those with varicose veins and, diaphragmatic breathing is easily observed and learned. The posture also causes higher blood pressure and simple mechanical pressure in the neck to rejuvenate the thyroid and parathyroid glands, making them function optimally; reduces the occurrence of acute and chronic throat ailments; increases blood supply to all the important structures of the neck; and is a panacea for internal organ ailments, especially those of old age. The shoulderstand combats indigestion, constipation, degeneration of endocrine glands, problems occurring in the liver, the gall bladder, the kidney, the pancreas, the spleen, and the digestive system.[17]

Thus, each *asana* benefits many different organs and muscles in the body. However, hatha yoga soon becomes more than mere physical exercise. When done properly, it is a meditation and an act of worship. As Usharbudh Arya has written: "The entire practice of hatha yoga as an act of worship, as an act of ritual is an enactment of the cycle of creation and dissolution, an enactment of the cycle of birth and death. You start with a deep breath, and end with a corpse: [The last *asana* in daily yoga practice is the corpse pose which brings final relaxation and a meditative state.] You die daily, and thereby you become immortal."[18]

There are four direct connections between hatha yoga and meditative practice. First, in the corpse posture, "you become relaxed, and then that leads to meditation"; second, through breathing exercises you are led "to control of *prana* [energy] and that leads into meditation"; third, through the practice of *asanas* your body comes under control, the posture comes under control, and your mind "stops its fight and becomes still, and is led into meditation"; and fourth, *Kriyas* [purification practices] in hatha yoga start "with eye exercise, move on to gazing; gazing becomes concentration; and concentration, prolonged, becomes meditation."[19] The physical exercises prepare us for meditation and spiritual exercises.

The heart of yogic exercises is breathing. Gaining control over "involuntary" functions like our heartbeat depends upon learning to control our breath. Control of our breathing also opens the gateway to meditation and to effective physical actions. This can be seen in martial arts demonstrations but can also be true in tense political situations and in times of crisis.

Concentrating upon breathing allows us to alter our psychological moods. Through breathing exercises we dissipate the stress that is so endemic to modern life and in the tension-producing work of social justice.

The yogis discovered centuries ago that breathing is the elixir of life. They developed it into an empirical science and art that could be applied in different rhythmic patterns to every human need. There is a way to step up mental performance through a brisk supply of oxygen to the brain cells. By flushing the bloodstream with oxygen, the cells in the body are revitalized. A reservoir of energy can be slowly gathered, focused, and then directed through the body to strengthen the lungs and develop a strong, efficient heart. This builds up recuperative powers, calms the nerves, induces restful sleep, and slows down the aging process.[20]

As the *Hatha Yoga Pradipika* says, "Mind is the master of the senses, and breath is the master of the mind."[21] A principal goal of hatha yoga is control of the breath and, hence, control of the mind and emotions. This opens the pathway to higher spiritual disciplines such as meditation.

Aerobic Exercise

However beneficial yogic *asanas* may be, many Americans need to supplement their yoga practice with aerobic exercises. Chief among these are jogging, swimming, and biking, which burn calories effectively. Someone who weighs 170 pounds burns 10.4 calories a minute when jogging an eleven-minute mile, 9.8 calories a minute when swimming a crawl, and 9.2 calories a minute when biking at ten miles per hour. Thus, after jogging a mile, ll4 calories are burned off.[22] Aerobic exercises dramatically slim the waistline, build lung and heart capacity, improve blood circulation, help relieve mild forms of depression, and add to general strength and physical fitness. In addition, if practiced correctly, these exercises can also lead to meditation. Runners discover that after they hit their stride, they feel totally relaxed. If they close their eyes they may even see visions. Runners report that they experience clearer thinking on problems that have been bothering them. The same is true of swimmers after a half mile or so.

Running can be hard on the knees and joints, so care must be taken in adopting it as a regular exercise. Proper warm-up, proper equipment in the case of jogging and biking, and proper safeguards against accidents are required for all aerobic sports. Training should begin with small distances, gradually increasing the distance and speed. These exercises should be done at least three times a week for at least a half hour if they are to provide major health benefits. They require the same care and sustained practice as hatha yoga.

Aerobic exercises are useful in expelling negative energy and emotions — particularly in fighting mild depression. Because they require breathing a lot of fresh oxygen, they affect the emotions just like hatha yoga breathing exercises. The common emotional trap to be avoided in aerobic exercises is overcompetitiveness which can lead to overexertion, physical injuries, and elimination of the spiritual benefits of these disciplines. As with all disciplines, it is the spirit in which they are done that is critical to their positive benefits.

Because Western culture over several thousands of years has divorced mind and body and because modern fashion upholds an unrealistic image of the ideal young body which is unobtainable by people of different body types and ages; we often become alienated from our bodies. Although this is true for both men and women, the tyranny is especially great for women in a patriarchal society. Sandra Bartky has argued that there is a direct relationship between "infantilization" and the current "tyranny of slenderness."

> The youthful body presently in vogue is an infantilized body, the body of an adolescent girl. . . . And consider this: all these practices—beauty discipline, our graceful (yet sexy) styles of movement, dieting—produce the female body as a certain kind of *spectacle*. But a spectacle for whom? For an abstract, internalized patriarchal consciousness—for the gaze of the male connoisseur we carry within us. He is the subject for whom I must make myself a gorgeous object. This creates a profound dependency in women: validation of my body, of *myself* depends on pleasing him, of conforming to his standards.[23]

If external standards cause us to be alienated from our bodies, we develop a negative self-image and even self-loathing. This leads to fad diets and fad exercises. When we accept external standards for our bodies and our lives, we fail to fulfill our own potential. Thus, aerobic exercises can either be part of a faddish attempt to lose weight or they can be a discipline of health, depending, as always, upon the spirit in which we undertake these practices.

Many religious people are out of touch with their bodies. Some Christian sects even teach that the body is a source of sin, an instrument to be controlled. Religious activists who do not necessarily believe that the body is sinful become so caught up in efforts to help others that they neglect themselves. They care little for what they eat and do not get adequate exercise, often becoming mildly depressed. They tell themselves that they have "sacrificed" their health for some political or religious cause. Then they wonder why they are often ineffective in carrying out plans for improving the world. But great spiritual leaders who are able to perform miracles are supremely in touch with themselves, at harmony with the world, and one with God.

The practice of compassion can begin with physical awareness. As we become healthy and more aware of our own bodies, we are more likely to succeed in the emotional, mental, and spiritual disciplines that make possible a healthy and sustained politics of compassion and transformation. The politics of compassion and transformation requires, beyond all else, endurance. Great strength is needed to continue to press for changes in the world in spite of the inertia of human nature and human institutions. Because the politics of compassion is the hardest discipline to follow, we are well advised to prepare ourselves by developing physical disciplines. As we master higher disciplines, physical disciplines become easier, or we can, as in the case of Buddha, dispense with them. But, by then, we will be in touch with greater energies and able to make wise decisions based upon higher knowledge. As we experience personal, physical transformation, we begin to understand that social transformation is possible.

Mental and Emotional Disciplines

As diet and exercise are essential to the physical body, meditation (which quiets the mind and emotions) is essential for our mental and emotional development. For Jewish prophets, mystical meditation sealed their special relationship to God: "God spoke to them not because they had special abilities, but because they were willing to listen." Similarly, meditation is an integral part of Christian devotion as "a crucial preparation for and adjunct to the work of prayer."[24] Eastern religions depend upon meditation for self-realization or God-realization, and all religions depend upon some form of mental and emotional disciplines.

Meditation

Some authors suggest that there are differences between Christian and Eastern meditation. Richard Foster, for one, claims:

> Eastern meditation is an attempt to empty the mind; Christian meditation is an attempt to empty the mind in order to fill it. . . . Detachment is the final goal of Eastern religion. It is escaping from the miserable wheel of existence. . . . Christian meditation goes far beyond the notion of detachment. There is a need for detachment. But we must go on to *attachment*. The detachment from the confusion all around us is in order to have a richer attachment to God and to other human beings. Christian meditation leads us to the inner wholeness necessary to give ourselves to God freely, and to the spiritual perception necessary to attack social evils.[25]

Often Christian meditation focuses on a particular scriptural text. Dietrich Bonhoeffer describes this meditation as follows: "We go into the unfathomable depths of a particular sentence and word. . . . In our meditation we ponder the chosen text on the strength that it has something utterly personal to say to us for the day and for our Christian life. . . . We expose ourselves to the specific word until it addresses us personally."[26] This meditation on the Word leads to prayer and contemplation, which is very similar to Eastern meditation. But, instead of beginning with a Sanskrit mantra, Christian meditation begins with a word or passage from the Christian Bible.

Despite these differences, in most ways meditation is similar in diverse traditions. Here is how Lawrence LeShan describes the consistent purpose of various traditions:

> We meditate to find, to recover, to come back to something of ourselves we once dimly and unknowingly had and have lost without knowing what it was or where or when we lost it. We may call it access to more of our human potential or being closer to ourselves and to reality, or to more of our capacity for love and zest and enthusiasm, or our knowledge that we are part of the universe and can never be alienated or separated from it, or our ability to see and function in reality more effectively.[27]

However we express it, the result of meditation is increased effectiveness and a different view of reality.

What is meditation that produces these mystical, psychological, and physical results? Sri Swami Sivananda defined it as that "state of mind wherein there are no . . . sensual thoughts." It is attained by "keeping up an unceasing flow of God-consciousness" and by "making the mind blank." For Swami Sivananda, it "is the only way for attaining Immortality and Eternal Bliss"; it serves as "the royal road to attain Godhead."[28] Swami Muktananda, in *Meditate,* expands Sivananda's descriptions.

> What we are seeking is the Supreme Truth, and through meditation we can experience the Truth vibrating in the form of sublime happiness in the heart. . . . Truly speaking, a human being is divine. It is only our wrong understanding which keeps us small. . . . We meditate to unfold our inner being. The Brihadjaabaala Upanishad says, "Through meditation we reach a place where the wind does not blow, where the heat of the sun does not reach, where death can not penetrate." This is the country of eternal bliss. If a yogi becomes established there, he [or she] becomes liberated. Death can not touch him [or her].[29]

Meditation begins by quieting the body and focusing the mind on a single object. This one-pointedness releases and directs "latent internal energy," which eventually leads to discovering the *Self,* the knowledge of which "makes us one with God." Finding the self or the divine spark within is the ultimate purpose of meditation.

Just as this energy pervades the universe, it permeates the human body, filling it from head to toe. It is this *Shakti* which carries on all our life functions. It becomes the *prana* and *apana,* which makes our heart beat and which causes the blood to flow in our veins. In this way, this conscious energy powers our bodies.

However, in its spiritual aspect, the energy ordinarily lies dormant. The awakening of this latent inner energy is essential for all of us, because only when it is activated and unfolds within us are we truly able to experience the Self. According to the yogic scriptures, this inner *Kundalini Shakti* resides at a subtle energy center known as the *muladhara chakra,* located at the base of the spine. The awakening of this energy is the beginning of the subtle inner process which leads us ultimately to the state of union with the Self. . . . The Upanishads teach that we can not attain the Self by [diet] or by performing rituals. We can attain the Self only through direct knowledge; it is knowledge which makes us one with God. When our dormant *Shakti* is awakened, this knowledge arises, and very naturally we are able to see the Self.[30]

Many who practice meditation do not experience or expect these spiritual benefits, but all agree that there are psychological benefits. LeShan describes them as follows:

One psychological effect of serious meditation, then, is to comprehend a new way of perceiving and relating to the world. On the basis of the experience of those who have achieved it, this attainment, and the paths to it, bring a strong serenity and inner peace that remain stable even in the face of much adversity.

The second psychological effect grows out of the work itself. For this effect it is not so important how well you do at a meditation . . . but rather how hard you work at the job. It is the steady work . . . that strengthens the will, purpose, goal-oriented behavior, ability to bar distractions, etc., and facilitates the personality reorganization that is a part of our slow endless growth to real maturity. . . . Those who stay with this kind of work have increased competence and confidence.

Finally, meditation leads to deautomatization of perception and behavior, which is the reason for the remarkable freshness and clarity of perception that often occurs after serious meditation work. Things seem to have more "suchness." "Red is redder, water is wetter, and mud is muddier. We see again with fresh eyes from which the scales of inattention have dropped."[31]

There are many types of meditation. They include meditations of the body such as t'ai chi and hatha yoga, actions in everyday life with total concentration, meditation on concrete objects or forms of God, and abstract meditation without a concrete object. Two forms of meditation merit special attention for those concerned with a politics of compassion and transformation: Christian and Eastern meditation.

For Richard Foster, Christian meditation should be practiced in a place that is quiet and free from interruption, preferably in one designated place, in a position that is most comfortable and the least distracting. It is probably "best to sit in a straight chair, with the back correctly positioned in the chair and both feet flat on the floor. . . . Place the hands on the knees, palms up in a gesture of receptivity. Sometimes it is good to close the eyes in order to remove distractions and center attention on the living Christ. At other times it is helpful to ponder a picture of the Lord or look out at the lovely trees and plants for the same purpose. Regardless of how it is done, the aim is to center the attention of the body, the emotions, the mind and the spirit upon 'the glory of God in the face of Christ' (2 Cor. 4:6)."[32]

In the Eastern approach to meditation, one sits on the floor on a meditation cushion with the back straight and the legs crossed in front. More advanced students assume the "lotus posture" with the feet on top of the thighs. Beginning students who have difficulty in sitting with their backs straight without tiring may sit against a wall, on a couch, or in a chair with cushions for back support. The essential requirement of the posture is that the back be straight. The palms of the hands are open, resting on the knees, with the thumb and second finger touching to close the energy fields that circulate through the body. The eyes are either closed or unfocused.

Swami Muktananda discusses the four factors involved in Eastern meditation: "The object of meditation, which is the inner Self; the mantra [a Sanskrit phrase] is the vibration of the Self; the *asana,* the posture in which we can sit comfortably for a long time; and the natural *pranayama* [breathing which controls subtle energy flows] which arises when we repeat the mantra with love and reverence. These four factors are interrelated, and, when they come together, meditation occurs in a very natural manner."[33] Muktananda meditations begin by chanting the mantra *Om Namah Shivaya* which means "I bow to Shiva." The mantra may be chanted in a group or alone.

> This mantra will help you in meditation. Through the mantra, the mind which is always wandering, easily turns within, towards the pure Self [or God]. . . . It means "I bow to Shiva." Shiva is neither Hindu, nor Muslim, nor Buddhist, nor Christian. [Shiva] is your own Self. [Shiva] is the Self of all. Shiva is all powerful. Always repeat the mantra.
>
> The mantra received from a Guru who has attained full realization by its power is a live, conscious mantra. It vibrates with his [or her] Shakti. Such a mantra has the power to give you liberation by cutting through all the knots of your karma.[34]

After ten minutes chanting aloud, the mantra is chanted silently. Then breathing becomes regular and a deeper state of consciousness is reached. Visions may appear or the mind may wander. These images are simply observed and soon subside. The point of meditation is not primarily to have images, visions, or hallucinatory experiences but to go beyond them. Repeating the mantra stills the mind. "Along the way will be many experiences, and these experiences are fine. However, the true state is beyond them. As we go deeper into meditation, we reach a place where we see nothing and hear nothing. Here there is nothing but bliss. This is the place of the Self, and true meditation is to become immersed in that."[35] Thus, the task of meditation is not to see visions or reach a particular ecstatic state but "inner growth and becoming."[36] As Eckhart said, it is because of inner work that we can do great outward work. Meditation helps us to discover a part of ourselves and our hidden potential by quieting the mind and emotions so that the hidden side of ourselves, our connection with God, and our oneness with our fellow creatures can be experienced.

The process of meditation as practiced by both Christians and by Eastern religions is ultimately very similar. "The common factor uniting such disparate [meditation movements] is a tendency to go beyond the emotional and intellectual consciousness. That is why these forms of meditation have few words. And sometimes they have no words at all." Brainwaves are classified as beta (thirteen or more cycles per second), alpha (eight to twelve cycles), theta (four to seven cycles), and delta (zero to four cycles). Meditation produces clear physical results that can be measured by these brain waves. "Put in scientific terms, what the spiritual masters wanted was to bring their disciples into an alpha state and keep them there, intuitively realizing the value of this neurological conditioning."

However, those who actually practice meditation do not provide such a cold scientific description, but resort to contradictory, vivid images. They seem to be at a loss to give a straightforward, linear explanation of their experience. "In the meditation of the great religions one makes progress by going beyond thought, beyond concepts, images, beyond reasoning, thus entering a deeper state of consciousness or enhanced awareness that is characterized by profound silence. This is the *silentium mysticum*. It is a state of consciousness in which there may be no words or images."[37]

Meditation is not just a technique but a way of love and compassion. In *Silent Music,* William Johnston says: "My point is that whether one recites the *mantra* [words] or gazes at the *mandala* [a four-sided visual design] or wrestles with the *koan* [a Buddhist verbal puzzle], the whole process should be undergirded by love if the enlightenment is to go the whole way." Along this meditative path we encounter first the "prayer of quiet" when we first glimpse brief moments of enlightenment. These then become more habitual, and there is a more permanent mystical union or integration with divine energy. This brings a stage of ecstasy which leads to transforming union.

The meditator, now accustomed to the powerful inflow of spirit is able to control it. Hence no more suspension of the sensible faculties, no more loss of control, no more ligature, and in place of these a great freedom to act and to work and to love. This in some ways resembles the Zen "return to the market-place," a stage in which the enlightened person comes back to ordinary life to redeem all sentient beings.[38]

Thus, the deep inner work of meditation leads back to the real world. In our time, it leads back to a world on the brink of potential disasters.

Meditation is a preparation for compassionate action, not a retreat from action. Zen masters advise that "The superior work you have done so industriously in quietness should be applied when you are submerged in the tumult of your daily life. If you find it difficult to do so, it is most likely that you have not gained much from the work of quietude."[39] Dietrich Bonhoeffer comes to much the same conclusion: "Every day brings to the Christian many hours in which he [or she] will be alone in an unchristian environment. These are the times of *testing*. This is the test of true meditation and true Christian community. . . . This is the place where we find out whether the Christian's meditation . . . has led him [or her] into real contact with God, from which he [or she] emerges strengthened and purified."[40] The goal of meditation is not simply frenzied activity; rather, it is itself an *act* of compassion. Johnston concludes that meditation "is a love affair and that love is the most powerful energy in the universe. It is love that builds the earth and carries forward the thrust of evolution."[41]

There are many paths and practices of meditation. Let us consider two very different approaches set forth in *The Cloud of Unknowing* by an unknown fourteenth-century English monk and *The Secret of the Golden Flower* by eighteenth-century taoist monks compiled from sayings at least as old as the eighth century.

In *The Cloud of Unknowing* the ultimate goal, as with many meditation practices, "is union with God, not as God is thought of or as God is imagined to be, but as God is. . . . "By coming into contact with one's naked being" it becomes possible to come into contact with God. This is not achieved by thinking about God's attributes such as kindness, nor is it achieved by theological study. "For even though it is good to think about the kindness of God and to love [God] and to praise [God] for it, nevertheless it is far better to think about [God's] naked being and to praise . . . and to love [God] for [Godself]."

Union with God can not be achieved by ordinary consciousness, but in this Christian tradition it can be accomplished "by means of disciplined attention to the activities of the mind." This work is accomplished by withdrawing attention from our surroundings and by concentrating our energies within. An individual focuses upon how "separated by nature from God [he or she] can yet achieve unity with God." From this desire within "the cloud of unknowing, a spontaneous prayer may be called forth. It will not be an eloquent prayer, but a prayer of one word, perhaps of only one syllable, such as 'God' . . .".[42]

The unknown fourteenth-century monk further declares:

> Prayer in itself properly is nothing less than a devout intention directed toward God to receive good and remove evil. Since all evil is comprehended in sin, either by cause or being, let us therefore say, or think, or mean, when we wish to pray intently to remove evil, only this little word "sin." And if we wish to pray intently to receive good, let us cry either with word or thought, or desire no other word and no more words but this one word, "God." This is because all good is in God, either by cause or by being.[43]

This focus on a one-word mantra such as "God" or "Love" is enough because "the perfect apprentice does not seek to be released from pain nor to receive greater rewards, but . . . seeks simply nothing but God. . . ."[44] Through deep yearning, the gradual elimination of distractions, and this single syllable mantra or prayer repeated over and over union with God is achieved.

The Secret of the Golden Flower claims that "The Golden Flower alone, which grows out of inner detachment from all entanglement with things, is eternal. A [person] who reaches this stage transposes [his or her] ego; [he or she] is no longer limited to the monad but penetrates the magic circle of the polar duality of all phenomena and returns to the undivided One, the Tao." The Taoists teach further that "The Golden Flower is the light. . . . It is the true energy of the transcendent great One [God]."[45] Thus, as with many meditation techniques the Taoist purpose is to activate the divine energy so as to merge with God.

In this meditation tradition the disciple gains control of this light and energy by closing his or her eyes and looking inward. This process is aided by proper, rhythmic breathing. "Since heart and breath are mutually dependent, the circulation of light must be united with the rhythm of breathing." As the light and energy is collected, it is concentrated inwardly and disciples free themselves from outside entanglements. "Consciousness reverts to contemplation . . . a psychic state which can best be characterized as a detachment of consciousness from the world . . . . [a consciousness] no longer preoccupied with the images of things. . . ."

Reaching this stage of development allows life energy (what Hindus call Kundalini Energy) to be conserved. "A [person] who holds to the way of conservation [of life energy] all through life may reach the stage of the Golden

Flower [or immortal spirit-body], which then frees the ego from the conflict of opposites, and it again becomes part of the Tao, the undivided, great One [or God]."[46] Detachment, control of the breath, focusing inward, and consuming the divine energy within allows enlightenment.

Meditation, using any of these various methods, may allow us to achieve great outer deeds but it is, first of all, an inner path to God. Meditation begins in quiet and silence. Later, it becomes "meditation in action." Deeds become our prayer and our mantra. Our very lives become a meditation and have within them moments of meditative action.

Psychoanalysis and Dream Interpretation

A Western technique of self-discovery that differs substantially from meditation, psychoanalysis began as a method of treating hysteria. At first, hypnosis was used to help patients reveal their fantasies during their "absences"—when hysteria symptoms were manifested. The important finding from studying hysteria was that "symptoms of the disease would disappear when in hypnosis the patient could be made to remember the situation and the associative connections under which they first appeared, provided free vent was given to the emotions which they aroused." The key was uncovering emotions that had been repressed. Sigmund Freud thus concluded: "We feel justified in regarding 'emotion' as a quantity which may become increased, derived, and displaced. . . . The patient fell ill because the emotion developed in the pathogenic situation was prevented from escaping normally. . . . The essence of the sickness lies in the fact that these 'imprisoned' emotions undergo a series of abnormal changes."[47]

Freud's general theory, based upon his work with neurotic patients, was that they were driven by unconscious desires. Wishes from as far back as childhood still existed in the unconscious and manifested themselves in disguised and unrecognized ways. If we become aware and accept these urges, we can act them out, transform their energy by sublimation into the pursuit of a higher goal, or knowingly reject the original impulse.[48] There are a number of methods to achieve this "talking cure," and psychoanalysis is useful for more than treating neurotics. It is a method of self-discovery in which we learn about ourselves and discover our oneness with our fellow humans at the level of sexuality and personality.

Psychoanalysis begins with a model of the human personality. The Freudian model of an ego, id, and superego, in which sexual instinctual desires of the id are hidden from the ego and suppressed by the superego, is not entirely satisfactory. Although it is important to discover our repressed, societally unacceptable instincts, this is not enough to bring psychological health and wholeness. A more complete model was provided by C. G. Jung who distinguished between two basic psychological types, introvert and extrovert. In the first type, the psychic energy is directed inwardly. In the second, the energy is directed outwardly and the person is naturally more outgoing. These two types are further differentiated by four functions of consciousness, understood as two sets of opposites.

Figure 1. Four functions of consciousness.

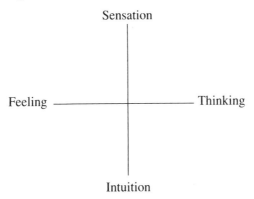

The four functions differ as to whether individuals favor thought or feelings to guide their judgment and whether they experience the world according to the impressions made upon their senses or by "intuiting" hidden relationships and connections. One of the four functions will be dominant for each personality type and, usually, only one other function will be highly developed. In modern Western society, thinking and sensation are usually dominant, leaving feeling and intuition "disregarded, undeveloped, or even repressed."[49]

Based on the Jungian model, part of our psychological task is to learn which of the personality types we possess and to develop our natural inclinations and abilities. But the Jungian approach is also concerned with the repressed aspects of the personality. Our maturation depends on incorporating the "shadow" parts into the conscious self.

> The shadow is a moral problem that challenges the whole ego-personality, for no one can become conscious of the shadow without considerable moral effort. To become conscious of it involves recognizing the dark aspects of the personality as present and real. This act is the essential condition for any kind of self-knowledge, and it therefore, as a rule, meets with considerable resistance. Indeed, self-knowledge as a psychotherapeutic measure frequently requires much painstaking work extending over a long period.[50]

For Jung, the psyche contains not only an individual's conscious and unconscious mind; in addition, each of us is inextricably tied to the whole of human history through a collective unconscious. "The psyche is not of today; its ancestry goes back many millions of years. Individual consciousness is only the flower and the fruit of a season, sprung from the perennial rhizome beneath the earth; and it would find itself in better accord with the truth if it took the existence of the rhizome into its calculations. For the root matter is the mother of all things."[51] The secrets of the collective unconscious are revealed in archetypal potentials, the images of which appear most obviously in myths and tales as recurring, basic patterns of experience. In short, there is a direct connection between ourselves and other people, including our ancestors. As Jung said in his autobiography, "It has always seemed to me that I had to answer questions which fate had posed to my forefathers, and which had not yet been answered, or as if I had to complete, or perhaps continue, things which previous ages had left unfinished."[52]

Moreover, as Jung demonstrated, the human psyche, rooted in the collective unconscious, struggles against the ego, personal masks, and social roles that tend to get us stuck in old habits. The aim of the progressive thrust of the psyche was called by Jung "individuation." It has as its goal the ongoing actualization of the Self as the reconciling center of all archetypes and as the source of all "symbols of unity and wholeness."[53] Jungian analyst John Giannini described it this way:

> A person is challenged to realize his/her uniqueness, as opposed to collective conformity, in a process that Jung called individuation. This process has a goal, a circling around a consciously experiencing center, the archetype of the self. Realizing one's selfhood, however, does not isolate one; rather the person's roles in society become more flexible, varied and sensitive to endless change. Rigid persona structures (social masks or games) are shed, as one's entire bodily presence, not just face or clothing, becomes the carrier and amplifier of the Self archetype. One's movements, feelings, ideas, relationships, as well as roles, become increasingly authentic, accurate mirrors of an otherwise hidden inner life.[54]

Thus, Jungian psychoanalysis is broader than Freudian approaches. Like Eastern meditation, it has as its goals the discovery of the Self, which is not only the personal self with simple instincts such as love, sex, and death. Jungian concepts link us through archetypes to our fundamental connections with our ancestors, other people, and all human history. The Self, found through individuation, is similar to the divine Self revealed by meditation. That Jung was profoundly influenced by Eastern thought and experience makes this connection even more understandable.

For our purposes, it is important to connect the general Jungian model to the lives of actual religious leaders. John Sanford in *The Kingdom Within* uses

Jesus of Nazareth as an example of a person who developed his personality along each of the dimensions specified by the Jungian model.

> A whole person . . . has achieved some development in both [the extrovert and introvert] realms. Without some development within himself [or herself], the life of the extrovert may be shallow; without some capacity to function in the world, the insights of the introvert may prove ineffectual. Only if a person has some development both inwardly and outwardly can he [or she] be said to approach wholeness.
> When we apply these categories to Jesus of Nazareth, we find that he appears to be equally developed in both the extroverted and introverted realms. We see his extroverted development in a life which involved him with people. . . . At the same time Jesus' introversion is equally well developed. . . . At crucial moments in his life he retires into solitude again in order to reorient himself and discover his inner direction. . . . The picture we get . . . is of a man well developed in all four functions [thinking, feeling, intuition, sensation]. It is not possible to isolate any one of the functions of Jesus as an inferior one, for examples can be drawn showing good development in each. It is as though in the personality of Jesus we are seeing a whole person. . . . It is apparent that we have here in Jesus of Nazareth the paradigm of the whole man, the prototype of all human development, a truly individual person, and therefore, someone unique.[55]

As the example of Jesus shows, there are important religious implications in personal psychological development. The religious purpose of psychoanalysis is to rid ourselves of the repressed complexes that inhibit individuation and mature psychological development, to discover our inferior functions and shadow aspects so that the negative impact of our projections onto others can be reduced, and to develop all aspects of our personality so that we can have the ego strength to act effectively in the world.

> There is an unconscious psychic reality which demonstrably influences consciousness and its contents. All of this is known, but no practical conclusions have been drawn from it. We still go on thinking and acting as before, as if we were *simplex* and not *duplex*. Accordingly, we imagine ourselves to be innocuous, reasonable and humane. We do not think of distrusting our motives or of asking ourselves how the inner [person] feels about the things we do in the outside world. But actually it is frivolous, superficial and unreasonable of us, as well as psychically unhygienic, to overlook the reaction and standpoint of the unconscious.[56]

The Jungian approach suggests that development of self-knowledge and withdrawal of our projections upon others will have long-term positive effects. There are social and political consequences of personal psychological development. We come to understand our own motives for acting, we confront the real people who oppose our will instead of projecting our "shadow" as their false image. Moreover, we influence other people at the psychic level. As Jung explained,

> What does lie within our reach . . . is the change of individuals who have, or create, an opportunity to influence others of like mind in their circle of acquaintance. . . . The deepening and broadening of this consciousness produce the kind of effect which the primitives call "mana." It is an unintentional influence on the unconscious of others, a sort of unconscious prestige, and its effect lasts only so long as it is not disturbed by conscious intention.[57]

One powerful tool to get at unconscious aspects of our lives is the interpretation of our dreams. In the symbols of our dreams and in our strong emotional reactions to them we get clues as to the repressed impulses that may determine much of our life without our conscious volition. Some dreams provide a basic map to our psyche with dream characters representing our anima/animus, our rational persona, our shadow, and inferior aspects. By noting our reactions to dreams and by dream elaboration through "day dreaming" or meditation, we can discover hidden aspects of our own psyche. Once we recognize these aspects, we can trace their development to events that may have occurred earlier in our lives as far back as childhood. When we then relive these events, we release emotions that may be blocking our effective and wholehearted pursuit of a politics of compassion and transformation. As we become "cured" of neurotic restraints, as we discover more about who we are, as we become more identified with the rest of humankind, as we are transformed, we are made whole. As we develop our inferior functions and as we release the immense energies that have gone into repressing "unacceptable" impulses, we become more effective. Dreams provide valuable clues to our hidden selves. The energy and power that flows from our true selves, when unimpeded by psychological defenses and cultural restrictions, can be enormous.

There is considerable dispute as to how dreams should be interpreted. Rather than adopting a fixed interpretation of dream images, interpretations consistent with an individual's dream patterns are best.

> Jung takes the position that there are no fixed meanings for the symbols of the unconscious. . . . In order to get at [the] context for the analysis of dreams, it is necessary to study not one but a series of

dreams. . . . In Jung's phrase, "the series is the context and the dreamer . . . supplies it". . . . In particular, given a long series of dreams to study, one can observe a change in the nature of the dream material at given stages in the dream series.[58]

Dream images, stories, and events provide clues to the structure of our personality, allow us to develop greater self-awareness, and free our psychic energy.

There are different types of psychoanalysis with different benefits. One use of "therapy" is "intervention" at the time of major loss such as the death of a parent or divorce. Similar practical therapy is marital or family counseling in a family undergoing crises. These interventions usually address a specific problem. They are often of short duration, perhaps lasting only a few weeks or a few months, and end when the "problem" is resolved satisfactorily.

Another common use of psychoanalysis requires several years spent with a single therapist in which the whole personality is explored, including early childhood years when "complexes" were formed which now manifest themselves in unwanted ways. The hope of more extended psychoanalysis is to uncover unrecognized aspects of the self and to release the emotional pressure of resistance to them. This should lead to further individuation and growth on our part. Ideally, after in-depth psychoanalysis, we should have the self-understanding to monitor ourselves, our moods, our dreams, and our behavior; to detect our deeper motives; and to channel these impulses into healthy and effective activity. Psychoanalysis and dream interpretation are in this way religious disciplines whose practice allows us to develop our whole life, including our spiritual life.

The problems of our psyche which dreams reveal and which psychoanalysis addresses are not only private, individual matters of individuation and personal self-development. There are also social and political consequences of learning to cooperate with our subconscious. There is, first of all, the need to face the major crises of our time and to conquer our despair in order to respond creatively. Moreover, ongoing political struggles mirror a more fundamental struggle between Eros and Thanatos, between the impulses of life and death. But there is more about the psychological nature of our political struggles.

In writing about the potential for nuclear destruction, Jung concluded that it is partially fueled by the unconscious.

> The many attacks on the unconscious [such as enlightenment and the development of science and technology] have forced it into a "defensive position which expresses itself in a universal will to destruction"; that is, the unconscious seeks in turn to destroy a world that seems bent on the destruction of the unconscious. In this respect Jung views the

development of nuclear weapons as partially the work of the unconscious; for the unconscious, through hunches and intuitions, collaborates in inventions and discoveries, and "if it puts a weapon in your hand it is aiming at some kind of violence."[59]

The psychological dimensions of current crises are greater than we realize. In addition to particular crises like the nuclear arms race, the "death of God" and the resulting loss of the religious underpinning of key institutions of our civilization are also psychological.

> Gods have died. New gods have not yet been born, although psychological labor pains are apparent in many areas. New gods will in time be brought to birth. . . . The human race can do nothing else, unless it exterminates itself. . . . The psychological problem is a problem of religious need, but not a need for religious rituals. It is a need for symbols that may be lived spontaneously, intensely and naturally, and that can be "alive" in the psyche; for only in the emergence of a new way of life which may be deeply experienced and lived can the modern [person] find his [or her] new soul.[60]

So one of the central tasks of our time is to find new religious symbols to rejuvenate ourselves and our civilization. These symbols will be born in our unconscious.

In addition, we must eliminate false projections upon the world.

> Just as primitive [peoples] externalized their inner psychological drives onto objects and movements in nature, so contemporary [peoples] externalize their psychological drives onto society and politics. Up to a point, the externalization is therapeutic and palliative of the more extreme symptoms of the psychological problems of the modern individual. But it is dangerous, for it is palliative only at the expense of the individual's relinquishing his [or her] responsibility for [their] destiny to the "gods" that [they] have created. . . . Jung insists that if the problems confronting modern society are to be solved, the externalization must cease, the projections must be withdrawn, and individuals must come face to face with [themselves], particularly with the still unknown, primitive forces of [their] unconscious. Only then can [we] begin to make a valid distinction between the problems that are soluble externally, or socially, and those that are only soluble internally or psychologically, and not confuse the two. With the resulting increase in consciousness and knowledge, [we] could begin to create [our] individual destiny, determine the nature of [our] society, and shape [our] history, instead of being threatened with destruction by natural

forces which [we do] not understand and over which [we have] no control.[61]

Our challenge is to discover our unconscious so that we may heal ourselves, withdraw our projections from the political arena, calculate how to act more effectively, and, by the "mana" which we thereby develop, provide the leadership necessary for a successful political transformation. Just as therapists are required to undergo psychoanalysis before practicing their profession, those who would practice a politics of compassion and transformation also need to undergo this painful process of self-discovery.

Journal Keeping

Dream interpretation requires recording our dreams so that they may be remembered and studied. A common complaint is: "I don't dream because I don't remember dreaming." But as single dream images are remembered and written down, it becomes easier to remember more of our dreams and the number of dreams increases. Remembering a dream is like pulling a fish out of water. You grab it by the tail and then as you pull, more and more of the dream emerges. Because writing down dreams is an essential discipline in the mapping of our unconscious, a "dream log" develops.

Similarly, scraps of poetry will be collected. A journal of daily events and reflections may be started at some significant time in our lives. From all these sources, creative people who seek to develop their interior life begin to keep a journal of some sort. Jungian analyst Ira Progoff noticed how often journal keeping emerged in the lives of creative people and how various journal techniques helped his patients. He developed a set of explicit journal exercises which he named "Intensive Journal" and "Life Context Journal." His techniques raised journals from a haphazard activity in the life of a few "creative" people to the level of a spiritual practice. The journal process becomes for Progoff "an instrument for self-guidance, to crystallize the decisions [individuals] need to make, to identify their goals, and to find the meaning of their own unique life." It provides therapy without a therapist. As a method of self-discovery it opens up the unconscious and allows us to discover the pattern our life has taken. This helps us to face the choices that lie before us.

The specific means of achieving this contact with the inner resources of one's life is by the regular and disciplined use of the *Intensive Journal* with its progressive exercises. The effective principle operating in this is that, when a person is shown how to reconnect himself [or herself] with the contents and the continuity of his [or her] life, the inner thread of movement by which [this] life has been unfolding reveals itself . . . by itself. Given the opportunity, a life crystallizes out of its own nature, revealing its meaning and its goal. This is the self-integrating principle of life which the Journal procedures make available to us. . . .

The procedures of the *Intensive Journal* method make it possible for all the events and relationships of our life to show us what they were *for,* what their purpose was in our lives and what they wish to tell us for our future. Thus we gradually discover that our life has been going somewhere, however blind we have been to its direction and however unhelpful to it we ourselves may have been. We find that a connective thread has been forming beneath the surface of our lives; carrying the meaning that has been trying to establish itself in our existence. It is the inner continuity of our lives. As we recognize and identify with it, we see an inner myth that has been guiding our lives unknown to ourselves.[62]

The purpose of journal writing is not a literary product but a private road map that can put us in touch with the unconscious aspects of our lives—with the specific purpose of our life of which we may not consciously have been aware. Our journal allows us to extend the dreams, visions, and images of the unconscious in ways that uncover this hidden aspect of our lives.

The Progoff "Intensive Journal" has different sections. There are several "logs"—analogous to a ship's log—that allow us to record exterior and interior events. They include, among others, a daily log of events and our first reflections upon them, a dream log, and a log of discrete periods in our lives.

Journal keeping formally begins with an entry into the period log and, when we return to work in our journal after a lapse in time, we begin with it again. As Progoff explains the period log,

> Our focus and starting point is always the present moment in time, for it is by means of that that we can position ourselves in the time movement of our lives. . . . The *Period Log* is the section of the Journal in which we make the entries, succinct and objective as can be, to record this [present] period as a whole. We describe the main outer and inner events that come to the fore of our minds when we reflect on the period and recall its primary aspects.[63]

In the period log we record "the salient and specific details of this now period in our lives." The now period is subjective and can range from a time that is just now beginning to a period that has been years in duration. Whatever the time span, the memories, events, arguments, friendships, love affairs, family relationships, work, inner experiences, and dreams are all considered briefly in the period log.

After these "facts" have been jotted down for the current period we move to the "twilight imagery" section of the journal. By means of a brief meditation we search for representative and symbolic images to sum up the period we have just described. "Having described in the Period Log the main factors that come to our mind, we now do nothing further on the conscious level. We merely sit in quietness, our eyes closed, our attention turned to the twilight level of experience. Here we let images come to us again, images of every kind." After the images are recorded, the period log and the images are compared in order to see the relationship between them and "to establish an *inner correlation* between our life events and the imagery that reflects the movement of our experience and comments upon it in symbolic form."[64]

In addition to the logs, there are four other journal dimensions with separate exercises. The "Dialogue Dimension" contains imaginary dialogues written like short play scripts including dialogues with key persons in our lives, work, society, events, and our body. The "Depth Dimension" probes our unconscious inner life and includes a dream log, dream enlargements which interpret and complete our dreams, "twilight imagery" extensions, and inner wisdom dialogues in which we imagine conversations with teachers who can provide wisdom and perspective. These exercises reveal the broader meaning of our lives. A "Life/Time Dimension" explores other periods of our life and includes a life history log for recording our memories, "stepping stones" to identify individual steps or stages of earlier periods, and "intersections" to identify turning points in our lives which allow us once again to consider taking some abandoned paths. This dimension concludes with a section, "Now: The Open Moment," which summarizes lessons learned from the journal and in which we may make resolutions as to our future actions. Finally, the "Process Meditation Dimension" of our journal attempts to integrate the inner and outer events of our lives. It includes visions which arise from our meditations, a "mantra" section in which we develop a seven-syllable mantra to crystallize the spiritual dimension of our life, a record our peak and depth experiences, and a "testament" which attempts to sum up our lives.

The importance of the journal does not lie in any single exercise but in its nonanalytical method for integrating different threads of our lives. This brings a greater awareness of our life's pattern. Journal keeping requires recording different aspects in various sections. Then, exercises, meditations, and reflections upon these aspects allow a new integration by revealing patterns and continuing life processes. Our purpose is to gain a deeper understanding so as to be able to move consciously to the next stage of our own life process. By considering so many aspects, illusive parts of ourselves are brought to consciousness. We come to see how different interior and exterior events fit together to provide a coherent pattern. By reintegrating all aspects of our lives into new patterns, we accelerate our inner development, we drop elements of our personality that are no longer needed, and we prepare ourselves for the time which we are entering.

Mental and emotional disciplines such as meditation, psychoanalysis, dream interpretation, and journal keeping have an important role in the politics of compassion and transformation. As they reveal who we really are to the conscious mind, we can become acutely conscious of what we think, of what we feel, and of the effect of our life experiences. Just as physical exercises bring bodily awareness and control, these exercises let us experience feelings and fears of our hidden shadow selves. But mental and emotional disciplines not only allow us to discover ourselves, they also allow us to clear away inhibitions, impediments, fantasies, and self-deceptions. Through meditation we find the quiet inner core where the Self resides. Through psychoanalysis and dream interpretation we release repressed emotions that secretly direct our attitudes and actions. Through journal keeping we find hidden threads of our life, strengthen our sense of our life purpose, and discover the spiritual journey we have already begun. Mental and emotional disciplines prepare us to practice wholeheartedly the spiritual disciplines necessary for a warrior of compassion. Personal transformation paves the way for social transformation.

Spiritual Disciplines

The practice of physical, mental, and emotional disciplines are important in developing our capacity for compassion. But, by themselves, they are incomplete. We must also practice spiritual disciplines. Two of the most important are prayer and corporate worship. For compassion connects us not only with our neighbor but also with the *Holy,* with God. To be in relationship with God we must individually and corporately connect with the animating force of the cosmos. Individually, we do this through prayer. As a community we achieve this through worship.

Prayer

Foremost of all spiritual disciplines is prayer. As Richard Foster says, "It is the discipline of prayer itself that brings us into the deepest and highest work of the human spirit." Religious people have always had prayers as the cornerstone of their religious life. Prayers are not simply requests for divine favors and gifts, but they also provide the opportunity for gaining divine perspective and understanding. "In prayer, real prayer, we begin to think God's thoughts after [God]; to desire the things [God] desires, to love the things [God] loves. Progressively, we are taught to see things from [God's] point of view." Because our God is a God of compassion, intercessory prayers for others are often our focus. But where do we begin? "We begin praying for others by first centering down and listening to the quiet thunder of the Lord of Hosts. Attuning ourselves to divine breathings is spiritual work, but without it our praying is vain repetition." We quiet ourselves through meditation; we listen for the inner voice of command. When we then pray for others, we imagine the desired result, which is a step towards its realization. We visualize them healed and whole. "Imagination opens the door to faith. If we 'see' in our mind's eye a shattered marriage whole or a sick person well, it is only a short step to believing that it will be so."[65] From willing that it be so, we are able to direct our energy and our efforts to make it come to pass. We begin to cooperate with God in creating the future. In this we remain open to God's will. Our vision is limited as to how justice, health, and healing can be achieved. Nor will all of our visions be achieved. Thus, we end our prayer with the religious conclusion—God's will, not ours, be done.

Consider the Jewish tradition of worship during Rosh Hashanah, Yom Kippur, and Sukkot to learn more of prayer. Rosh Hashanah is the joyous beginning of the new year, followed ten days later by the service of Yom Kippur (called the day of atonement), and completed by Sukkot, the harvest festival of first fruits. The Yom Kippur service at home begins with each member of the household contributing to some worthy charity and with the saying: "Happy are those who consider the poor." Then comes the prayer:

> As we begin this day of holiness we shall not forget the words of your prophet, who called us to share our bread with the hungry, to clothe the naked, and never hide ourselves from our own kin.
>
> May we, together with the whole House of Israel, be mindful of the needs of others, sharing with them the fruits of our labor, helping to sustain them in body and soul. . . .

The Service continues,

> The holiest day of the year is about to begin. Let us use it well. May it be for each of us a day of renewal. May it help us to overcome what is evil in us, and to strengthen what is good. May it bring us closer to one another and make us more loyal to our community, our faith and our God.[66]

The following day is spent in fasting, community worship, and prayer in which individual and collective sins are admitted. With sunset comes the grateful recognition of a truly new beginning. This is culminated a week later in the harvest festival.

The day of Yom Kippur includes the prayer:

> Lord our God, we turn now to You once more
> to cry out our longing
> and the longing of all men and women
> for a beginning of that wholeness
> we call peace.
> Ever and again, we now admit,
> we have turned our backs on You,
> and on our sisters and brothers:
> forsaking Your Law,
> denying Your truth,
> ignoring Your will,
> defacing Your beauty.
> The intelligence You have implanted within us
> we have applied to the arts of war;
> with the skill we have from You
> we make engines of terror and pain.
> We have prayed for peace
> even as we laughed at truth;
> for blessing
> but did not care to do Your will;
> for mercy
> and have shown none to others.
> We have prayed for impossible things:
> peace without justice,
> forgiveness without restitution,
> love without sacrifice. . . .

Yom Kippur ends with the prayer:

> Aware of our weakness, Eternal God, we have come before You
> longing for Your Presence, Your light, Your peace. We have reflected
> with anguish on a life misused and filled with regrets, on opportunities
> neglected and promises unfulfilled. We have struggled to reach You, to
> turn back to You and to Your Law. Accept then our penitent spirits; be
> with us as our hope for the future.
> Now, as evening falls, light dawns within us; hope and trust revive. The
> shadow that darkened our spirit is vanished; and through the passing
> cloud there breaks, with the last rays of the setting sun, the radiance of
> Your forgiving peace. We are restored and renewed by Your love.[67]

The Jewish cycle for welcoming the new year, atoning for sins, and
celebrating the gifts of the earth provides a model of prayer and worship. It

need to do good deeds, to act with charity and justice for all. In these services we recognize that we have not lived in a right relationship with God and our neighbors, and we begin the New Year in a renewed covenant to live in compassion, mercy, peace, and justice.

In Christian tradition, the "Lord's Prayer" provides a further model of how to pray.

> Our [Mother] Father who art in heaven, hallowed be thy name. Thy kingdom [realm] come, thy will be done on earth as it is in heaven. Give us this day our daily bread. Forgive us our debts as we forgive our debtors. And lead us not into temptation but deliver us from evil. For thine is the kingdom and the power and the glory forever. Amen.

What are the elements of such a prayer? This prayer, given to us by Jesus, begins by addressing God as *Abba* or Daddy. Translating the prayer as our Father, our Mother, or our Parent does not reflect the direct personal relationship that Jesus taught. But, having recognized our personal relationship to God, the prayer then recognizes God's holiness—"hallowed be thy name."

The first petition of the prayer is that God's kingdom or reign on earth will come and that "God's will" will be done. Later petitions are simple ones—give us this day, and our daily bread; forgive our debts, our trespasses, and our sins. But for our debts and sins to be forgiven we recognize that we must be willing to forgive debts and sins against us. In the conclusion we pray that we may be led from evil and from temptation. And the prayer ends, as it begins, with a recognition of the power and glory of God.

Notice that this prayer does not petition God for wealth, for victory over enemies, or for earthly glory. We ask only for our basic needs and for our spiritual needs. We ask that we might be a part of the Realm of God here on earth. We recognize our continuing dependence upon God for our strength, for our spiritual development, and for life itself. It is a prayer of petition and celebration combined.

We learn about prayer from other teachers of compassion. It is worth repeating Meister Eckhart:

> If the only prayer
> you say in your entire life
> is 'Thank you,'
> that would suffice.[68]

Eckhart understands that there are many types of prayer but that the basic attitude of thankfulness is critical to prayer. Those who turn to God only to ask favors or to haggle over what they want—"God, I'll be good if you give me a million dollars"—miss the point of prayer.

Sathya Sai Baba teaches a universal prayer in Hindu tradition:

The *Gayathri* is the universal prayer enshrined in the Vedas, the most ancient scriptures . . . It is addressed to the Immanent and Transcendent Divine. . . . The *Gayathri* may be considered as having three parts—(1) Praise, (2) Meditation, and (3) Prayer. First the Divine is praised, then it is meditated upon in reverence, and lastly, an appeal is made to the Divine to awaken and strengthen the intellect, the discriminating faculty of man. . . . And also repeat *"Santhi"* thrice at the end, for that repetition will give *santhi* or peace to three entities in you—body, mind, and soul.[69]

The Gayathri is similar to the Lord's Prayer in that both begin with praise, meditate on the glory of God, ask for spiritual awareness, and end with a final affirmation and blessing.

Another Universal Prayer is taught by Swami Sivananda:

O Adorable Lord of Mercy and Love.
Salutations and prostrations unto Thee.
Thou art Omnipresent, Omnipotent, and Omniscient.
Thou art *Sat Chid Ananda.*
Thou art Existence, Knowledge, and Bliss Absolute.
Thou art the Indweller of all beings.
Grant us an understanding heart, equal vision,
Balanced mind, faith, devotion and wisdom,
Grant us inner spiritual strength to resist
Temptation and to control the mind.
Free us from egoism, lust, greed, hatred and jealousy.
Fill our hearts with Divine Virtues.
Let us behold Thee in all these names and forms,
Let us serve Thee in all these names and forms,
Let us ever remember Thee,
Let us ever sing Thy glories,
Let Thy Name be ever on our lips,
Let us abide in Thee for ever and ever.

This prayer, like the other universal prayers, begins and ends with praise of God. It contains a petition in the middle but does not have the usual intercessory requests. Instead, we request the purification and necessary virtues to lead a holy life of service. If we can resist temptation and control our mind, then we will have the strength and serenity to accept our fate and to serve God and our fellow beings.

One of Gandhi's frequently repeated teachings was on the nature of prayer. "Prayer is nothing else but an intense longing of the heart. You may express yourself through the lips; you may express yourself in the private closet or in public; but to be genuine, the expression must come from the deepest recesses of the heart." Gandhi also helps us to understand the petitional aspects of prayer.

> Prayer is either petitional or in its wider sense is inward communion. In either case, the ultimate result is the same. Even when it is petitional, the petition should be for the cleansing and purification of the soul, for freeing it from the layers of ignorance and darkness that envelop it. . . . Do not worry about the form of prayer. Let it be any form, it should be such as can put us into communion with the divine.

Prayer is not an optional discipline for persons of faith. Rather, it provides a necessary path to peace and spiritual strength. As Gandhi testifies:

> Prayer has been the saving of my life. . . . I have had my fair share of the bitterest public and private experiences. They threw me into temporary despair, but if I was able to get rid of it, it was because of prayer. Now I may tell you that prayer has not been part of my life in the sense that truth has been. It came out of sheer necessity, as I found myself in a plight when I could not possibly be happy without it. . . .
> In spite of despair staring me in the face on the political horizon, I never lost my peace. In fact, I have found people who envy my peace. That peace, I tell you comes from prayer. I am not a man of learning but I humbly claim to be a man of prayer. . . .
> Once you accept the existence of God, the necessity for prayer is unescapable.[70]

Gandhi offers two additional lessons. The first is on the purpose of prayer: "The object of prayer is not to please God, who does not want our prayers or praise, but to purify ourselves. The process of self-purification consists in a conscious realization of [God's] presence within us. There is no strength greater than that which such realization gives." Gandhi, like Eckhart, stresses the spontaneous upwelling of gratitude that is the hallmark of prayer: "Prayer should be a spontaneous upwelling of the heart. One should not pray if one feels that the prayer is a burden. God is not hungry for [our] prayer or praise. [God] tolerates all because [God] is all Love. If we feel that we owe a debt to [God], who is the giver of all things, we should remember [God] and pray to [God] out of sheer gratitude.[71]

Prayers may be divided into three basic types, although universal prayers like the Lord's Prayer combine the elements. Following Sai Baba's teachings on the different parts of a prayer, we may describe them as prayers of meditation, intercession, and praise.

In the Benedictine method of Christian prayer, attributed to Saint Benedict, all three elements are present, but it focuses principally on meditation.[72] Like Saint Benedict, Dietrich Bonhoeffer affirmed that the starting point for prayer is the study of sacred Scriptures:

> The Scripture meditation leads to prayer. We have already said that the most promising method of prayer is to allow oneself to be guided by the Word of Scripture, to pray on the basis of a word of Scripture. . . . Because God's Word has found its fulfillment in Jesus Christ, all prayers that we pray conforming to this Word are certainly heard and answered in Jesus Christ.[73]

The Benedictine prayer moves from a contemplation of Scriptures to a deep meditation.

> Start by quieting yourself in the presence of God. . . . Then take up a book for sacred reading, *lectio,* and begin reading until you alight upon a word, a phrase, a sentence that appeals to you, that attracts you. . . . The first part of the exercise is now over and the second part, the meditation, must begin. . . .
>
> Repeat this sentence again and again. You may do this mentally; there is no need to pronounce the words with your mouth or to say them aloud. What is important, however, is that you keep repeating these words (even if you do so mentally) and reduce your reflection on their meaning to the barest minimum. In fact, it is better not to reflect on them at all. You know what they mean. Now, through repetition of them, allow them to sink into your heart and mind, to become a part of you. . . .
>
> Once you have done this for a while, you will have relished the words sufficiently. You will feel saturated with them, touched by the unction they give. Now is the time to stop the meditation and start the prayer, the *oratio.*
>
> How is the oratio made? Either by speaking spontaneously to the Lord in whose presence you are, or by maintaining a loving silence in [God's] presence, filled as you are with the grace, the unction, the attitude that these words have induced in you.[74]

Prayer need not stay as meditation. Frequently, the prayers will involve intercession for ourselves and others. Anthony de Mello, in *Sadhana: A Way to God: Christian Exercises in Eastern Form,* describes intercession this way:

Spend some time in becoming aware of the presence of Jesus and in getting in touch with him. . . .

Imagine that Jesus floods you with his life and light and power. . . . See the whole of your being, in imagination, lit up by this light that comes from him. . . .

Now conjure up in imagination, one by one, the persons you wish to pray for. Lay your hands on each person, communicating to him or her all the life and power that you have just received from Christ. . . . Take your time over each individual. . . . Call down Christ's love on him [or her] wordlessly. . . . See him light up with Christ's life and love. . . . See him [or her] transformed. . . .[75]

Christians focus on Jesus as a manifestation of God as Hindus focus on Sai Baba or Krishna or Rama to intercede for themselves or for others in need of spiritual help or healing. However, there are also secular techniques for utilizing meditation and visualization to achieve specific goals for our lives. One method called DMA (the initials stand for Creative Force, Higher Consciousness, and Life Breath or Prana) was developed by Robert Fritz and is based on the simple principle that "there is a direct connection between what in your consciousness and what occurs in your external life, and that if you initiate change internally a corresponding change will happen externally."[76] This principle has been recognized by many creative people. For example, Goethe wrote:

Until one is committed
there is hesitancy, the chance to draw back,
always ineffectiveness.
Concerning all acts of initiative (and creation)
there is one elementary truth
the ignorance of which kills countless ideas
and splendid plans:
That the moment one definitely commits oneself
then Providence moves too.
All sorts of things occur to help one
that would never otherwise have occurred.
A whole stream of events issues from the decision
raising in one's favour all manner
of unforeseen incidents and meetings
and material assistance
which no [one] could have dreamt
would have come [their] way.
Whatever you can do or dream you can, begin it.
Boldness has genius, power and magic in it.
Begin it now.

Picasso adds his account of how a painting emerges from an original vision.

> It would be very interesting to record photographically, not the
> stages of a painting, but its metamorphoses. One would see perhaps by
> what course a mind finds its way *toward the crystallization of its dream.*
> But what is really very serious is to see that the picture does not change
> basically, that the initial vision remains almost intact in spite of the
> appearance.[77]

DMA focuses upon crystallizing our inner visions so as to bring them into
existence despite opposition or obstacles. DMA is a practical way of selecting
visions and using them to remake our lives. "The structures of creativity may
be used for more than creating new works of art or technology. They may be
used to help you create the life you want. You can use them to see what is not
yet present in your life, to reach beyond today's circumstances, to conceive a
new and more effective 'self' for your life that has not yet come into
existence."[78] This method of meditation requires us to sit quietly, to decide
what we want—regardless of whether it seems possible. To be sure that we
have chosen correctly, we put the choice into words and then ask ourselves,
"If I could have that, would I take it?" If the answer is yes, we write it down
on a list of a few choices. Our choice will often differ from current reality.
The elements we would like to see may not be present yet. Nonetheless, we
create a clear vision or mental photograph of our choice and of achieving our
goal. It may include visualizing our whole life the way we want it to be. Time
is spent each day meditating upon and rechoosing our goal. Appropriate
actions are taken toward our goal to convince our subconscious that we are
really committed to it. Then, as Goethe and Picasso described, our inner
vision is often realized.[79]

Thus visualization can be used in either formal prayer or in secular
meditation. When we make positive choices for others, such as that they be
healed of illness or that they receive relief from grief and suffering, it is called
intercessory prayer. But we can use similar techniques to achieve positive
goals in our own lives.

Dietrich Bonhoeffer points out that intercessory prayers are also a critical
part of corporate worship. They have an especially important function for
communities of compassion such as the seminary which he led in Hitler's
Germany. Just as an individual's intercessory prayer may begin with a focus
upon a particular scriptural passage, and continue with prayers for all the
persons committed to our care, in corporate worship, intercessory prayers
arise as an integral part of the service.

A Christian fellowship lives and exists by intercession of its members for one another, or it collapses. I can no longer condemn or hate a brother [or sister] for whom I pray no matter how much trouble he [or she] causes me. His [or her] face, that hitherto may have been strange and intolerable to me, is transformed in intercession into the countenance of a brother [or sister] for whom Christ died, the face of a forgiven sinner. . . . To make intercession means to grant our [sister or] brother the same right that we have received, namely, to stand before Christ and share in his mercy.[80]

The final type of prayer, the prayer of praise, emerges from the prayers of meditation and intercession. For example, Hindus sing Bajans (hymns repeating the various names of God) and pray Japas (reciting the "thousand names of God"). This is one simple Hindu hymn: "Hare Rama, Hare Rama, Rama Rama, Hare Hare. Hare Krishna, Hare Krishna, Krishna Krishna, Hare Hare." The meaning of the hymn is simply "Hail God Rama, Hail God Krishna." Repetition of God's names and remembering of God's different aspects is enough to fix our mind on God and to attune us to God's will.

Christian hymns and prayers of praise may differ, but they have similar effects.

The prayer [of praise] consists, quite simply, of praising and thanking God for everything. It is based on the belief that nothing happens in our lives that is not foreseen and planned by God—just nothing, not even our sins. . . .

This is something we hardly dare think of: to thank and praise God even for our sins! It is right that we regret our sins. But, having done this, we must also learn to praise God for them.

Thus, the purpose of the prayers of praise is to recognize our dependence upon God in all things and to realign our life to God's purposes rather than to see our life as a means of fulfilling selfish desires. As de Mello promises from his own experience with such prayers of praise,

Peace and joy will become a fairly habitual disposition with us as we become accustomed to praise and thank God constantly. Where formerly we would have grown tense and worried over the many disappointments that life brings with it, even in minor situations (a train comes late, bad weather when we are about to go outdoors, an unfortunate remark we inadvertently make in conversation . . .), we now set about calmly to do what we can on our part and cheerfully leave all the rest in God's hands, knowing that all shall be well, even though *at the moment* it doesn't seem to be so.[81]

Prayers of praise and thanksgiving allow us to celebrate life, to align our life to the higher forces, and to become peaceful and secure in the knowledge of our place in the world.

Charles Elliott in *Praying the Kingdom: Towards a Political Spirituality* provides an explanation of how our prayers become political and lead to transformation:

> Prayer for the Kingdom, then, begins with a psychic, spiritual opening to the poor, which is likely to be dialectically related to an actual process of becoming acquainted with the poor. This inward opening to the poor is held in counterpoint to an inward opening to God, to [God's] infinite love and [God's] infinite power of tranformation. It is thus a simultaneous standing in the presence of the poor and of God; a baring of the deepest parts of one's being to the stuff of the Kingdom and the King. . . .
>
> Whatever language one uses, and all at this point are inadequate, there are four elements: the poor (a shorthand for all who suffer from the sin of their fellow [humans]); the power of sin; the love of God; and you or me or whoever. At its most abstract, prayer for the Kingdom is confronting the power of sin in the love of God to liberate the poor.

Thus, prayer for the coming of the Kingdom or Realm of God, what Martin Luther King, Jr., called the Beloved Community, requires "standing in all our weakness before God on the side of the poor, and offering our psychic energies in the great battle against evil in ourselves, in our environment and in the whole cosmos."[82] When this stance is taken then all of the techniques of prayer such as purification, meditation, visualization, petition, and praise may be applied. But be warned. To visualize in prayer the coming of the Beloved Community—liberating the poor, eliminating evil in ourselves, and transforming the planet—is to commit ourselves to act to bring it about.

Worship

Private prayer is an important discipline, but public prayer in the midst of corporate worship is also essential in deepening and strengthening our compassion. Corporate worship strengthens us so that we may follow the difficult path of compassion and transformation in the world. Voicing praise, petition, contemplation, and worship of God aloud is powerful. Eastern religions claim that the very act of saying the words aloud sets up a vibrational pattern that helps empower us and make us one with God. In any case, corporate worship certainly has the power to move us emotionally.

Richard Foster declares that "worship is human response to divine initiative." Neither the structure nor the components of worship are the most critical element.

> Forms and rituals do not produce worship, nor does the formal disuse of forms and rituals. We can use all the right techniques and methods, we can have the best possible liturgy, but we have not worshiped the Lord until Spirit touches spirit. . . . Our spirit must be ignited by divine fire.
>
> As a result, we can be indifferent to the question of correct form for worship. The issue of high liturgy or low liturgy, this form or that form, is peripheral rather than central.[83]

Still, there must be a pattern to worship, some common elements that make the rituals, the symbols, the activities meaningful. These are reinforced by their repetition from service to service. Worship becomes the common ritual of a congregation.

Yoga worship services held each morning and night by the followers of Swami Vishnudevananda take this form:

1. Meditation in silence together which may last for thirty to forty minutes
2. Chanting and singing of hymns in Sanskrit
3. Reading from a text of Hindu origin or from the writings of Swami Sivananda and Swami Vishnudevananda
4. A talk by Swami Vishnudevananda or another swami
5. The Universal Prayer said in unison as taught by Swami Sivananda
6. A final hymn of benediction and blessing including symbolic purification by incense

The final hymn of benediction includes the words "O Lord! Thou art the Light in the sun, moon, and fire. Remove the darkness in me by bestowing your Divine Light." Another hymn petitions: "Lead me from the unreal to the Real; from darkness unto light; from death to immortality." These hymns, coupled with meditation, teaching, and the Universal Prayer, create a worship pattern of praise, contemplation, and joy.

The parallel pattern of worship common to many Protestant Christian churches is:

1. Call to worship
2. Hymn of worship
3. Call to confession (read in unison or responsively)
4. Words of assurance
5. Hymn of assurance

6. Sharing of joys, concerns, and announcements by the congregation
7. Reading of the Scripture
8. Sermon
9. Intercessory Prayer
10. Lord's Prayer
11. Offering
12. Hymn of Closing
13. Benediction

In all religious worship services, there is a similar pattern that includes meditation; singing or chanting; common prayers; the use of a spiritual text; a discourse, sermon, or teaching on the text; and a final benediction. These move a congregation through a worship process, but the ultimate point of worship is communal contact with the "Holy," with God. "A striking feature of worship in the Bible is that people gathered in what we could call only a 'holy expectancy.' They believed they would actually hear the *Kol Yahweh,* the voice of God." The presence of a gathered people heightens spiritual energy so that each of us is able to reach greater spiritual heights than we can alone. And, as a worshiping community, we are transformed by this common experience. That is the final test and purpose of worship.

If worship does not change us, it has not been worship. To stand before the Holy One of eternity is to change. . . . In worship an increased power steals its way into the heart of sanctuary, an increased compassion grows in the soul. To worship is to change.
If worship does not propel us into greater obedience, it has not been worship. Just as worship begins in holy expectancy, it ends in holy obedience. Holy obedience saves worship from becoming an opiate, an escape from the pressing needs of modern life. Worship enables us to hear the call to service clearly so we respond, "Here I am! Send Me." (Isaiah 6:8)[84]

Worship is a spiritual discipline that allows us, as a community of people, to contact God and to know God's will. In keeping with our whole enlarged sense of compassion, worship is not a permanent withdrawal from the problems of the world but an energizing, healing, supporting, and empowering experience to allow us to take up the tasks of service in the world. It is a process that should lead to personal and to social transformation. But many people find their experience of corporate worship hollow and meaningless. It is not surprising, therefore, that for most of us our spiritual quest begins with our search for the right congregation and the specific form of liturgy in which we can worship. We search for the community and form of worship that completes us—that develops our physical, mental, and emotional awareness; that supports our attempts at discipline; that encourages us, embraces us, forgives us, and lifts us to a higher plane of consciousness and existence. In short, we look for the community of people and the worship form that transforms us.

The Prevention of Burnout

The physical, mental, emotional, and spiritual disciplines are meant to enlarge our compassion and our effectiveness. But these disciplines are also needed to keep us from "burning out" and to restore our health if we do burn out. People of compassion are particularly susceptible to this emotional disease.

There are, of course, rewards for people in "helping professions" such as education, health services, and ministry. There is the social prestige of being a professor, teacher, physician, nurse, or minister. There is applause and appreciation for giving a fine speech, lecture, or sermon. There is the sense that people really need your services, that you are able to help individuals directly in ways that change their lives. There may even be a sense of being in touch with God, of doing God's work, of being a part of a "communion of saints," or, at least, of being part of a humane tradition stretching back across centuries of civilization. This can sometimes lead to the "sin of pride," but there are genuine rewards for work of compassion. There are also resources available to people who serve in these professions. Unfortunately, these may be insufficient to keep us from "burning out."

In *Ministry Burnout,* John Sanford identifies nine "root difficulties" that we face in our work of compassion. The problems apply to compassionate people who provide services or lead movements and organizations:

> 1. *The job of the ministering person is never finished.* People in many jobs and professions can feel that they have taken on a task and completed it. . . . Not so the ministering person. His [or her] work is never finished for he [or she] faces a continuous onslaught of services, weddings, funerals, crises, parish conflicts, holy day celebrations, sick persons to see, shut-ins to visit. . . .
> 2. *The ministering person cannot always tell if his [or her] work is having any results.* . . .
> 3. *The work of the ministering person is repetitive.* . . .
> 4. *The ministering person is dealing constantly with people's expectations.* . . . The expectations people place upon the ministering person vary enormously. . . . The ministering person pays a price in energy if [she or] he ignores these expectations just as

[she or] he does in fulfilling them. It takes energy to contend with the rejection, criticism, or hostility of people, just as it does to please them by doing what they want us to do. . . .

5. *The ministering person must work with the same people year in and year out.* . . .

6. *Because he [or she] works with people in need, there is a particularly great drain on energy of the ministering person.* . . . It is like having a small but constant loss of blood. . . . His [or her] energy is used up in supplying energy to the other person. . . .

7. *The ministering person deals with many people who come to [him or] her or the church not for solid spiritual food but for "strokes".* . . .

8. *The ministering person must function a great deal of the time on his [or her] "persona."* The persona is the front or mask we assume in order to meet and relate to the outer world. . . . When we have to cover up part of our genuine feelings, or, worse yet, assume a posture that does not belong to us at all, a lot of energy is required.

9. *The ministering person may become exhausted by failure.* [85]

The four most difficult causes of burnout are the never-ending job, uncertainty of results, the drain of working with people in need, and our sense of failure in our mission. To start a new program or undertake some bold political action can be invigorating. But continuing to work day after day with the homeless, hungry, unemployed, mentally ill, or refugees and to continue to confront uncaring, unsympathetic members of the upper and middle classes can be a terrible drain.

Despite our best efforts, we often experience a sense of failure. The civil rights movement won great victories twenty years ago, but more minority people are in poverty than ever before in our history. The wealthiest nation on earth has three million homeless people and at least twelve million hungry. Thus, we sometimes wonder if all the sacrifices and acts of compassion haven't ultimately failed. In a matter of a few minutes, a war may begin that will end all life on this planet forever. Such reflections can drive us to despair.

Disciplines help us to continue our efforts not for a day, a week, or a year, but for a lifetime. As in a good yoga class, after hours of exercise, we are stronger and more energized than when we began. Disciplines of the body provide the health and physical energy we need, and they discharge negative emotions. Developing our underdeveloped selves through psychoanalysis, dream interpretation, and journal keeping makes us sensitive, creative, and less judgmental. The hidden aspects of ourselves become known and reliance on our persona is decreased. We recognize our own psychic wounds and weaknesses. In Henri Nouwen's phrase, we become "wounded healers" better able to be compassionate and effective because we have recognized our own pain, suffering, and shortcomings. Lastly, spiritual disciplines put us in touch with God and restore our soul.

It must be emphasized that narrow "spiritual" disciplines of "self-denial or self-suppression as a basic secret for attaining the state of selfhood" will not prevent burnout or provide health, wholeness, and holiness. William Stringfellow reminds us in *The Politics of Spirituality* that

> Holiness is not an an attainment, in any sense of the term, but is a gift of . . . God. Holiness is not a badge of achievement for a saint but is wrought in the life, in the very being of an ordinary person by . . . God. Holiness, from the vantage of the person who may truthfully be said to be holy, is, in the most elementary meaning, the restoration of integrity and wholeness to a person. . . . Thus, instead of self-denial, what is taking place is more nearly the opposite of self-denial: in place of denial there is fulfillment.[86]

The Protestant perspective is that we achieve our wholeness and our sense of peace by the grace of God and not as an award for proper diet, exercise, prayer, or worship. We surrender our will and our striving ultimately to God. Disciplines may help us to do this, but grace comes from beyond discipline as God's gift.

John Sanford retells the story of Elijah who, with exhaustion and a sense of failure, went off in the desert alone. He was renewed and enabled to continue his work, "but only because he had been able to talk with God. That is, his exhausted ego had found a way to contact the source of renewal, for in his pilgrimage to Mount Sinai, and in his dialogue with God, Elijah's vital energies were replenished."[87] Ultimately, spiritual disciplines allowing contact with God are necessary to sustain us in our politics of compassion and transformation.

Ram Das and Paul Gorman, following Eastern teachings and Western experience, suggest that the ultimate discipline necessary for a people of compassion is to let go of the fruits of our action and to trust God.

> So, at some level we care with all our heart . . . and then we finally let go. We give it all we have . . . and trust the rest to God, to Nature, and to the Universe. We do everything we can to relieve someone's suffering—our dearest's, our beloved's, anyone's—but we are willing to surrender attachment to how we want things to be, attachment even to the relief of their suffering. Our heart may break . . . and then we surrender that too.

Although we want to relieve suffering of others, we cannot always succeed. "The pain of the world will sear and break our hearts because we can no longer keep them closed. . . . [We] are willing to pay the price of compassion." We experience joy in "a single, caring act. . . . With it comes the simple, singular grace of being an instrument of love, in whatever form, to whatever end."[88]

Thus, we grow in the path of compassion. Our original instincts are reinforced; our capacity to feel, to suffer, and to act are enlarged. We do not need to practice every discipline of compassion every day. Often our practice of a particular discipline will lapse for months or years. But practice of these disciplines, as we grow and develop, will provide us the strength we need as long as we practice with love and devotion. These disciplines help us develop compassion for ourselves as well as for others.[89] They have as their ultimate goal preparing us to practice the politics of compassion and transformation, which is the most demanding discipline of all. Joining together with God and with other people of compassion, we receive new energy that enables us to overcome enormous physical and emotional demands. We learn to live with grace and strength. This is what it means to be religious. We do the inner work of compassion that makes the outer work of transformation possible.

Chapter 6
COMPASSIONATE ACTION

It has lately come to pass that America has entered upon a dark age . . . an authentic dark age; that is, a time in which the power of death is pervasive and militant and in which people exist without hope or else in pursuit of transient, fraudulent, or delusive hopes. . . . It is an era of chaotic activity, disoriented priorities, banal redundancy. . . . The infrastructure of great institutions crumble. For those who consider that there is a God, there is a widespread suspicion of abandonment. It is a period marked by intense animosity toward human life and, indeed, intransigent hostility toward all of created life.
William Stringfellow, The Politics of
Spirituality

The crises of our time are not only to be seen in global problems of starvation, unemployment, war, and the general decline of our civilization. They are also present now in our towns and cities, in our workplaces, in our churches and synagogues, in our families, and in our own psyches. This is the sense in which we live in a truly dark age. In the face of these problems, there is still the possibility of birthing a better civilization. The beginnings can already be seen in individual lives and in local efforts by which people join together to fight against the darkness.

L. S. Stavrianos wrote in *The Promise of the Coming Dark Age:*

The prospect emerges of a new Dark Age that, like the medieval original will witness deterioration and demolition, but that will also generate amidst the wreckage new values and new institutions heralding a new epoch in human history. . . .

Just as green shoots took root amid the ruins of imperial Rome, they are growing now amid the wreckage of contemporary civilization. But to see today's green shoots we must discard the perspective of many modern observers who, like their Roman predecessors, perceive only the darkness around them.[1]

Let us consider a single city, Chicago, to see evidence not only of deterioration but also evidence of these "green shoots." By focusing upon a single city it is easier to ask the concrete, political question compassion

185

requires: Is it possible in a city like Chicago to create those new religious and political institutions necessary to prevent the collapse of this civilization, or failing that, those institutions and values necessary to birth a better civilization?

The social, economic, and political crises sketched earlier are not merely theoretical problems that may someday affect the future of our planet. They already manifest themselves in our daily lives. In Chicago the problems of hunger, violence, resources wasted on war preparations, resources depleted in producing unneeded products, pollution, inflation, unemployment, and autocratic government are already a reality. Yet, successful attempts to solve local manifestations of these problems must take account of the global pressures that exacerbate them. On the other hand, any attempt to cope with global problems must be undertaken in local communities like Chicago.

Wars Come Home To Chicago

Chicago is a multiracial, multiethnic city. It is inevitably an integral part of the wider world. More Poles live in Chicago than in any other city except Warsaw. For many ethnic groups it is the same. Because more than 40 percent of Chicago's three million people are black, we cannot but be concerned with liberation struggles in South Africa or with starvation in Ethiopia. Because more than 18 percent of our population are Latinos, we are directly involved with the wars and repression in Central America.

The former mayor of Chicago, Harold Washington, alluded to the positive aspects of living in a multiracial city in a speech entitled "Chicago's Future": "By the year 2000 Chicago will have a population that is one-third White, one-third Black, and one-third Hispanic and Asian. Because of our diverse population we will have a golden opportunity to expand into world trade with Latin America, Africa, and Asia as well as Europe. Chicago will not be the third or the second city of the nation, it will be restored to its rightful position as a premier city in the broader world."[2] This also means that local struggles in Chicago have meaning for the rest of the world. If Chicago can solve its problems, so can the rest of the world. Moreover, we in Chicago are involved with the world. For example, our racial composition guaranteed that the black community would bring pressure to bear on the Chicago City Council to pass a South African divestiture ordinance. Similarly, the Mexican community organized fund-raising for relief of the victims of the Mexican earthquake of 1986, the Jewish community focuses on Israel and problems of Russian Jewry, and the Hispanic community makes sure that stories of the Central American wars are brought home to Chicago.

Our response to wars and other world problems is not inevitable. Chicagoans could ignore them. But the actions of two small religious groups made this impossible in the case of Central America. One group was the Wellington Avenue United Church of Christ and the other was the Chicago Religious Task Force on Central America. The task force is an informal interreligious organization with only a dozen "members" and a handful of staff members. The Wellington Avenue church has only 125 members; its unique feature has been its development of lay leadership in recent years. Many of its members, yearning for deeper religious education, have also gone to seminary and have been ordained. In its neighborhood for seventy-five years, Wellington Avenue church has been a liberal congregation supporting liberal causes since the 1960s. In 1980 in a divided vote of the membership, the church condemned Reaganomics and joined the Illinois Coalition Against Reagan Economics (ICARE) to protest Reagan's new budgetary policies. Still, in its previous political and religious stands, it had stayed within the law.

In March 1982, South Side Presbyterian Church in Tucson, Arizona (along with five churches in California), publicly declared itself a "Sanctuary" for refugees from Central America. But the number of Central American refugees crossing the border soon became too numerous for these churches to handle. Moreover, the church members believed it was important that people in other parts of the country know firsthand about wars and oppression in Central America as well as the U.S. involvement in them. It quickly became clear to these churches in Tucson and California that the only solution to the refugee problem was to stop the wars that were creating the refugees. So the Tucson religious leaders asked for a church in the North to spread the Sanctuary movement from the Southwest to the rest of the country. The Chicago Religious Task Force on Central America took their request to several Chicago churches. Among them was Wellington Avenue United Church of Christ.

When the Religious Task Force approached the church council at Wellington regarding Sanctuary, the council responded by naming a fact-finding committee, as well as setting forth a process for decision-making. . . . The decision-making process set forth by the council called for two informal meetings in which the fact-finding committee made presentations, articulating the need for such a project, the possible legal ramifications, as well as the faith tradition which called Christian communities of faith to such action. After these preliminary meetings, a formal meeting would be held and a congregational vote taken. A vote of two-thirds would be needed for the project to be approved, thereby insuring broad based congregational support.

The reason sanctuary was a serious issue was that "harboring" Salvadorans or Guatemalans is deemed by our government to be contrary to federal law and punishable by a fine and jail sentence. Section 274 (a) of the Immigration and Nationality Act reads:

> Any person . . . who . . . willfully or knowingly conceals, harbors, or shields from detection, or attempts to conceal, harbor, or shield from detection, in any place, including any building or any means of transportation . . . any alien . . . not duly admitted by an immigration officer or not lawfully entitled to enter or reside within the United States . . . shall be guilty of a felony, and upon conviction thereof shall be punished by a fine not exceeding $2,000 or by imprisonment for a term not exceeding five years, or both. . . . [3]

Despite the potential dangers of arrest and punishment, the Wellington Avenue church remembered the tradition of sanctuary. We thought about God's commandment to the Jews that before they entered the Promised Land, they establish "cities of sanctuary," the purpose of which was to provide a refuge where victims of blood feuds could flee until they could obtain justice. We remembered that under Roman law and during the Middle Ages, Christian churches were safe places to flee feudal wars. We were reminded that the original U.S. colonies were sanctuaries for those fleeing religious persecution, and Congregationalist churches like ours were part of the Underground Railroad before the Civil War. But the discussion on whether to become a sanctuary for Central Americans was decided on even more basic grounds.

The Ten Commandments say "Thou shall not kill." To let our government send back Salvadorans or Guatemalans to their torture and death is to be accomplices in killings just as Germans let the Jews be killed during World War II. The issues for our church became simply the legal consequences and the practical problems of housing refugees, because the moral issues seemed very clear-cut to us. The legal consequences also seemed clear, although we could not know whether our national government would enforce the laws. They might not choose to come and arrest a whole church, but if they did, we would be convicted and jailed.

The practical problems were also substantial. We had to convert rooms on the top floor of the church; repair plumbing that wasn't working; recruit volunteers to serve as around-the-clock security monitors for the refugees; raise several thousand dollars for food; and gather furniture, clothing, and blankets. These practical problems were lessened when the task force agreed to help recruit the volunteers, repair the building, and raise the necessary funds. But the ultimate risk and responsibility would still be that of the Wellington Avenue church.

In the end, the possible legal consequences and practical problems did not weigh as heavily on us as the simple moral demand "to choose life, not death." The basic humanitarian and religious instincts of the congregation won over our fears by a vote of fifty-nine to four. In the years ahead, a similar vote would be taken by over three hundred churches and synagogues as well as by national denominations. More than three hundred times the result was the same, a vote to affirm life and to defy our government.

Soon after the vote at the church, arrangements were made to receive a refugee family, and a letter was sent to the attorney general, the Immigration and Naturalization Service, and the U.S. district attorney, telling them of our decision. The letter read in part:

> We are writing to inform you that today our congregation voted to declare our church as a sanctuary for undocumented refugees from El Salvador. On Saturday, July 24, we will openly receive a refugee family into the care and protection of the church. We realize in so doing that we will be in violation of the Immigration and Nationality Act Section 274(A).
>
> This action, which we take after months of prayer and deliberation, reflects our belief that the current policy and practice of the United States Government with regard to Central American refugees is illegal and immoral. We believe our government is in violation of the 1980 Refugee Act and International Law by continuing to arrest, detain and forcibly return refugees to the terror, persecution and murder in El Salvador and Guatemala.[4]

So in July 1982, the Wellington Avenue United Church of Christ formally became a "sanctuary." Asked why, Church Council President Barbara Lagoni said that "these are dangerous times. When thousands of innocent people are still being victimized by U.S. supported violence in El Salvador and Guatemala, it is time to escalate the struggle for justice. Dangerous times call for risky responses. The consequences that may happen to Wellington are minimal in comparison to the pain that happens every day to the people of El Salvador and Guatemala."[5] The first refugee to claim sanctuary at Wellington was a young Salvadoran given the name "Juan" to hide his identity. Here is Juan's story, recounted in Renny Golden and Michael McConnell's *Sanctuary: The New Underground Railroad:*

> It was during his student days at the University of San Salvador that Juan was picked up. One day after class, while he was waiting for a bus, a security policeman came up behind him, yanking his hair and throwing him to the ground. At first, because he was not "political," he was bewildered and hoped that mistaken identity would be established when his papers were checked.

But the police did not ask for his papers. They threw him on the floor of a jeep; a policeman pressed one boot against his head and another on his back. When he tried to move, one of them slammed a rifle butt against the side of his face. . . .

During Juan's imprisonment, his father "disappeared." Neighbors saw the security forces come to the house. Three months later his mother died of a heart attack. Juan never has located any of his six brothers. . . .

They began his torture in a place that was not a jail. He remembered hallways and torture rooms. He never saw other prisoners, because he was always blindfolded when taken from his room, but he heard screams daily. For eight months he held on; others went mad or committed suicide. Near the end he was delirious, and his hope was waning.

They pounded his hands with heavy metal rods, demanding responses to questions he could not answer. They asked for names. When he would not answer, they hit him on the chest over and over. He still has continual pain in his chest and occasional lack of sensation in his spine. They used electric shock, pulled out his fingernails, hung him by his wrists, burned him with acid, broke his arms.

"But what were they after?" we asked. "Was it your student activities?" His answer:

No, it wasn't that. It's true I was part of a student movement demanding curriculum change, an overhaul of the educational system, and student participation in university decisions. But their interest was in my truck driving years before the university. I had a route that ran into Guatemala toward the Atlantic coast. In both El Salvador and Guatemala I saw many cadavers lying on the roads. Back then, when they bothered to disguise things, they threw the bodies in the road so that high-speed trucks or cars would run over them, making their death appear to be accidents. But if you stopped, you could see the bodies had been tortured. I think they thought I knew something from my travels.

Juan was unaware that a general amnesty had been granted prisoners when they blindfolded him and drove him to what was clearly a jail. The next day he was released in San Salvador. It was 1979. . . .

He stayed [at the home of a friend] three days before the National Guard came looking for him. He learned later that four of the five prisoners released with him had been apprehended and their decapitated bodies thrown into the streets. When the guard came to his friend's front door, Juan leapt out a back window, scampered over a row of rooftops toward Rio Acelhuate, a city drainage river, where he dropped into the water and thus covered his tracks.

He slept on the riverbank when he could walk no longer. Under the sun, and under the stars, he forced himself to walk toward Aguilares, where friends would feed him and he could move on toward the mountains to hide. For months he traveled from town to town in the Chalatenango area, seeking the whereabouts of his brothers. He was taken in by friends. Then he made his way to the mountains where time healed his wounds. . . .

As a final question to Juan, almost as an afterthought, we asked him why he came [to Wellington], prepared for possible arrest by the INS.

"It is because of the children," he said, the same innocence in his eyes. "They don't die just from guns. They are hungry. I don't want them just to grow up to a strong adulthood; I want them to have an infancy. That's part of why I'm here, to demonstrate that all of us must be willing, not just one person, to stop this suffering. It's a call."[6]

Juan's presence and story made concrete for the members of the Wellington congregation that we really had been making a choice between life and death. We had chosen to protect the lives and safety of Juan and several other refugee families who stayed with us, and they taught us faith. As Bishop Oscar Romero of El Salvador said before his assassination, "We either serve the life of Salvadorans or we are accomplices in their death. . . . We either believe in a God of Life or we serve the idols of death." Michael McConnell (a minister and member of the Wellington congregation) and Renny Golden (a member of the Chicago Religious Task Force on Central America) put the choice made by Sanctuary churches this way: "The choice between life and death became for [them] as concrete and clear as the choice for or against military aid to Central America. Churches, synagogues, Quaker meetings had to choose sides: the refugees or secular authority, God or Caesar, life or death. . . . The refugees themselves finally compelled the faithful to engage in the widest form of resistance since the civil rights era." And this choice had consequences for the members of Sanctuary congregations just as it had had terrible consequences for the refugees, for base communities in their home country, and for the secret church shelters in Mexico. Jim Corbett, one of the founders of the Sanctuary movement and convicted in the Tucson Sanctuary trial, said that "choosing to serve the poor and powerless, not just as an intellectual posture or a charitable gesture, but in spirit and truth, we will soon be stripped of our wealth and position. And just as the refugees are outlawed, hunted down, and imprisoned, if we choose to serve them in spirit and truth, we will also be outlawed."[7]

The Wellington congregation has more than its share of heroic individuals who have lead political movements, participated in protest demonstrations, and undertaken individual acts of resistance such as the refusal to pay "war taxes" to the federal government. It has a legacy of good preachers and strong be a sense of community—a trust in the other members and in God. This is also reflected nationally in the Sanctuary movement. As Golden and McConnell report:

> What sustains sanctuary workers' ability to stand firm is their discovery of themselves as a community. Under the menacing sweep of Reagan's deadly eagle, a people's church is being born. Community is understood by this new liberation movement as the result of faith actions. It is a discovery made in the process of becoming a church, when religious persons choose sides and embrace the God of history among the poor and oppressed. This spiritual conviction is the combustive moral force Reagan cannot jail, infiltrate or kill.[8]

What the refugees and our actions as a community have taught us is exemplified in the experiences of a very few days in March 1984 when a caravan of religious people took a Guatemalan family from Wellington Avenue church to sanctuary in Weston Priory, Vermont.[9] On 17 February 1984, a non-Catholic lay worker, along with a reporter and three Salvadoran refugees, were arrested in Texas. A few weeks later, similar arrests were made in Arizona. It had become clear that the underground railroad that had carried refugees from deep inside Central America through Mexico to sanctuary churches in the United States had finally become the target of government attack. On 24 March 1984, the 100th sanctuary was to be opened in Weston Priory, Vermont, a Benedictine monastery whose order has provided sanctuary since the sixth century. The family that was to be part of the sanctuary was a Guatemalan family of seven.

The father, Felipe, was a Catholic catechist in Guatemala who left the country because seventeen of his co-workers had been killed. Felipe; his wife, Elena; and their children, Mark, Julio, Alicia, Juanita, and Inez, crossed the border into the United States in January of 1984.

By the winter of 1984, the underground railroad (which had been built across the country after the Wellington church's decision) was no longer a safe way to travel, so approximately fifty religious people from Chicago provided a guard for the family as they journeyed to Weston Priory, Vermont. We stopped in many towns and cities for press conferences and for the celebration of sanctuary projects. We also stopped in Washington, D.C, to confront the government. The trip itself was a spiritual journey for the participants, and something important was learned by us all. In a few days, the transforming experiences of sanctuary at a church like Wellington were to be experienced by the caravan and thousands of local church people visited on our journey.

Felipe is a campesino, a peasant farmer who was trained at an institute established by Roman Catholic priests. He incarnates liberation theology, and for this, the Guatemalan government labeled him a Communist, a guerilla. After seventeen of his co-workers were killed for helping teach peasants to read and write, he was forced to flee, so, with his family, he crossed the border into the United States in January 1984. On this trip to Western Priory Felipe shared his views of compassion and solidarity, saying that "compassion is giving a poor man a dollar when you see him on the side of the road; solidarity is going on a trip with him." We wanted to be in solidarity not only with Felipe, but also with other Guatemalans and Salvadorans, and we wanted not just to respond to the problem by charity. We saw the caravan to Weston Priory as a journey for ourselves as much as for Felipe and Elena and their family. We wanted to protest what our government was doing because seldom has it been so wrong on humanitarian grounds as it has in its foreign policy in Central America and its policy concerning refugees here in the United States.

A couple of experiences influenced the decision of members of the Wellington church to go on the caravan. First, it was the deep searching eyes of the young Inez as she gazed in our eyes while we shared wine and papaya bread around our communion table at the church—bread that Elena, Inez's mother, had made from corn flour and shared with us as a gesture of friendship and gratitude. We wanted Inez's eyes to see life's beauty, not death and destruction. Second, Felipe's remark that solidarity was traveling the path with the poor made the choice clear for us. The caravan gave us an opportunity to be in solidarity not only with Felipe, but also with other oppressed people in Central America struggling for peace and justice and with church workers here who have taken their side. The only reason not to go was our fears.

The caravan began on Saint Patrick's Day 1984 with a parade, but it was a very different parade from the one going on in downtown Chicago. We left from Markham, Illinois after a worship service in a Mennonite church which was a sanctuary. Another Salvadoran refugee named Jose spoke of the bombs and weapons which were destroying Central America. He told us how his wife, now here in the United States, is dying from the chemicals used in the war. We sang for the first time a hymn we would sing many times in the course of the journey, "Be Not Afraid," based upon explicit images from Isaiah and the Exodus: Crossing the deserts without being thirsty, going through raging waters without drowning, going through burning flames without harm. That wasn't what the experience was for us on the caravan who were Americans, but we could visualize what it had been like for the Guatemalans and Salvadorans who had been through so much in their lands and who had fled to the United States. To them the United States seemed a strange land with so many people and new modern technology so far away from their home.

After traveling about three and a half hours from Markham, our first stop was at Indianapolis. We came into a wealthy section of town with big homes, big yards. Some of these homes could easily house twenty of the refugees who were fleeing the violence in Central America. Our stop included what was to be the first of many home-cooked meals prepared by loving and concerned hands that helped us on our journey. Our presence there helped to nurture the idea that they too could begin a sanctuary. Felipe and Elena shared, both with the press and the community, why this journey was so important during the time of Lent.

From Indianapolis we traveled to Cincinnati. When we arrived, there were a hundred or more people standing outside the Friends Meeting House singing songs and hymns, carrying banners, clapping vigorously, hugging, and making everyone welcome. To be greeted by this sort of celebration in the United States when we were breaking the law and could go to jail for five years for doing so, or when Felipe and Elena could be seized by our government agents and sent back to Guatemala to be killed, was an ecstatic experience. During the worship service in Cincinnati, Felipe delivered the longest homily that we had yet heard from him. After making the graphic parallel between the crucifixion of Christ and the suffering of the Christs in Latin America today, Felipe declared that, indeed, there was a Pontius Pilate sitting in the White House washing his hands of the whole event. In this country and in other countries, there were the Herods who were supporting the puppet governments of Central America. Felipe reminded us of our religious obligation to act. We ended the service with the hymn, "We Shall Not Be Moved," in Spanish.

What we experienced in Cincinnati was the incredible sense of community which had existed there and which had been extended to those of us in the caravan. We gathered in a small room for our worship service—we could see one another's eyes as Felipe spoke—and we sang together. Later that evening, we spoke with Gabriella, a Salvadoran in sanctuary at the Quaker House. She was fearful that violence would accompany the upcoming Salvadoran elections, and she was very worried about her five-year-old daughter left behind in El Salvador.

The second day's journey was physically harder than the first. We had farther to drive and we were already tired from the first day. But as we began to move away from Chicago, from our normal life, we also found that we began to shed our rigidity and the structures that keep us apart. Somehow we began to merge this disparate group of Americans and Guatemalans into a single caravan that cared for each other and developed a spirit of camaraderie. Felipe spoke again as he was recorded by TV cameras at a church in Columbus, Ohio. Afterwards, one elderly woman confronted the TV crew to ask them who had given them permission to film the church service. She was very unhappy about having a public political event in her church. As we left the church after lunch, we found that its leaders—one of whom was a tax resister—were indeed going to try to convince the congregation to become a sanctuary.

We went on to Pittsburgh, eventually arriving at an American Friends Meeting House where another Salvadoran refugee family met with Felipe and Elena. It was particularly touching moment because this family had had to leave their nine children behind in El Salvador and their oldest son was old enough to be drafted. They are considering leaving sanctuary here in the United States and taking all the risks and dangers of going back to El Salvador to get their children out. Even though they are working and studying in the U.S., they grieve and miss their children very much. They saw Felipe and Elena with their children intact, and it was a poignant, tearful time for them. The Quaker House had only twenty-five members, but, as in many cities, they are supported by a larger coalition that makes it possible for them to create sanctuary for refugees from far away. After the press conference, worship service, and dinner in Pittsburgh, we were on to Harrisburg where we were to spend the night. During that whole day, what I remember most was Elena speaking for the first time of the suffering of the women and children in Guatemala. Almost more eloquent than her words were her liquid brown eyes which had seen so much suffering. Yet she still had faith, and her children played happy games along the trip.

When we arrived at Harrisburg around eleven, we were very tired. People welcomed us warmly and were thankful that we had arrived safely as we had been delayed. That evening our bedroom was a large gym floor. We were all snuggled in our sleeping bags sharing the days reflections when we heard giggling and laughter from Elena and Felipe's children. Felipe tried to quiet them. At one point, he put on a Salvadoran tape on his recorder, and the entire family started to sing along with the music, lulling us all into sleep. We arose early as we had on previous mornings and began our journey to Washington, D.C. There was something exciting about having the caravan move toward our nation's capital because it is there that the policies we are protesting originate, and it is there that we hoped we would influence changing these policies.

After we arrived in Washington, D.C., Felipe's family was safely sent to an apartment in order to spend some time alone. We went to the National Religious Convocation on Central America which involved several thousand people in the Washington area in a series of workshops on how to change our foreign policy on Central America. Then we went off to lobby with our senators, Percy and Dixon, who were back in Illinois because the 1984 primary election was the next day. We met, instead, with Dr. Margaret Hayes Smith, a political scientist who was the lead staff member on the Senate Foreign Relations Committee, then chaired by Senator Charles Percy (since defeated and replaced by liberal democrat Paul Simon). Smith's area of expertise was Central America, and some in our group were amazed to hear the arguments the Reagan administration and the Foreign Relations Committee make about Central America. In the Senate, they are willing to aid Central American countries militarily but admit they are unwilling to give such aid to Guatemala, which was viewed as having the worst human rights record in Central America. Besides fueling the wars in Central America by our aid, Congress is unwilling to grant voluntary departure status for refugees. It was hard for us to understand this, because, from our viewpoint, not to grant voluntary departure status was to consign to jail or death the refugees who were sent back to their countries. A study by the American Civil Liberties Union documenting returning Salvadorans who were "killed, arrested, or tortured" failed to change U.S. policy.[10] We made no progress in arguing these issues with Washington officials, and it is clear there would be no progress in the near future regarding the wars in Central America or our immigration policies. It was 1988 before the Congress began to reject even military aid to the Nicaraguan contras.

Fortunately, the day didn't end with our visit to Senate staffs. We gathered with hundreds of other religious people for an interfaith service on Central America with lay leaders and clergy from various denominations. We heard homilies from Oscar Romero, the archbishop of San Salvador who was murdered while celebrating Mass with the campesinos. At the service, Felipe spoke of how his people are people of corn and corn is disappearing. The rich who own most of the land are not growing corn to feed the people. Rather, they are growing other crops for export for bigger and better profits. The people themselves find it hard to grow corn given the disruption and violence that is part of their everyday lives. The oppressor's attempt to withhold corn from the people symbolizes their attempt to deny the oppressed their liberation. Corn was passed out to everyone in the service to remind us of our role in the struggle to build a just society.

At the end of the religious service, we joined a candlelight parade through Washington, D.C., ending at the White House. There, we were a few hundred flickering candles in the dark night, voices lifted up together in prayer and song in the hope that things would be different and in a challenge to our government. That challenge was carried forward the next day when we gathered for a final rally on the Capitol steps. Felipe and Elena spoke. We were at the heart of the government, we were saying, "No," the policies of the U.S. government will not go unchallenged. Although we didn't overturn those policies that day, we began to build a consensus of people from throughout the country that it was time to change. Years later the successes of the Central American Peace Process and the cut off of aid to the Nicaraguan contras would offer more hope.

The caravan was a spiritual as well as a physical journey. It involved personal transformation, particularly for the Americans, because it was a chance for us to reintegrate our lives around different principles—not only the principles of political struggle but also a new understanding of how precious life is. When the laws of a nation are evil laws and do harm, when institutions in society seem large, so out of control, so dangerous to human life and to the planet itself—life is indeed precious. This experience was a turning point, an opening, a new beginning. We promised ourselves we would be part of a new people who would struggle to bring about a new civilization, based on the Hebrew and Christian scriptures and simple ideals such as we should not kill and we should not steal. We began to see how offering sanctuary to refugees was also offering sanctuary for ourselves.

In the caravan we moved sanctuary from a safe building, with quick access to help of all sorts—to the open road and its inherent uncertainties. As Michael McConnell, a leader of the national Sanctuary movement, has said, "Our goal is not to have a thousand sanctuaries. Rather, it is to eliminate the need for sanctuaries."

Transformation comes from such events. Everyone involved in sanctuary or caravans directly helping refugees of Central America, has received a great blessing. We felt our own lives improve; we have seen our congregations and church organizations transformed into more vibrant groups. There is an immediacy and urgency about these tasks that simply can't be put off to another time. For what is at stake is the lives of many people. It is really very much like the holocaust in Germany during World War II, and yet so few people see it that way. Thousands and thousands of people are being murdered and tortured in Central America today. We know in many ways that our own government is directly at fault, but we have not been able to get the government to open the borders. Instead, our government sends people back to be killed. These are policies that no religious person, no person of conscience, can ignore.

The process of declaring sanctuary or of going on illegal caravans of the overground railroad profoundly affected individuals and congregations. As Golden and McConnell have written:

> Something happens to people in their encounter with sanctuary. On one level it is mysterious and inexplicable, a movement of the spirit. On another level, it is a shift of consciousness.
>
> The process of sanctuary—the learning process and the wrestling with faith that occur before a declaration of sanctuary, and the conscientization that comes after a refugee family arrives—is a conversion experience. It is a change of understanding and a change of heart that leads to deeper commitment.
>
> Conscientization is a process of critical reflection at deeper and deeper levels about how human beings live and die in this world. It invariably destroys old assumptions and breaks down mythologies that no longer explain reality because of new information. We all need to

"make sense" of our world. We all construct a "worldview" or "ideology" that explains reality to us in a coherent fashion. Encounters with refugees, their story, and a more intensive study of the history and present reality of Central America have shaken the dominant worldview of many in the religious community.[11]

The experience of declaring sanctuary, along with the direct contact with refugees from the churches of Central America, deepens our concept of compassionate politics and the transformation that follows from it. As Felipe said: "If compassion is understood only as charity, we must opt for solidarity instead." Two other refugees, Raul and Alejandro, in sanctuary in Detroit and New York, have written eloquently against limiting the Sanctuary movement to mere charity.

> You are working for charity only if you deny that a crime is being committed and that the guiltiest party is your government. To fall into the idea of sanctuary as merely an act of charity is to fail to make the historical response. The repression will increase as much in Guatemala as in El Salvador. The number of refugees will continue growing in large proportion and no one will be able to help them. All of us want to live in our countries without the danger of death. Christian love must not only be charitable, but must understand the roots of the problem.
> To continue sanctuary only at the level of charity is to be deceitful. It is to deceive and be at the service of the powerful. It is treason to the gospel. . . . [It] is to be accomplices in the system of lies and repression.

Mary Ann Corely of the Chicago Religious Task Force on Central America has echoed this theme:

> Liberation without charity is only a power struggle. Charity without liberation is only self-serving pietism. But when charity is truly effective, it acts to stop the deprivation of charity, entering a struggle for liberation. . . . [We must] risk challenging the root causes of people's hunger, nakedness, and homelessness. . . . If not, our "charity" will remain unbiblical, a historical pietism. . . .

These are some of the refugees' definitions of compassion as solidarity: "Solidarity is doing all that we can to stop the suffering of others. And solidarity is the total identification with suffering people."

Based upon the teaching of the refugees and their own experience of sanctuary churches, like the Wellington church, discovered that solidarity is essential.

"Solidarity is not in equivocation or moderation; it is found on the road. It is made not by talking, but by walking. . . . As the poet Antonio Machado writes, 'There is no way; the way is made by walking.' "[12] In the Sanctuary movement members of local congregations in cities like Chicago declared their existence as a special community—"the People of God"—linked by compassion and solidarity with their suffering brothers and sisters. Their actions caused them to understand themselves, their world, and their faith differently. The original declaration of sanctuary led to the later caravans, to opposing contra aid, and to refusing to file official employee reports as required by the new Immigration Act. The wars had come home to Chicago, Tucson, Indianapolis, Cincinnati, and Washington, D.C.

Creating Nuclear Weapon Free Zones

Chicago is not only drawn into the wars of Central America, the crises of the Middle East, and the repression in South Africa. It is also a part of the nuclear armament buildup and would be totally destroyed in a major nuclear war. Thus, religious groups in Chicago have had to respond to the threat of nuclear war as well as to existing and potential wars.

The increase in the U.S. Defense Department's budget of 1.6 trillion dollars from 1981 to 1986 has had a direct impact upon the city. Former mayor Harold Washington summarized the financial impact of President Reagan's proposed 1987 federal budget this way:

The 1987 federal budget proposed by President Reagan includes drastic cuts in funding America's cities. In Chicago, these cuts would create a huge $440 million budgetary hole, threatening citizens, rich and poor, young and old alike.

The President's recommendations, combined with cuts we are facing in 1986, would tear the guts out of local government. We would be left with essential services only: police, fire, sanitation, health and bare social services. Our development agencies—Housing, Economic Development and Planning—would face elimination. We would have nothing left with which to build a future for our youth.

The elimination of Revenue Sharing alone, which provided us $67 million in 1985, would mean that a dozen city departments would lose about one-third of their funding—severely affecting health care, garbage pick-up, emergency services, services to the elderly, and consumer programs.

The one-third cut of $37 million we anticipate in the Community Development Block Grant program will force cuts in literally dozens of programs, including elimination of major neighborhood health centers, the end to our home-delivered meal program for seniors, cuts in day care centers, food packages, and so on.

We estimate that $100 million in private sector funds and as many as 7,400 jobs will be lost with the elimination of Urban Development Action Grants, which have been creatively used to help businesses grow in Chicago.[13]

The long-term effects of the 1987 proposed budget by President Reagan was calculated to create city program losses of $1,583,300,000 between 1985 and 1989. While Congress blocked some of the proposed budget cuts, the financial losses for Chicago in 1988 were still very bad.

Fear of future nuclear war, as well as the devastating financial impacts of preparing for war, caused churches and synagogues in Chicago to seek positive actions to resist both nuclear war and the nuclear armament buildup. A first major step was to create Nuclear Weapon Free Zones at local churches and synagogues. As one national pamphlet put it,

> Nuclear warfare and all related institutions and support systems represent a fundamental violation of [the] holiness of creation because they threaten its very survival. To declare a city, a community, a synagogue, church, mosque or home a Nuclear [Weapon] Free Zone and to work towards making this a reality is to affirm God's loving domination over this particular piece of creation. It is an act of faith by which we declare this space to be holy ground.
>
> In so doing, we are healing the earth by rejecting all the destructive forces which militate against its sacred character.

The first church in the Chicago metropolitan area to declare itself a Nuclear Weapon Free Zone was Wheadon United Methodist Church. Here is their story:

> In the spring of 1982, the members of our church in Evanston, out of deep concern for the state of our nation and of the world, established a "strategic response task force." Its charge was to recommend to the congregation a priority program for the Wheadon community. The task force was made up of representatives of the various work areas in the church.
>
> Members of the church spent a number of meetings discussing concerns and priorities, and at a meeting of the Administrative Council in early summer, a consensus was reached that the immediate priority was the issue of world peace, with related concerns of racism and hierarchicalism.

In August, two members of the church met with a young Methodist minister from New Zealand who was visiting the United States seeking to establish "networks of faith" around the issues of world peace. From that meeting came the idea of declaring the Wheadon United Methodist Church property a NUCLEAR WEAPON FREE ZONE. A four by six foot sign was painted by members of the congregation, and on October 2, 1982, the sign was erected. Posters were made available to members of the community and presentations were made to a number of other Evanston churches, with an offer to supply posters to their members.

More than 3,000 posters have been distributed (including 500 with the Declaration in Spanish) across the country. A special Christmas card was prepared, and used by many members of the church.

The sign stands at the corner of Ridge Avenue and Noyes Street in Evanston. During the winter and spring of 1983, two more signs were erected on Ridge Avenue: The Unitarian Church in Evanston and Temple Beth Emmet, the Free Synagogue. Since that time, five more churches in the Chicago area have erected signs, as has St. Scholastica High School in Chicago. Others have been erected on homes in Evanston. They stand as declarations of faith in an unfaithful world.[14]

As the Nuclear Weapon Free Zone campaign grew in Chicago, more conservative churches also joined in the campaign. By 1985, for example, Saint Paul's Congregational Church had also taken a stand. According to an account supplied by their pastor:

> During the 11:00 a.m. worship service on March 3, 1985, St. Paul's Congregational Church declared itself a Nuclear Weapon Free Zone. For this church comprised of white ethnics mainly over the age of 60 who had never before made a commitment in the social action field, this was a major new development in its faith life.
>
> Its genesis took place in mid-November the previous year. The members noticed that for the first time street people began walking through the neighborhood to members' homes begging for money for milk for the baby or for a chance to earn a few dollars doing work around the yard. On one zero night, a bedraggled fellow pleaded for a chance to wash the outside of a member's windows for 34 cents apiece. The members were very distressed by such examples of personal suffering, and they talked about it a lot before and after church. They were already giving food to a pantry, but they wanted to do more.
>
> On Thursday, December 6, a mailing arrived from the Chicago Metropolitan Association office dealing with the Nuclear [Weapon] Free Zone issue. It lifted up the linkage between arms spending and social service spending in the U.S. and the cooperation between churches in a community, and food sharing. Sunday, December 9, was

the church's Family Day celebration when the attendance would be double the normal amount. It would be only two weeks to Christmas Sunday. Events were pulling together in a remarkable array of coincidences. God seemed to be very much at work here. The pastor devoted his entire sermon that week to the Nuclear Weapon Free Zone issue with the above linkages heavily emphasized, and he passed out copies of the Wellington Avenue church's resolution as the proposal for consideration. A call for a congregational meeting signed by six members was read.

Afterwards, silence. That night Ethel Bruneau, one of the signatories who usually has her finger on the pulse of the church, felt that the proposed draft needed some changes. At the pastor's urging she added some paragraphs about human needs, softened some language, and called for "curtailing" instead of "eliminating" nuclear weapons. A revised proposal along with Ethel's call for a letter-writing campaign to Congress were introduced on December 16. The response? Favorable.

The Cabinet met the next evening. The pastor handed out copies of the proposal and declared his willingness to accept any revisions that were within the general parameters previously discussed. Almost every member contributed their suggestions and support.

At the brief meeting on Christmas Sunday, only one person spoke against the declaration. By secret ballot only two people voted against it. Through this overwhelming action of the congregation, God had worked mightily to make Christ real in the church's ministry this Christmas, 1984.[15]

Between the first churches like Wheadon United Methodist and the later churches like Saint Paul's was the declaration of Wellington Avenue United Church of Christ on 30 September 1984. In that declaration, the theology became more explicit and the tactics more political. This is the Wellington church's declaration:

DECLARATION OF WELLINGTON AVENUE UNITED CHURCH OF CHRIST AS A NUCLEAR WEAPON FREE ZONE

Because the poor and oppressed of the world suffer due to the massive excesses of the rich,

Because *all* children of this world have been robbed of a secure future,

Because of the heritage of those of our foreparents, who within the vision of their times lived and worked for justice and freedom, and their work should not be in vain,

Because there are people all over the world whose lives and relationships have been disrupted and destroyed by the intruding forces of other nations,

Because *all* people in this world live under the threat of nuclear holocaust,

We, the people in this place, declare the following:

We choose a life for ourselves that will also allow and ensure life for all others.

We demand that we not be "defended" by dropping nuclear bombs on other people and other living things.

We believe that neither we, nor anything that is ours, is made safe by threatening to use such weapons.

We will oppose our government's political commitment to these systems and use of our money to build and maintain them.

We commit ourselves and our possessions to dismantling nuclear weapons and nuclear weapons systems, and to replacing them with human sharing, work, friendship, and understanding.

We will not leave this to other people to do for us. We will join with others to actively oppose this insanity and obscenity.

We hold sacred all God's creation. It must not be destroyed.

We name this community of faith and this place where we stand as a nuclear weapon free zone forever.

In the name of God, nuclear hell shall not be built, stored, or launched from at least this place.[16]

The news coverage of the Wellington church declaration was less than the coverage of its declaration of sanctuary, but the story was on the evening news on one television station, announced on most radio news programs, and a photograph appeared prominently in the *Chicago Sun-Times*.

The sermon that Sunday filled in the theological and practical framework necessary for the broader campaign. The text was from Deuteronomy 30:19. "I call heaven and earth to witness against you this day, that I have set before you life and death, blessing and curse; therefore choose life that you and your descendents may live. . . . " The sermon proclaimed:

As a community of faith, here at Wellington Avenue Church, we are today signing the covenant of peace with God. We are agreeing to be God's agent of peace and to bring peace to this planet. . . .

As we say today when we declare Wellington Avenue Church a Nuclear Weapon Free Zone forever, we have come to the point of action. We are choosing life for ourselves and acting to ensure life for all others. We are no longer seeking to be even "protected" or "defended" by nuclear weapons. We want to dismantle all nuclear weapons. We oppose building further nuclear weapons by our government.

Because this church is holy ground and a sanctuary for life, we will never house, build, deploy, or allow any nuclear weapons here. Nuclear hell will not be launched from this sanctuary. We are creating a shelter for humanity within these bounds and we seek to expand this holy ground to other churches, synagogues, temples, schools and public buildings. And we dedicate ourselves to fighting to make the entire city of Chicago a Nuclear [Weapon] Free Zone by city ordinance.

Some may say that this is only a symbolic act. But then the writing of the Ten Commandments and the Crucifixion of Jesus were also "symbolic" acts. We trust God to take our action here today and to transform it into an act of meaning, of saving grace and purpose. We act not only for ourselves but for all people, for all creatures, for the whole earth. And we act by vowing that we will never build, house, or use nuclear weapons. From this day we declare ourselves unalterably opposed to nuclear arms and as we say in our declaration: "We commit ourselves and our possessions to dismantling nuclear weapons and nuclear weapons systems."

Today we declare again this a holy ground. Today we declare again that we are a people of God who will act with God in saving this creation. We will trust and leave the final result of our actions in the hands of our God who is the God of history. We will answer God's call. We will shout warning to the world, we will pursue peace, and we shall abolish war from this building and from an ever larger space in this city until a holy shield is raised against nuclear war large enough to protect the whole earth. May God be with us in this task and may we be faithfully with our God.[17]

The declaration of the individual churches, synagogues, and schools, as well as the appearance of several thousand nuclear weapon free zone posters in individual homes and apartments, was part of a much broader campaign undertaken by the Metro Chicago Clergy and Laity Concerned (CALC). The campaign was originally planned to run from Hiroshima Day, 6 August 1984, to 6 August 1985. It was actually successfully completed on Palm Sunday, 23 March 1986.

The larger purpose of the campaign was "to pressure the American government to move toward nuclear disarmament through treaties and the passage of a Nuclear Freeze Resolution in Congress." The campaign's method was "to expand the number of Nuclear [Weapon] Free Zones in the churches and schools of Metropolitan Chicago with the intent of publicizing the nuclear war issue in ways that affect the Presidential and Illinois Senatorial Election [of 1984] and, after the election, to cause the City of Chicago to declare the entire city a nuclear [weapon] free zone by City

Council Ordinance."[18] The campaign planned to declare an additional five churches and one school district as Nuclear Weapon Free Zones by the election on 6 November 1984. A total of ten churches and ten schools were to be declared Nuclear Weapon Free Zones before seeking passage of the city ordinance. The school campaign never really heated up although two Catholic high schools did play a role in the later effort to pass the city ordinance. However, twenty-two churches, synagogues, and schools, along with the city of Evanston (a Chicago suburb), were declared Nuclear Weapon Free Zones before the Chicago City Council campaign came to fruition. In addition, various denominational leaders, church agencies, and peace groups were approached for their support. Representatives of the Nuclear Weapon Free Zone churches also began to meet together to develop a legislative campaign strategy. Subgroups, developed under CALC's leadership, met on the North, South, and West sides of the city.

Because political divisions in the Chicago City Council between the Vrdolyak and Washington factions had held all controversial legislation captive for three years, finding sponsors from each faction was critical. During the summer of 1985, CALC worked with Alderman David Orr (Forty-ninth Ward supporter of Mayor Washington) to draft a suitable ordinance. Then, in the fall, CALC and individual church leaders convinced Alderman Bernard Hansen (Forty-fourth Ward member of the Vrdolyak bloc) to become a cosponsor.

The legislative campaign timetable for 1986 then became:

14 January: Opening press conference announcing introduction of ordinance.

16 January: Ordinance introduced into Chicago City Council and referred to Committee on Economic Development, chaired by Alderman Hansen.

January and February: Meetings by religious groups and constituents with all aldermen on the Committee on Economic Development.

20 February: Press Conference on study by city's Department of Economic Development on economic impact of the proposed ordinance and legal study by law firm of Sachnoff, Weaver and Rubenstein.

25 February: First hearing by the committee. Ten witnesses, including a city councilman from Jersey City, New Jersey; an economics professor; a lawyer; a spokesperson for the city Department of Economic Development; a physics professor; and religious leaders in support of the ordinance. No opposing witnesses appeared and one hundred supporters were present.

12 March: Second comittee hearing. No opposition. Additional witnesses spoke in favor, and 10,000 signed petitions of support presented to committee. Passed committee unanimously. Legislation brought to the floor of the city council and passed unanimously by voice vote on the same day.

Palm Sunday, 23 March: Mayor signed ordinance into law at a CALC rally and celebration.

The Chicago ordinance was substantial legislation. It contained the following provisions:

● The City Council ordered that no person shall engage in, or commence work within the City of Chicago the purpose of which is the design, production, deployment, launching, maintenance, or storage of nuclear weapons or their component parts.

● A Chicago Peace Conversion Commission shall prepare a detailed plan for the conversion of factories to peaceful uses and develop alternative sources of employment for persons currently employed in the nuclear weapons industry.

● The city will post and maintain signs at entrances to the city and in City Hall proclaiming the city's status as a Nuclear Weapon Free Zone.

● In recognition of the first use of nuclear weapons against Hiroshima in 1945, August 6 shall be declared "Nuclear Weapon Free Zone Commemoration Day" within the City of Chicago. The city shall sponsor an appropriate observation annually on this date which shall include a report by the Mayor on the city's activities to enforce this ordinance.[19]

A Department of Economic Development study, presented in testimony before the City Council, concluded that "the federally-induced nuclear weapons 'industry' in Chicago is very small—there are no nuclear weapons labs or companies that deal exclusively in nuclear weapons work." It was possible that up to $1.5 million of the 1984–85 Department of Defense and Department of Energy weapons contracts spent in Chicago might go toward the construction of nuclear weapons or nuclear weapon components. But, the study concluded that less than forty-five jobs would be lost by passage of the ordinance. The department reached the conclusion that "a ban on direct nuclear weapons work will not harm the city economy nor impede future high tech development and job opportunities.[20] Despite the lack of major defense contractors in Chicago, which made its passage easier, the ordinance was still a major challenge to federal government policy.

The importance of this ordinance was made clear by Alderman Orr at the press conference introducing the legislation on 14 January 1986:

This ordinance would make Chicago the largest city in the nation to prohibit the design, production, storage and deployment of nuclear weapons and their components within its boundaries. Specifically, the ordinance requires that all such work be phased out within two years. It immediately prohibits any new start-ups of such work. The ordinance also creates a Peace Conversion Commission to plan for the conversion of existing nuclear weapons facilities to peaceful and productive uses, and to find alternative employment for persons now engaged in nuclear weapons production.

It is appropriate that Chicago should lead the way on this crucial issue. It was here in Chicago that Enrico Fermi performed the pioneering work that unleashed the power of the atom and ushered in the nuclear age. Let us again make history, by becoming the first major American city to pass a binding ordinance establishing itself as a Nuclear Weapon Free Zone.[21]

These sentiments were echoed at the press conference by Ron Freund, former executive director of CALC:

We are announcing today a city-wide campaign to make Chicago a Nuclear Weapon Free Zone. The goal of this campaign is to gradually phase out any existing, and prohibit any future, participation in the production of nuclear weapons or their components within Chicago. If this campaign is successful, the City of Chicago would become the largest community in the country to become a Nuclear Weapon Free Zone through binding legislation . . .

The purpose of this campaign is threefold:

(1) To stabilize and improve the long-term economic health of the city, without serious harm to current employment . . .

(2) To prevent the diversion of needed public and private resources from human resources to the nuclear weapons industry;

(3) To carry out the will of the people of Chicago expressed in the 1982 referendum in which they gave overwhelming support for a freeze on nuclear weapons production and deployment.[22]

Like the Sanctuary movement, the Nuclear Weapon Free Zone Campaign grew from individual congregations to a network embracing suburban towns and then the city of Chicago. More towns in the metropolitan region are now in the process of declaring themselves Nuclear Weapon Free Zones. In 1987 CALC was successful in passing a county ordinance making all the unincorporated areas in Cook County a part of the Nuclear Weapon Free Zone. By 1988 the city of Chicago, Cook County, and six suburban towns had joined together to create the largest Nuclear Weapon Free Zone in North

America. Eventually, a state law outlawing the construction of nuclear weapons will be attempted. The state contains a number of major weapons manufacturers, and this legislative effort may well encounter more opposition.

The response to these efforts in Chicago has continued to broaden. The Third Unitarian Church on the western edge of the city provides a good example of a growing sense of compassion politics and congregational growth. The church has declared itself as holy ground three different times—as a sanctuary for refugees, as a Nuclear Weapon Free Zone, and as a shelter for the homeless. Its members have seen their task as not only being a sanctuary but also as "spreading the light from this sacred place. . . . " They "created a tiny open space of life in the midst of a city, a nation, and a world . . . filled with the forces of darkness . . . because [they] were filled with compassion for the actual suffering of the homeless and the refugees, and the potential suffering of us all in the event of nuclear war."[23]

From the Sanctuary movement we can learn to redefine compassion not as charity but as solidarity. From the Nuclear Weapon Free Zone movement we can learn to see how the forces of life can spread not only through a network of like-minded congregations and agencies but also to politicians, government officials, and leaders of mainline institutions. The umbrella of light can be expanded outward from linked communities to provide an ever larger "holy space," which guarantees the sanctity of life.

Sheltering the Homeless and Feeding the Hungry

In Chicago today there are over twenty-five thousand homeless people, and in 1984 the Greater Chicago Food Depository had to distribute more than eight hundred thousand meals to the hungry through free food pantries and soup kitchens run by churches and settlement houses. The number of hungry people continues to grow each year. Although the city population is continuing to decline, dropping to below three million people by the 1980 census, the impoverished population continues to expand. Meanwhile, workers leave the city to seek jobs elsewhere, and the rich move to the suburbs or to the wealthy enclaves of housing along Chicago's beautiful lakefront. It is estimated that as many as eight hundred thousand Chicagoans may be in jeopardy of going hungry at least part of every month.[24] Because less than three million people live in Chicago, the hungry have become a very large percentage of the population. And, as a further index of misery, the rate of infant mortality and the number of deaths due to malnutrition continue to be as high in Chicago as in many of the less developed countries of the world.

Many churches and synagogues as well as units of local government have attempted to respond to the "epidemic" of homelessness and hunger in

Chicago. Hundreds of food pantries and soup kitchens have been established; dozens of emergency shelters for the homeless have opened in church basements. The city has moved from allocating no money in the city budget for the homeless to allocating more than three million dollars a year in its corporate budget and several million dollars of Community Development Block Grant funds from the federal government. Still, at the beginning of the winter of 1985-86, there were only 1,660 emergency shelter beds for the homeless. A special "emergency warming center" program added another 500 beds whenever the temperature dropped below eleven degrees (theoretically, the temperature when street people are more likely to freeze to death unsheltered). The situation by 1987–88 was only slightly improved with 2,100 shelter beds, with warming centers operating whenever the temperature dropped below thirty-two degrees, and with the availability of a few more daytime drop-in centers.

More than social service programs have been attempted. An Anti-Hunger Coalition, Chicago Coalition for the Homeless, and Interfaith Council for the Homeless have formed to exert political pressure to eliminate the roots of hunger and homelessness. Short-term groups of the homeless themselves, such as the Chicago Homeless Caucus and a Union of the Homeless, have come into existence. Traditional groups such as the Public Welfare Coalition and the Welfare Rights Organization, as well as newer Unemployment Councils, continue. Religious groups and leaders are deeply involved in all these efforts. And they have had some success in loosening the ordinance restricting churches from opening shelters and in drawing more public attention to the problems.

But the number of the hungry and the homeless continue to grow in Chicago. The number of people freezing to death on the street per year has climbed to four hundred, and the number dying of malnutrition go uncounted. Compassion has demanded a response and there have been many unsung, heroic efforts to change things for the poor in Chicago.

Consider the efforts of a single individual. James Harper was a black, recovering alcoholic, living in the Uptown Community. "In the saloons and flophouses of Uptown, where memories are short and faith is fleeting, they still talk about James Harper. Some say he had the light of God in his eyes." In 1974, Harper founded an agency funded by a shoestring budget which he named Save the Alcoholic. Later the name was changed to the Center for Street People. Harper's personal name for the center was "Save the Alcoholic from Professional Treatment." The center was founded on the philosophy that only caring and acceptance would help street people, that paperwork, appointments, and outside interference by uncaring professionals would never work. The center did not intend to "reform" street people. As Doug Doabmeyer, a later director of the center, put it: "The things we're doing prolong life. That's what the Center is about—it's there to be supportive, not of a particular life-style in the sense of endorsing it, but supporting people, giving them the minimal respect due a human being, and recognizing that some people will make changes."[25]

Harper got the start-up money of $5,000 from the Chicago-Uptown Ministry. The Wellington Avenue United Church of Christ, which he and his wife Ann attended, acted as fiscal agent for the project. The center grew from a nonmedical detoxification center to a daytime and early evening drop-in center for several hundred street people. A number of the street people serve as staff, and several recovering alcoholics such as James have been key outreach workers. Not long after it was a drop-in center, it began to be "a thoroughly illegal overnight shelter, with mattresses packed in for as many as 100 men on below-zero nights." The police knew about it, "but they also knew it was the best solution available. A building inspector once asked Harper, 'You're not sleeping people here, are you?' Harper smiled and said, 'That would be illegal, wouldn't it?' and the building inspector smiled too and that was the end of that."[26]

Later the shelter was moved to the People's Church, which still provides shelter for up to sixty men at night, and a second shelter opened at Uptown Baptist Church for thirty women. An evening "warming center" for sixty more men was begun at the nearby Salvation Army. An entire system for the homeless grew from the Center for Street People in Uptown.

From the center's original illegal overnight sheltering of the homeless, a legal shelter system has developed in Edgewater and Uptown under Residents for Emergency Shelter (REST), which operates the shelters at the People's Church and the Uptown Baptist Church. In the winter of 1984–85 REST provided 22,412 bed nights of shelter—123 men and women per night. Moreover, REST provided a full-time housing counselor to work with the homeless to find them permanent housing and was able to move 75 shelter guests into permanent housing during 1984–85. Other services were provided to assist the homeless in securing welfare program benefits, jobs, and medical services. A medical clinic to serve the homeless was also initiated.

By the late 1970s, Harper began to recognize that his work with derelicts was a ministry and that he wanted to become an ordained minister. After earning a high school diploma in an adult education program (he had previously only completed the eighth grade), Harper entered Garrett Theological Seminary as a special student. Despite the fact that he was now in great physical pain with cancer of the stomach, he finished seminary. Chemotherapy provided another year of nearly normal life.

As he studied in seminary and prepared for ordination, Harper began to articulate a special relationship between the poor and Jesus. "Who else but the unloved could truly identify with a message of love? Who else but the unforgiven could truly understand words of forgiveness? I have come to recognize just how important the poor are to Christ. Without the poor there would be no message; without the message there would be no Christ."[27] Harper called his theology, born of his own poverty, lack of formal education, crime, sickness, and threat of death, "a theology of the lost."[28] It was not a spiritualized theology.

In his paper written for the Church and Ministry Committee which would determine whether to ordain him as a minister in the United Church of Christ, Harper wrote:

> To spiritualize Christ is to deprive Him of His humanity; but worse still, it is to deprive humanity of Christ. I know that He has the power to forgive, because He has forgiven me. It is Christ within me that would not allow me to surrender my identity in the face of overwhelming odds, to those who were interested only in saving my soul. It is to Him that I owe my life; and it is to Him that I have surrendered. My theology was born of suffering, but it is hope born of Christ which gives it expression.

He concluded:

> I believe that God called me to the Ordained Ministry when He inspired me to develop the Center For Street People. I believe He called me through the mouths of homeless and alcoholic persons to present their cases to the powers that be. . . .
>
> To me, more than anything else, Holy Communion is a ritual of compassion; to be filled with Christ is to also be filled with a loving relationship with those who are counted among the least of us.[29]

On 8 May 1983, with James Harper near death from the raging cancer in his body, several hundred people gathered in a hospital chapel to ordain him. At the service, Rev. David Chevrier of the Wellington Avenue Church of Christ said that James Harper was not only ordained because the church recognized his existing ministry at the Center for Street People but also because the church needed to ordain him, that for the church's good it needed to affirm that this was what Christianity was all about.[30] James Harper died the morning after his ordination at 3 a.m.

The Center for Street People in Chicago, which James Harper founded, continues today. Its goals are: to give street people a sense of self-worth through caring for others as well as meeting those who care for them, to maintain the health and dignity of people coming in the door, to refer people to appropriate agencies, to continue opportunities to reinforce the participants' positive self-image through responsibility, and to defend the lives and health of street people through advocacy.

To achieve these goals, the Center for Street People has continued to operate a drop-in center for an average of 150 people a day seven days a week. During 1986, the center received several grants to renovate its existing facility and to expand into a new building next door to its current site. This expansion allows it to serve even more street people more comfortably. The center has added showers and now serves meals four nights a week. In 1983 alone, 10,000 meals were provided. The center has continued a strong advocacy program for the homeless citywide including providing leadership for the Chicago Coalition for the Homeless. Most of all, its own facilities continue to provide an atmosphere of caring that is missing in the lives of the homeless. Its motto remains "Fall down seven times, get up eight."

In the Lake View Community, closer to the Wellington Avenue church, a shelter was opened at Lake View Lutheran Church. In 1984–85, the shelter provided 3,819 bed nights for men and women; however, the overflow meant 198 individuals had to be turned away. Obviously, the one overnight shelter site was insufficient for the Lake View Community. During the summer of 1985, the Wellington Avenue church applied for grants to the city of Chicago and the Interfaith Council for the Homeless to become a legal overnight shelter. The city grant was turned down, but the Interfaith Council was willing to make available $2,500, and the existing Lake View Emergency Winter Shelter Team, which ran the Lake View Shelter, was willing to provide the organizational base from which to operate a second shelter. The city of Chicago did certify the Wellington site as part of its "Emergency Warming Center" system. After considerable discussion about potential problems in operating the program, the congregation agreed to open the shelter on 2 January 1986, as a shelter for fifteen homeless women.

It turned out that there was not as much demand for shelter for homeless women as was thought to be the case in 1985, and later a shelter was opened to serve homeless women in a nearby community. So the shelter was expanded on 30 January 1986, to include men. The rest of the winter it operated with about 25 homeless men and 5 women each night. During the winter of 1985–86 the original Lake View Shelter provided 3,954 nights of shelter for men and 443 for women, and the Wellington site provided 1,800 shelter nights for men and 425 for women. In addition, hot meals were provided both in the evening and in the morning, and a social worker was available to help the guests with their other problems at both Lake View sites.

But statistics simply can't convey the importance of the shelters for the homeless or the effect on volunteers. Altogether, fifty members of the Wellington congregation worked overnight as volunteers at the shelter, and others brought in food and blankets. Here are some of their comments on their experiences:

> I was really glad on nights during a blizzard to be able to open our church doors and invite the homeless in to warmth and safety.
>
> I made friends with the guests and little things meant a lot to them.

One of them really thanked me just for calling him by his name. He said, "It's been so long since anyone called my name." Obviously, it made him feel that he was a real person, a human being. It was the little things that really made the Wellington shelter special. . . .

I remember during the last morning cleanup when we were closing the shelter one of the women guests who had so many problems. She just sat down at the piano and played for maybe forty minutes while we cleaned. For the first time she seemed completely at peace.

I remember my surprise when the guests themselves brought food for others in the shelters. One of the guests, Helene, used her food stamps to buy pizza for everyone one night. A number of the guests by the end were helping to set up the shelter and most helped with the cleanup. It became their home.

I remember how guests got to meet each other in a safe atmosphere and then helped each other out on the street. They made friends amongst themselves here.

I remember one night at the shelter a woman who lost her shoe. It was freezing out and I was so worried for her. I think maybe she really just wanted to talk.

I remember so many of the women guests without socks or stockings in the dead of winter. I am glad we were able to provide socks, gloves, sweaters, and coats for them.

One of the shelter volunteers put applesauce in the oatmeal. And a guest confessed the next night—"That's just how my grandmother used to cook oatmeal." Even the homeless once had a family, once had a home, once were loved.

I got a lot out of the shelter as a volunteer. It sharpened my focus on how much I have to be thankful for. And I learned from the guests.

Once I served a man who was really dirty from being out on the street all day. The guests were really shocked when we served them. He said, "How can you be so kind to an animal like me?" The poor man, he felt he had been reduced to being just an animal.

Another guest cried when I told him he could have two small bottles of real juice we had been given by the health food store.

Every week I would dread coming. By the time I had been here for only three minutes I was so glad though to be here. I would sail home. That lasted until about 9 a.m. when I would crash from too little sleep. But it was worth it.

I remember pictures: One woman washing her hair in the bathroom sink even though it was bitter cold. The hunger in the eyes of a man who begged, "Can you give me a second helping?"

The guests really loved having the children around. Rita would always ask when we came "Where is Bo?" "Where is Kate?" Their eyes would really light up when the children were here. The children *always* treated them like real people.

Before I volunteered here I had no idea that you woke up guests at 3 a.m. so they could go sell newspapers for a little money or that others got up at 5 a.m. to stand in lines for day labor.

The homeless are not like we think. We had a tax consultant and a data processor among our guests. They were even working some of the time and couldn't get enough money to live on their own.

I remember one night just after we opened the shelter for men that I let a man in late, about midnight. His hands were gloveless and nearly frozen. They were very close to frostbite. I had to get a pan of lukewarm water to help him to thaw them gradually. Without our shelter that night he would clearly have had frostbite and probably frozen to death on the street.[31]

After the shelter had been open in the 1985–86 winter, the Wellington Avenue church voted unanimously at its June 1986 congregational meeting to reopen its shelter for the homeless despite the fact that it would still be technically only an "Emergency Warming Center." Thus, every night it was over thirty-two degrees during the winter it would be operating contrary to city law. However, for a church which defied federal laws to provide sanctuary for Central Americans, violating zoning ordinances was a minor consideration. The Wellington shelter has opened each year since it began in 1985.

More churches and synagogues run shelters, drop-in centers, pantries, and soup kitchens than are sanctuaries or Nuclear Weapon Free Zones, for the need is clear-cut and, seemingly, less political. The Community for Creative Non-Violence in Washington, D.C., has phrased the call to act this way:

Something is very wrong. What is wrong is that the walking homeless, the street people, have become missing persons: missing from our consciousness and our deliberations. Therefore, they stand outside the range of institutional possibilities; they have become America's untouchables.

As a result, human beings, God's children all, freeze to death for lack of shelter, or more accurately they are killed by lack of concern. Some die quickly in abandoned buildings, during snowstorms; some die by degrees, slowly tortured on the rack of poverty. Human suffering, which should be concrete and visible, has become abstract and unseen.

We have built a wall between ourselves and those who have no place to lay their heads. That wall must come down, and it must come down now. The homeless demand shelter, not excuses. They demand dignity and ending the demeaning that comes from sleeping on the street. They demand that the insulation of our lives be broken by paying the debt of our neglect. They demand that here and now, in the capital of the wealthiest nation on earth, basic shelter and adequate nutrition be recognized politically, philosophically, and programmatically as an absolute and inalienable human right.[32]

Members of churches and religious groups working with the homeless, hungry, and unemployed have felt their guts wrenched by compassion. Their eyes have been opened. Where before they saw only empty rooms in their church they now see a space to house those without a home. Where they pursued only their own success in society they now see the need to help their brothers and sisters. They have had to confront the structures of society. Can a nation which has three million homeless people and thirty-six million people living below the poverty line be called democratic? Can we as a people exist half well-off and half in misery? Can we be proud of an economy that destroys so many human lives? These questions are fueled by the passion of direct contact with those who suffer—those without livelihood, dignity, or hope. The poor cry out in their pain. We hear. We respond. But what we do is not enough. So we join with the poor themselves to do more. If from the Sanctuary movement we learn to redefine compassion as solidarity, if from the Nuclear Weapon Free Zone Campaign we learn how sacred space can be spread, we learn from the struggle with the poor and homeless that our institutions can and must be changed. The homeless demonstrate by their existence and their suffering the fundamental flaws of our society.

Other Crises

Chicago is not just a microcosm of the issues of war and homelessness. It also mirrors many other conflicts of our civilization. Chicago is made more violent and less governable by racial and ethnic conflicts in the same way that wars make the world more violent and less governable. Just as superpowers hoard international resources, whites in Chicago benefit from their privileged position. Chicago remains the most segregated large city in America.[33] Its housing, its schools, and its jobs are all segregated. Each ethnic group tends to live in its own segregated community, and hostility, especially between white and black communities, is intense. In the past, Chicago has been a center for race riots, and, today, racial tensions are running high once more. The attempt to end racial segregation by the election of a black mayor has been only partially successful. First, there was a political stalemate between Mayor Washington and a white, machine-controlled city council. Then, with Mayor Washington's death, the political machine attempted to regain control despite the election of another black, Mayor Eugene Sawyer, as acting mayor until 1989. Before wars of race, religion, nationality, and economic self-interest can be eliminated on an international scale, it will be necessary to learn how to eliminate racial and ethnic conflict at the local level. Clearly, problems of racial, ethnic, and religious conflict have not yet been solved in Chicago.

Like the hunger and the homelessness crisis, resource depletion/pollution is visible in Chicago. Before 1970 there were no ordinances governing the forms of pollution endemic to modern urban areas. Since 1970 there have been a series of local laws, as well as state and federal regulations, seeking to contain the worst forms of air and water pollution. Today Chicago's air has less sulfur dioxide than before 1970 because of these new laws. But cars are only beginning to be regulated, and soot, particulate matter, and carbon dioxide from automobile exhaust remain at such a high level that Chicagoans are far less healthy than Americans living in rural areas or in small towns. Ozone alerts still occur and the water in Lake Michigan is so dangerous that we must limit the number of lake fish we eat or risk polychlorinated biphenyl and mercury poisoning. Many traditionally polluting industries of the past, such as steel mills, are closing, but the city is now ringed by the Commonwealth Edison Company's nuclear power plants, which provide our electric power. A single incident at a plant like the Zion, Illinois, nuclear power plant could contaminate Chicago's air and water forever. Trucks transporting nuclear and toxic waste still drive unannounced on Chicago's expressways, and toxic cargo is transported on our rail system. Spills and accidents remain a constant hazard. Finally, disposing of thousands of tons of garbage each day is an ever-greater problem despite the introduction of waste recycling programs by the city government.

Just as Chicago suffers from racism, hunger, pollution, and resource depletion, it is also heavily hit by global economic crises. One proposal to meet the crisis is to replace the old Chicago "stockyards" and outdated steel plants, which were the heart of industrial Chicago, with new industries developed by the University of Illinois, the state of Illinois, and the city of Chicago at a "high-tech" park west of the downtown Chicago area. These new biological industries sponsored by drug companies are meant to rival the "Silicon Valley" computer plants in California. Yet, these new potential biological factories are unable to replace the many jobs lost when the gigantic factories closed over the last decade and a half. Chicago continues to lose jobs and lose businesses, while supporting polluting firms that remain in the city. There is no real attempt to switch to an alternative technology based upon neighborhood companies, employing local employees and using nonpolluting methods to produce the necessary products for people living in the city. Unfortunately, Chicago has no long-range vision of creating resource-efficient, nonpolluting industries for a more healthy economic future.

Certainly, the negative aspects of the recent economic cycle are seen in Chicago. For the last decade and a half, Chicago has been losing up to 60,000 people, 25,000 jobs, and 12,500 homes a year. Only in the late 1980s have these losses of population, jobs, and homes slowed. Despite many years of double-digit inflation, the assessed valuation of all property in Chicago scarcely changed during the 1970s because of the enormous losses of businesses and homes. For a while, the exodus was only to the suburban area of metropolitan Chicago, but now people and jobs are moving out of state, following the companies fleeing the city. Some companies have even moved overseas, hiring cheaper foreign workers to produce steel, automobiles, and television sets formerly made in Chicago.

One result is a high level of unemployment. Unemployment in Cook County has rarely dropped below 12 percent since 1980. Unemployment in many Chicago ghettos is from 30 to 40 percent, and unemployment among minority youth has remained higher than 50 percent. The number of poor people in Chicago has grown as a consequence, creating the high number of hungry, homeless, and hopeless souls in the city today. Those who were not physically and mentally ill before they lost their jobs, possessions, families, and pride are quickly destroyed living on Chicago's bitter streets. The Chicago economy has created 200,000 new jobs since the worst of the 1982–83 recession, but most of them are in the service or retail sectors of the economy. In the six-county metropolitan area, manufacturing jobs fell by 135,000 from 1979 to 1985. The result of switching to a service economy has been mostly negative: "Average household income has risen only slightly during the current economic expansion and remains below the mid-1970s peak, despite the massive influx of women into the labor force and the rise in two-income families. Earnings per job have fallen even faster. . . . Key poverty indicators remain stubbornly high. . . . Two years of economic expansion [has not changed the extent] of economic hardship.[34]

Although new condominium high-rise buildings have been built along the lakefront and new service corporations have opened offices in downtown Chicago, these new jobs have not been enough to offset the ill effects of a national economy of inflation/recession nor to eliminate the high levels of unemployment and poverty in the city. To make matters worse, federal budget cutbacks since President Reagan took office have cost the Chicago local governments losses of several hundred million dollars in subsidies. The federal budget has also cut millions of dollars in direct aid to individual recipients of welfare, unemployment, and social security programs. All this has taken money and purchasing power out of Chicago and made economic recovery for the city difficult. With private industries going bankrupt or leaving the city, and with federal assistance to both individuals and local government being cut back, the prospects of combating unemployment are bleak.

In addition to the crises of hunger, racial conflict, wasted military expenditures, decreased federal government aid, and unemployment, Chicago today is also a battleground between democracy (in the form of greater citizen participation and a more just distribution of government services) and machine control (autocratic government favoring particular races, ethnic groups, and individuals). This is not new for Chicago. Ever since the Chicago fire of 1871 the city has been the home of machine politics. At first there were separate fiefdoms controlled by aldermen and ward committeemen who shared the spoils among themselves. They were supported by keepers of saloons, gambling dens, and houses of prostitution who gave them votes in return for protection from the police. In later years, machine politics became organized on a citywide basis—first dominated by Republicans and, after 1932, by Democrats. As machine politics grew stronger and corruption and vice more rampant, reformers and reform organizations developed to challenge the corruption, waste, and inefficiency of machine-dominated government.

The defense of machine politics in Chicago has always been that Chicago is "the city that works." That is to say, machine politics, especially under the legendary Mayor Daley, "got things done" including building expressways, developing the downtown Loop area, and insuring that basic city services like garbage collection and police protection were provided. Moreover, it was the politics of the immigrant groups—it helped to acculturate and to advance the poorest and newest members of society. Reformers attacked the machine because it circumvented democracy to have the decisions made by the machine "bosses" and influential businesspeople with "clout"; it led to high levels of corruption and waste in government; and it discriminated in the delivery of city services so that the Irish got more city jobs and better city services than minority groups. But for over a hundred years, most Chicago citizens were prepared to trade the purer forms of democracy for a reasonably efficient autocracy. Those who weren't were crushed by the powers of the government including threats to cut off welfare payments.

Now the city of Chicago is engaged in a great political battle to determine whether the old machine or the new reform movement, which was headed until his death in 1987 by Mayor Washington, will succeed in controlling the city. The "reform" movement in Chicago is composed of three elements: (1) traditional advocates of good government reform dedicated to economy, honesty, and efficiency in government; (2) those favoring citizen participation by creating open processes at city hall and neighborhood government in communities in order to give citizens a voice in those decisions that most affect them; and (3) minority groups seeking empowerment to open up government jobs and power to blacks, latinos, and women. The Washington administration at times faltered in pursuing these goals but the goals remained. Because of this, liberal religious groups in Chicago supported and worked with the Washington administration and the movement that brought him to power. Since Mayor Washington's death, however, progress in achieving these reforms has slowed.

There has been no permanent or comprehensive alliance between the religious groups and the reform movement in Chicago. Local Chicago problems remain disconnected from the international crises of which they are a local manifestation. Churches and synagogues have been able to react effectively only to one issue at a time, such as sanctuary, nuclear war, and homelessness. Solidarity, the importance of increasing sacred space, extending the sphere of life and light, and the depth of the flaws of our civilization are key lessons learned by local congregations. How to apply these lessons more broadly and comprehensively is still to be learned.

Compassionate Action Beyond Chicago

The crucial fact about what has happened in Chicago and what has been occurring in Central America, South Africa, the Philippines, and in many other spots around the globe is the discovery that compassion can effectively be practiced in a congregation or in a small community. The international crises which are building and which are already manifesting themselves locally can only be met by those with a faith commitment and with a support group that can provide the physical and psychological resources necessary for bold action. Old laws will have to be broken and new laws made, institutions overthrown and new institutions built. Only such collective actions will be sufficient to transform either a city like Chicago or the broader world.

David Roozen, William McKinney, and Jackson Carroll in *Varieties of Religious Presence* conclude that activist congregations that undertake compassionate action share several characteristics. They have strong pastoral leadership and a clear theology. As the authors put it, "the activist orientation is grounded in a theology that makes commitment to social justice an explicit and central priority." That meant for the Christian congregations they studied, "an emphasis on Christian responsibility for working for change in society as a means of serving God. For [these congregations], God meets a person in his or her spiritual pilgrimmage, not simply in the privacy of his or her interior life, but in the world, in the struggle for love and justice."[35] All accounts of compassionate action by congregations emphasize that they are not simply activist organizations. They are balanced by worship and liturgy, by support for individual members [called in the Christian tradition "pastoral care"], and by attention to developing spiritual disciplines including prayer.[36]

Often congregations, groups of congregations, and "base communities" are the critical building blocks for compassionate action. Yet they are often overlooked or thought to be of only minor significance. A Hindu social worker once explained the importance of congregations to a Christian missionary this way:

Did you ever stop to think that this is Christianity's most unique contribution to the religions [of the world]? Every religion has God, and an altar, and a holy book, a worshiper, and a sacrifice. Yours is the only religion—your Judeo-Christian faith—which has a congregation. It's a unique idea, that. But you see, *a congregation is never just an audience.* It's never people in a row sitting, listening, praying, worshiping. It's a little group made one in the power of the Savior. . . . I have heard Christians weigh the church's worth by the total of its resources and the richness of its property, and I have said to myself, "but what has this to do with the congregation, that little welded fellowship in which the power works?" For you see, he said, "the power of the Savior must be *in the congregation,* driving them out to meet their fellow men [and women]. That's the way [God] reaches the world."[37]

While this Hindu fails to point out that Ashrams, temples, and mosques also create "congregations," he is correct in emphasizing the special nature of such groups. As places where religion can inspire more radical political and social action, where social transformation can begin, and where group support can be provided for individuals undergoing their own radical personal transformations, congregations are little noticed seedbeds of the politics of compassion and transformation.

The development of religiously based compassionate action and the engagement in political struggles by religious people is, of course, not limited to local congregations. Nor is it limited to a single city like Chicago. Rather, compassionate action is occurring in Third World countries, in Europe, and in socialist bloc countries. It is also occurring in international religious organizations such as the Vatican Councils of the Catholic Church and in the World Council of Churches.

At the New Delhi Assembly of the World Council of Churches in 1961 Masao Takenaka sounded the call for a "revolutionary renewal": "What we need today is to accept this decisive service of Christ and to make the decisive change within ourselves and in the structure of our churches to respond to the transforming and redemptive power of God which is going on in our changing world."[38] By 1986, twenty-five years of supporting peoples' struggles had radicalized at least the Urban Rural Mission of the World Council. The original goal of the Urban Rural Mission had been "to make real the saving presence of Christ in those parts of society which are formed by industrialization and urbanization." This was soon enlarged to include "the need to advocate and secure social justice . . . " By the 1970s the Urban Rural Mission had developed "its insistence on local actions and organizing people for empowerment." It worked with the marginalized sectors of society, including "slum-dwellers, the unemployed, indigenous people, fish-workers, migrant workers . . . " The Urban Rural Mission participated "in their struggles and political actions to transform existing political, economic and social structures."[39]

The Urban Rural Mission is dedicated today to liberation and justice. Its members believe that "Liberation is no mere overturning of one particular set of power roles only to be replaced by another. Its goal is nothing less than the peace (Shalom) of God in a qualitatively new community in which the role of the oppressor and oppressed is completely done away with."[40] Being dedicated to this goal has also meant that these Christians are called to resist the forces of evil, including national governments.

> Resistance is an attitude of vigilance in the defense of the fullness of life. It is in every attitude and action, individual and corporate, which goes against powers which threaten people and God's creative work in the world . . .
>
> That Christians are called to resistance, therefore, should not even be regarded as a matter of debate in the Christian community. Wherever the laws of a society consistently and grossly violate the laws of God, there should be no doubt where the Christian duty lies. There are many situations in life where obedience to God requires disobedience to Caesar. Civil disobedience will become a necessary quality of Christian mission wherever the laws of a society do gross damage to human beings.[41]

It is just such theological premises that cause the Urban Rural Mission and the World Council of Churches as a whole to support peoples' struggles for justice and empowerment through local organizing of the exploited, by building up networks of communication between movements for change, by assisting in the training of local leaders, and by supporting local leaders when they are victimized or denied human rights. The Urban Rural Mission seeks to encourage deeper study of the bible and theological reflection, and it works to reshape the broader mission of the institutional church throughout the world.

In the United States the commitments of participants in the World Council of Churches were paralleled by the involvement of congregations in the civil rights movement, the peace movement, the sanctuary movement, and the struggle to alleviate poverty. Moreover, special "action training" programs to assist in "urban mission" were created by the predominantly white, mainline Protestant denominations during the 1960s. Twenty-seven training centers were begun, each training several thousand church people. But by the 1980s these centers had virtually all disappeared. As they sought to change both the religious denominations that sponsored them and the broader society, their funding was eliminated.[42] Their elimination demonstrates, once again, that the effort to transform the larger institutions of society is hard to sustain. But change continues to bubble up from local congregations and communities, nonetheless. The commitment to a politics of compassion and transformation inevitably leads to compassionate action at both the local and international levels. But there is no guarantee that these actions will succeed in transforming cities like Chicago or in averting the global crises we face. More will be required if we are to avoid the coming dark age.

Part IV

TRANSFORMATION

Chapter 7
A NEW PEOPLE

In that day the remnant of Israel and the survivors of the house of Jacob will no more lean upon him that smote them, but will lean upon the Lord, the Holy One of Israel, in truth. A remnant will return, the remnant of Jacob, to the mighty God. For though your people Israel be as the sand of the sea, only a remnant of them will return. Destruction is decreed, overflowing with righteousness. For the Lord, the Lord of hosts, will make a full end, as decreed, in the midst of all the earth.

Isaiah 10:23-24

Then I will gather the remnant of my flock out of all the countries where I have driven them, and I will bring them back to their fold, and they shall be fruitful and multiply. I will set shepherds over them who will care for them, and they shall fear no more. . . .

Jeremiah 23:3-4

The transformation of our culture and our society would have to happen at a number of levels. If it occurred only in the minds of individuals (as to some degree it already has), it would be powerless. If it came only from the initiative of the state, it would be tyrannical. Personal transformation among large numbers is essential and it must not only be a transformation of consciousness but must also involve individual action. . . . Out of existing groups and organizations, there would also have to develop a social movement dedicated to the idea of such a transformation.

Robert Bellah et al., Habits of the Heart: Individualism and Commitment in American Life

What is at stake in our time is nothing less than the fate of our civilization. *Individual* development and transformation is a necessary but insufficient response. Responses to current crises by congregations and local communities are only building blocks in the required larger transformation. Change must grow from individuals to small groups to larger networks of individuals to a full-fledged political/religious/cultural movement. Ultimately, a "new people of God" must emerge. The Hebrews who were led out of Egypt by Moses, the

225

later kingdoms of Judah and Israel, early Christians, Moslems, and Hindus have been such a people. All empires, kingdoms, and nations attempt to be such a people.

Basically, a nation and a civilization are unified by a common culture, a common history, a common religion, and, often, a common government. But it is their shared culture, history, and faith that make them a "people." The Hebrew prophets spoke of a faithful remnant from which the "people of God" would be built. Elijah told of the seven thousand Hebrews who had not worshiped Baal who would be the foundation of a new Israel. Isaiah and Jeremiah spoke of a remnant who would survive Assyrian and Babylonian conquests and would return to rebuild Jerusalem. Jesus began the Christian Church with twelve disciples and only a few hundred followers. In all these cases a faithful remnant was the building block from which a religion and a civilization was constructed.

Our civilization is at a crisis point, a time of great danger, which, paradoxically, provides great potential for transformation. But how is this transformation to be achieved? How are a new people to be cocreators with God of a new heaven and a new earth?

Personal Transformation

Psychoanalysts, "New Age" advocates, and many religious people believe that transformation must be primarily individual. This is something each of us individually can do: develop our individual consciousness, heal our own psychological wounds, and enlarge our own spiritual capacities. Then we can withdraw our negative projections from others and face the problems of our time maturely and creatively. It is assumed that when a critical mass of individuals has made this personal transformation, societal and cultural transformation will inevitably follow.

The importance of a greater personal awareness has long been the teaching of Zen Buddhism. In Zen-related art, for example, there are four dominant modes. They are *Sabi, Wabi, Aware,* and *Yugen.*

> *Sabi* may be defined as the feeling of isolation, or rather at a mid-point of the emotion when it is both welcome and unwelcome, source of both ease and unease . . . [associated with] the sense of being detached. . . .
>
> *Wabi* is the spirit of poverty, the poignant appreciation of what most consider the commonplace. . . . How much more real, how much more relevant to the spiritual quest that even the wisest words is Nature's least manifestation when accepted for the profound thing it is. . . .
>
> *Aware* is the sadness that comes with the sense of the impermanence

of things . . . [As Kenko Yoshida wrote,] "the beauty of life is in its impermanence . . . even one year lived peacefully seems very long. Yet for such as love the world, a thousand years would fade like the dream of one night." . . .

Yugen . . . is the sense of a mysterious depth in all that makes up nature . . . "true beauty and gentleness" a "realm of tranquility and elegance" . . . the mystic calm in things.[1]

The development of greater personal awareness opens our perception of the world and as one learns the teachings of Zen, "calm replaces restless ego." As Buddha taught:

And what is it, monks, that I have revealed? Why, that this is suffering, that is the arising of suffering, this is the ceasing of suffering, this the practice leading to the cessation of suffering. And why did I reveal this alone? Because, monks, this is concerned with profit and is the beginning of the holy life; this conduces to aversion, detachment, cessation, tranquility, comprehension, wisdom, Nirvana. Therefore have I revealed it.[2]

Thus, for centuries Buddhists have taught the path to self-realization, enlightenment, and personal transformation can make transforming the world possible. Being conscious of every aspect of one's life and every aspect of the world is the beginning of wisdom, and a person of wisdom can transform the world. From the awareness of *Sabi, Wabi, Aware,* and *Yugen* a new creative consciousness is born.

In *A Vision of the Aquarian Age,* Sir George Trevelyan explains in more modern terms of the "New Age" movement, how personal transformation (which both Buddhists and New Age gurus advocate) leads to world transformation: "Change [individuals] and you change society. Try to change society without the inner change in individuals, and confusion will be the sole result." Trevelyan suggests that a primary method for this transformation is meditation. Preparation of our bodies is an appropriate first step, but our primary task as individuals is to discover our oneness with the planet and the universe. "Behind disaster is a transforming power at work out of the Living Whole, which can cleanse the planet, sweep away much that is negative and bring in a New Age." We come to see our situation this way when we develop a new consciousness of our relationship with the Living Whole. Once this holistic view is adopted, "everything alive becomes sacred." As Teilhard de Chardin, Thomas Berry, and Brian Swimme confirm, we "discover that Planet Earth is truly alive, a sentient creature with her own breathing, bloodstream, glands, and consciousness."[3] With our coming to consciousness the earth is enabled to reflect upon herself.

The disintegration of our civilization can lead to gloom or it can cause us to see "the first bursting of spring." Trevelyan takes the positive view because he believes that personal transformation is taking place more frequently now as the barrier between the eternal and temporal planes, the spiritual and the mundane, are melting.[4] He suggests that the Age of Aquarius is transforming our access to the spiritual planes. New Age spirituality generally assumes that, as we become more attuned to the positive energy available to us in our time, we will be able to create a new civilization. The old civilization will simply disintegrate under its own weight.

Trevelyan recommends a meditation to open us to higher planes of light. In a meditative state we are to visualize divine light flowing from the top of our head, passing through our heart all the way through our body down to the earth. This opens our heart center, or chakra. The heart acts as a transformer sending out light as love for all life in the four directions of the compass. The resulting, three-dimensional Celtic cross of love becomes "an archetypal symbol for the New Age."[5] Regular meditation allows us to develop inner peace and the wisdom necessary to cope with the crises of our time. Our meditation aligns us with higher energies, creates the stillness necessary to gain new insights, and allows our love to flow out into the world.

New Age advocates recognize that individuals with higher levels of consciousness must not only work on meditation and personal spiritual development, but they must also form groups. Trevelyan is impressed with New Age communities like Findhorn founded in 1962 in northern Scotland. With its more than 200 permanent residents (and visitors staying for shorter periods), Findhorn attempts to develop the new institutions, ideas, art, crafts, rituals, and symbols of the New Age. It becomes a model of what a future New Age civilization might be like. "With joy, recognition will ensue, and groups will form by the attraction of mutual affinity. . .These seed groups, contacting each other, are the matrix of a new society into which the power and quality of the spirit can work down into every aspect of daily life. It is . . . a *new* society forming within the heart of the old."[6]

So the New Age moves from a "thinning of the veils between planes of being," to growth in individuals through meditation, to forming new groups and communities, to creation of "a veritable network of light linking the groups." This network makes possible the coming New Age.

Trevelyan ends with a prayer that sums up his hope for the future.

> From the point of Light within the Mind of God
> Let Light stream forth into [our] minds.
> Let Light descend on Earth.
> From the point of Love within the Heart of God
> Let Love stream forth into [our] hearts.
> May Christ return to Earth.

From the center where the Will of God is known
Let purpose guide [our] little wills—
The purpose which the Masters know and serve.
From the center which we call [our] race
Let the Plan of Love and Light work out.
And may it seal the door where evil dwells.
Let Light and Love and Power restore the Plan on Earth.[7]

From God to a New People positive energy flows.

The same conception of transformation occurs in other religious and spiritual traditions. For instance, William Stringfellow, in *The Politics of Spirituality,* argues for a Christian biblical spirituality that takes the form of a political resistance to death. In face of our "authentic dark age" he urges transformation to holiness or "sainthood." "Being holy, becoming and being a saint does not mean being perfect but being whole; it does not mean being exceptionally religious, or being religious at all, it means being liberated from religiosity and religious pietism of any sort; it does not mean being morally better, it means being exemplary; it does not mean being godly, but rather being truly human; it does not mean being otherworldly, but it means being deeply implicated in the practical existence of this world without succumbing to this world. . . . "[8]

For Stringfellow, development of ourselves as whole and holy leads inevitably to resisting the dominant technocratic regime characterized by the idolatry of science and the power of the Pentagon. A holy person is led by the twin faculties of sanity and consciousness. Christians are further guided by their faith that "Jesus Christ is Lord or that . . . God in history is active *now.*" The resulting "witness of resistance" incorporates two monastic traditions.

> The first of these is [intercessory prayer]—the *work* of intercession and, if you will, the *politics* of intercession [is] the solemn offering to Almighty God of all the cares of this world. . . . The one who *intercedes* for another is confessing that his or her trust in the vitality of the Word of God is so serious that he or she volunteers [to risk] sharing the burden of the one for whom intercession is offered. . . .
>
> [The second monastic tradition] is sustained . . . praise of . . . God.[9]

Stringfellow does not explicitly extend individual transformation to acts of resistance by congregations and the development of movements like the Sanctuary movement or the Nuclear Weapon Free Zone campaign but they are logical extensions of his thought and his own life of political involvement.

Sacred Scriptures, of course, frequently refer to the possibility of a God-human, an incarnation of God, or a transformed individual saving the world. Hindus believe that when crises on earth become too great an avatar is born. The Hindu God, Vishnu, reincarnates as a human being. Rama and Krishna were two such incarnations at about the time Indian civilization began five thousand years ago. Today Sathya Sai Baba claims to be living avatar, a reincarnation of the saint Sai Baba who died in the 1920s.

Similarly, Isaiah prophesies the coming of a "suffering servant" who will redeem Israel and the world.

> Behold, my servant shall prosper,
>   he shall be exalted and lifted up,
>   and shall be very high.
> As many were astonished at him—
>   his appearance was so marred,
>   beyond human semblance
>   and his form beyond that of the sons of men—
> so he shall startle many nations. . . .
> He was despised and rejected by [people];
>   a man of sorrows and acquainted with grief,
> and as one from whom [people] hide their faces
>   he was despised, and we esteemed him not.
> Surely he has borne our griefs
>   and carried our sorrows.
> yet we esteemed him stricken,
>   smitten by God, and afflicted.
> But he was wounded for our transgressions . . .
>   he poured out his soul to death . . .
> he bore the sins of [humans],
>   and made intercession for the transgressors.
>   (Isaiah 52:13-14; 53:3-5,12)

Christians believe that this prophecy was fulfilled in the life of Jesus of Nazareth. But, whether or not we give the passage a Christian interpretation, Isaiah prophesied that an individual "suffering servant" or that an entire people such as the Jews would come to redeem the world.

With such religious expectations that individual transformation can lead to world transformation, it is not surprising that in our current time of crises religious people often look to self-realization or the rediscovery of divine potential as a way to save the world. New Age, Buddhist, and Christian spirituality begin with individual transformation. Practical disciplines like meditation and prayer are used to attune the individual to higher forces. Transformed individuals then join together in congregations or communities and become a part of broader planetary networks. At a minimum, these transformed individuals, communities, and networks resist the institutions of death in our civilization. At best, they become strong enough to birth a New Age.

But why should we believe that individuals and networks will succeed in their efforts to transform our civilization? In addition, to the New Age argument for transformation because of a "thinning of the veils" or different galactic energy,[10] cultural arguments have been advanced as to why major change may be possible. Riane Eisler in *The Chalice and the Blade: Our History, Our Future* claims that ancient civilizations from about 7000-2500 B.C.E. throughout the world were matriarchal or gyclanic ("partnership") civilizations in which men and women shared the key roles in society and relations between peoples were mostly peaceful. From 4300-2800 B.C.E male-dominated societies or androcracies ("man-ruled") began to arise and domination and war became more frequent. After androcracies come to dominate their cultural patterns continued to the current day and have led to the crises which we currently face. But this is now changing. As Eisler writes, "the progressive modern ideologies can be seen as part of one mounting and continuing revolution against androcracy. . . . In our time of growing system disequilibrium, feminism could become the nucleus for a new fully integrated gyclanic ideology." The myths which have supported male domination and war are unraveling. The rediscovery of the peaceful period of earlier human history encourages the belief that a societal shift to a better civilization is possible. But a sufficient "critical mass" of new images and myths have not been adopted and acted upon by enough people yet. When enough individuals change, the social transformations will be profound.

> The most dramatic change as we move from a dominator to a partnership world will be that we, and our children and grandchildren, will again know what it means to live free of the war. In a world rid of the mandate that to be "masculine" men must dominate, and along with the rising status of women and more "feminine" social priorities, the danger of nuclear annihilation will gradually diminish. At the same time, as women gain more equality of social and economic opportunities—so that birthrates can come into better balance with our resources—the Malthusian "necessity" for famine, disease, and war will progressively lessen.[11]

Even if we do not believe in galactic or cultural cycles encouraging change, the strategies of individual and cultural transformation have the great advantage of allowing each of us to begin the process now. Such strategies assume that our heightened compassion and consciousness will inevitably lead to transformation. Although the necessary politics of resistance and birthing of a new civilization are not as well developed in these movements, it is believed that such a politics will naturally be produced by transformed individuals. In these strategies, compassion leads to personal transformation. Unfortunately, the politics of compassion and social transformation remains underdeveloped.

Political Leadership

An alternative to creating a new people through individual transformation is political leadership. In *Politics As Leadership* Robert Tucker defines a political leader as "one who gives direction, or meaningfully participates in the giving of direction, to the activities of a political community." Leadership is most obvious when a political community faces a crisis or a critical choice. This type of leadership, Tucker writes, has three functions:

> First, leadership has a diagnostic function: Leaders are expected to define the situation authoritatively for the group. Second, they must prescribe a course of group action, or of action on the group's behalf, that will meet the situation as defined. They must formulate a plan of action designed to resolve the problem in a manner that will serve group purposes. . . . Third, leadership has a mobilizing function. Leaders must gain the group's support or predominant support, for the definition of the group situation that they have advanced and for the plan of action that they have prescribed.[12]

Although all these functions are critical, the central function for leadership is defining the situation creatively.[13]

Tucker recognizes that we face major international crises. As he puts it, humans have "become an endangered species. A crisis of human survival is emerging." Yet "constituted leaders" who head the 150 national governments of the world "show little tendency toward forms of thinking and acting that would meet the challenge."[14] Constituted leaders tend to deal with immediate problems rather than looking at long-range trends or at potential catastrophes on a planetary level. Because constituted political leaders are forced to be parochial in furthering the interest of their nations, they automatically work against global peace and the global effort necessary for survival of the planet.

What then of nonconstituted leaders of movements, people like Mahatma Gandhi and Martin Luther King, Jr.? Tucker recognizes a "party of humanity" similar to philosophers of the eighteenth-century Enlightenment. They are "a scattered company of twentieth-century people who have acted as nonconstituted leaders of a still nonexistent community of [humans] by diagnosing the crisis of survival from a global perspective and envisioning ways of overcoming it." They are not a political party. "It is not a power-seeking group but a leadership cohort. It could be described as a moral party with a shared ethic." These people have diagnosed the problems, educated the public, and at least begun to mobilize the public for ecological solutions. They have called for a common set of actions: "The underlying leitmotif is that [humans] must place [their] planetary existence on an equilibrium, bringing levels of consumption and modes of living into balance with the potentialities of the environment, the finiteness of some resources and the renewability of others, the preservation of our natural surroundings, and the needs of equity."[15] Unfortunately, the people in the Third World who suffer most from wars, starvation, and resource scarcity have been unable to join effective ecological movements led by nonconstituted leaders. Those of us living in the First World who could join have not been sufficiently motivated to change our relatively comfortable lives. The "party of humanity" has failed to provide a compelling strategic analysis of how their shared goals could be achieved politically. They have not been able to redefine successfully our allegiance to "specieshood" in the place of our current identification with more limited cultures and nations.

Given this situation, Tucker makes an interim proposal for a Russo-American trusteeship "under which the two governments would jointly act as guarantors of international order pending the creation of a workable formal system of order. It would be a holding operation to help [us] survive long enough to develop the world society that is needed but does not yet exist."[16] Only these two superpowers have sufficient resources to prevent the approaching disasters in Tucker's view.

This secular approach begins with the assumption that what is required in our current situation is leadership to diagnose the planetary crises; formulate a policy of world order, gradual disarmament, and organic growth on the planet within our limited resources; promote more equity in distributing these resources; and mobilize people in support of those policies. An embryonic movement now exists in the "party of humanity," but it is not yet strong enough to play the leadership role nor has it created "a people" to support and to implement the necessary programs. Tucker's interim alternative focuses on the two great superpowers—the Soviet Union and the United States. However, this strategy requires that new leaders come to power, that they appropriately transform and mobilize their own societies, and that they jointly undertake a trusteeship mission until a new international order can be created that would be more adequate to the task.

Gaining leadership positions for the "party of humanity" in a totalitarian nation like the Soviet Union and in the firmly conservative United States, which has emerged under President Reagan, is difficult. However, it would not be entirely impossible as ecological and military crises loom greater in the years ahead. Tucker's approach specifies in a practical and concrete way how development in planetary consciousness is linked to specific institutional mechanisms sufficient to save and transform the civilization. His approach does not require any specific religious beliefs nor does it depend upon spiritual forces. In short, he develops the political dimension more fully than do the advocates of individual transformation. Tucker simply assumes that compassionate individuals have gained a level of higher consciousness and that they will be available to assume the necessary leadership roles. Whereas advocates of individual transformation focus upon compassion and transformation but neglect politics, advocates of secular political leadership focus on political strategies but neglect the question of how the necessary leaders are to be developed.

Some pragmatists do not put their faith in the leaders of the Soviet Union and the United States but trust, instead, the United Nations. There is good reason for doing so. First of all, it has often been led by outstanding public officials with a deep spiritual commitment to the planet and its peoples. Nor do they neglect the inner work necessary for significant outer deeds. The publication of *Markings* after Dag Hammarskjold's death makes that clear. In his private journal he wrote: "The more faithfully you listen to the voice within you, the better you will hear what is sounding outside. And only he who listens can speak." One of his poems includes the line, "the longest journey is the journey inwards." And he concluded that "in our era, the road to holiness necessarily passes through the world of action."[17]

Robert Muller, currently Assistant Secretary General of the U.N., continues the tradition of linking optimism and faith with the belief that global problems can be solved. He has faith in the U.N. because it has:

- Helped one billion people gain independence with a minimum of bloodshed, thus completing the historical movement started two hundred years ago by the Declaration of Independence;
- Helped the emergence of the poorer countries into the modern age, providing a safety lid for the explosive feelings of our less fortunate brethren at the injustices which prevail in the world;
- Provided a talking place and a meeting ground during the worst periods of the cold war;
- Provided for the first time in history a code of ethics for relations between the most powerful entities on earth: armed nations;
- Prevented, by its mere existence, even more national political and military adventures; . . .

Moreover, the U.N. is:

- The first universal, global instrument humanity has ever had; . . .
- The place where new ethical values for nations and humanity are being formulated.[18]

Muller concludes that:

> It is high time for humanity to accept and to work out the full consequences of the total global and interdependent nature of our planetary home and of our species. Our survival and further progress will depend largely on the advent of global visions and of proper global education in all countries of the world. We must effectuate a giant leap forward into the future and henceforth see ourselves and our actions in the endless stream of time.[19]

It may well be that the United Nations is the best institution yet created to cope with the global crises we face.

However, instead of beginning with global institutions, some advocate more local, grassroots movements. Such a secular movement that attempts to gain political power in order to transform the world is "Green Politics" in which "green movements" and "green political parties" are developed in western nations such as Germany, the United Kingdom and the United States. Jonathan Porritt in *Seeing Green: The Politics of Ecology Explained* contrasts green politics and traditional politics:

> It should by now be apparent that green politics is not just another dimension of the disintegrating industrial world order; it is something qualitatively different. . . . [In comparison to the politics of industrialism it has the following characteristics:]

The politics of industrialism	*The politics of ecology*
A deterministic view of the future	Flexibility and an emphasis on personal autonomy
An ethos of aggressive individualism	A co-operatively based, communitarian society
Materialism, pure and simple	A move towards spiritual, non-material values
Divisive, reductionist analysis	Holistic synthesis and integration
Anthropocentrism	Biocentrism
Rationality and packaged knowledge	Intuition and understanding
Outer-directed motivation	Inner-directed motivation and personal growth
Patriarchal values	Post-patriarchal, feminist values
Institutionalized violence	Non-violence
Economic growth and GNP	Sustainability and quality of life

The politics of industrialism	*The politics of ecology*
Production for exchange and profit	Production for use
High income differentials	Low income differentials
A 'free-market' economy	Local production for local need
Ever-expanding world trade	Self-reliance
Demand stimulation	Voluntary simplicity
Employment as a means to an end	Work as an end in itself
Capital-intensive production	Labour-intensive production
Unquestioning acceptance of the technological fix	Discriminating use and development of science and technology
Centralization, economies of scale	Decentralization, human scale
Hierarchical structure	Non-hierarchical structure
Dependence upon experts	Participative involvement
Representative democracy	Direct democracy
Emphasis on law and order	Libertarianism
Sovereignty of nation-state	Internationalism and global solidarity
Domination over nature	Harmony with nature
Environmentalism	Ecology
Environment managed as a resource	Resources regarded as strictly finite
Nuclear power	Renewable sources of energy
High energy, high consumption	Low energy, low consumption

Even the most cursory glance at such a comparison should demonstrate that the old age is giving way to the new, that the turning point is already with us.[20]

In describing the Green party in West Germany (which won 27 seats in the 1983 parliament) Charlene Spretnak and Fritjof Capra explain, "The Greens consider themselves the political voice of the citizens' movements, that is, ecology, anti-nuclear power, peace, feminist, and others. Most members of the Green party are also activists in one or more of those movements, and this diverse orientation is reflected in loose and overlapping alignments within the party." The Greens of West Germany have said of themselves:

We represent a total concept, as opposed to the one-dimensional still more production brand of politics. Our policies are guided by long-term visions for the future and are founded on four basic principles: ecology, social responsibility, grassroots democracy, and nonviolence.

U.S. Greens have identified ten key values which guide their politics and parallel the principles of the German Greens. They are: 1. Ecological Wisdom, 2. Grassroots Democracy, 3. Personal and Social Responsibility, 4. Nonviolence, 5. Decentralization, 6. Community-Based Economics, 7. Post-patriarchal Values, 8. Respect for Diversity, 9. Global Responsibility, and 10. Future Focus.

Few Greens in West Germany expect to become the majority or ruling party. U.S. Greens are not even a full political party but are only organized into "Committees of Correspondence" that regard themselves as "a regionally based political organization that can operate in many directions." While the Greens in West Germany have become a significant parliamentary faction, in the U.S. thus far they have captured 22% of the vote in the Amherst, Massachusetts municipal election of 1985 and helped to pass a Maine Nuclear Referendum on radioactive waste disposal. Still they claim that "What is evolving from Green efforts in this country and around the world is an earth-based politics of wisdom and compassion."[21] Nonetheless, at their current level of organization, the Greens are not strong enough to gain control of national governments or to enact the necessary policies to alleviate the global crises we face.

The possibility of a Russo-American Trusteeship, an expanded leadership role for the United Nations, and strengthened local or national political movements such as green political parties each have a contribution to make in confronting the global crises we face. None of these secular political approaches seems adequate by themselves to transform our civilization in time to avoid disaster.

Politics of Compassion

Jack Nelson-Pallmeyer proposes "the politics of compassion" as a better response to world crises. In *The Politics of Compassion,* he writes about worldwide hunger, the arms race, and U.S. policy in Central America. Rooted in biblical faith, his approach demands that "affluent Christians . . . let their faith and their politics, their economic and patriotic connections be challenged and transformed by the poor." He argues that we "can seriously hope for a world with more justice and less hunger only if we understand history, economics, and theology from the vantage point of the poor." Nelson-Pallmeyer asserts that, "massive hunger and the threat of nuclear holocaust call Christians to compassionate action that involves personal and social change."[22]

Thus, the politics of compassion combines the personal transformation characteristic of religion with the broader societal and institutional change characteristic of politics. It is based on a theology of liberation. It has the additional advantage of overcoming ethical dilemmas. Nelson-Pallmeyer writes that "biblical writers go beyond personal morality and abstract sin. They speak to *the disastrous consequences of personal complicity with social sin.* They understand that sin becomes embodied in social systems and economic relationships. . . . " People of compassion "become channels for kingdom [or realm] of God values within history." They fight against repressive forces and seek to alleviate suffering.

> They do not eliminate greed, hunger, or economic injustice. They do not create perfect societies or perfect economies or the full realization of the [realm] of God on earth. They do or can make life and economics *more* just, *more* compassionate, *more* hopeful. They see to it that social sins such as hunger and poverty are always met with confrontation and resistance rather than resignation.[23]

But what political strategy is to be followed to achieve these goals? Nelson-Pallmeyer proposes the following strategic principles:

> Our commitments must be long-term, informed by faith, and nurtured and strengthened with others. Secondly, the problems of hunger and the arms race will not be solved by heroes, heroines, experts, or technicians. Compassion and hope will live or die depending on the action or inaction of ordinary persons. Thirdly, the actions we take must reflect our primary commitments to God and to the family of God, while acknowledging special responsibility for working to transform the policies of the United States.

According to Nelson-Pallmeyer, these principles lead to a variety of possible actions:

1. Tax resistance
2. Refusal to participate in U.S. military service
3. Refusal to accept or continue employment in military industries
4. Peace conversion plans to convert industries involved in war production
5. Withdrawal of investments from military industries and other industries involved in socially irresponsible production
6. Support nuclear freeze legislation and treaties
7. Oppose development of first-strike nuclear weapons
8. Support unilateral steps to break the vicious cycle of escalating weapons expenditures
9. Support an international body to oversee a nuclear freeze and mutual reductions in nuclear and conventional weapons
10. Support and monitor the U.S. Peace Institute

11. Oppose all weapon sales, assistance and training to repressive governments
12. Support a new international economic order including debt relief for underdeveloped countries, more stable commodity prices, and international cooperation to produce and distribute goods to meet basic human needs
13. Participate in legislative action, boycotts, and civil disobedience
14. Become involved in local struggles with the poor
15. Adoption of simpler lifestyles in order to change economic priorities and the availability of resources to meet basic needs of present and future generations.[24]

These strategies make concrete the "politics of compassion." Warriors of compassion can use legislative strategies to change laws, participate in economic boycotts to change the behavior of multinational corporations, and engage in acts of civil disobedience—from tax resistance to mass demonstrations—in order to force changes by governments and private institutions. In these political actions they are required to obey "God's call to compassion" and to disobey "some laws of the state." These warriors of compassion join concrete local struggles of the poor in order to act *"with* rather than *for* the poor." Finally, this politics of compassion leads to a simpler life-style which *"frees us from* bondage to material things and *frees us for* social justice." Nelson-Pallmeyer concludes that "persons of faith [must] resist evil, build justice, and share love."[25]

This approach combines personal spiritual growth with political struggles to overcome societal problems. It leads to political action by both individuals and communities. It offers immediate actions to oppose hunger, the arms race, and oppression in Central America. These actions are ethically defensible and practical. They do not require the total transformation of U.S. leadership and policies as does Tucker's leadership model. Finally, Nelson-Pallmeyer recognizes the need to create "a people of hope." Even though he writes primarily for North American Christians (allied with the base communities in Central America), his message could easily be expanded to people of goodwill whatever their race, nationality, or creed.

Unfortunately, the strategy implied in his politics of compassion is insufficient. Even if it was embraced by thousands of "people of hope" it would still not prevent the potential catastrophes which we face. Limited nuclear wars, expanded wars in the Third World, ecological disasters, continued polluting and poisoning of the earth, and international economic collapse will overtake us before these strategies at their current level of support could succeed. The "politics of compassion" combines compassion, politics, and social transformation, but the actual political strategies that advocates like Nelson-Pallmeyer recommend are insufficient. In these strategies compassion leads to personal change and political action but not at the level necessary for civilization's transformation. Incremental changes are the most that can be achieved. However, the pressure of the looming crises may be enough to force even bolder actions and bring the necessary transformations.

Collapse and Transformation

We understand now the ancient Chinese curse: "May you live in interesting times." The birth and death of civilizations is always fascinating but seldom pleasant for the people who live in them. We live at a time when our contribution to history—determining the meaning of the present as well as shaping the future for generations—is critical. We hold the power of life or its extinction. We can consign billions of people to abject suffering or promote healthy, productive, and rewarding lives. Because of this power we also have a unique responsibility.

However, if we are to have any effect on the present or the future, we have to face certain facts. We confront a series of seemingly unavoidable, interrelated international crises *which are already occurring* on the planet and in our communities. The "causes" of these crises are embedded in the very fabric of our civilization. Personal consciousness raising is not occurring at a rate sufficient to avoid the catastrophes. From time to time we have political leaders and movements in different nations who are conscious of the international crises and who propose solutions. But leaders of larger nations and major international institutions (like the multinational corporations) have either ignored the problems or have adhered to conservative programs so as to preserve the existing balance of power, wealth, and resources from which they personally benefit. None of our constituted leaders are willing to change the patterns of industrialization, the nation-state system, high levels of wasteful consumption, inherited and unexamined religious traditions, the international economic system, or the political balance of power. On the other hand, those people drawn to a politics of compassion, or the more secular "Green Politics," which combine religion and politics, have neither the institutions nor the strategies necessary to transform our civilization.

It has often been noted about U.S. politics that voters usually vote against officials and parties in power when they are displeased rather than vote for positive candidates and programs in advance of when "the shoe pinches." It follows then that critical realigning elections in the United States, in which the balance of power between parties has changed, have all occurred at the time of war or economic depression.[26] This principle can be applied more broadly to human history. We personally grow most rapidly in times of conflict and personal crisis like adolescence, religious conversion, divorce, unemployment, or the death of a loved one. Anguish and suffering provide a special opportunity for personal growth. Similarly, empires, dictatorships, and democracies come into existence and are destroyed by their citizens' reactions to crises.

Although individuals may grow from suffering, civilizations have a difficult time changing in any fundamental way from the patterned responses developed to weather crises in the past. If America has entered a "truly dark age," we must also face the fact that no previous civilization has reached this stage of disintegration and survived. The civil rights, anti-Vietnam War, peace, ecological and political reform movements of the last three decades have not been able, as Lincoln was at the time of the Civil War, to refound this nation on either its former principles or upon new principles adequate to the "New Age" we now enter.

Realism would seem to lead only to despair. Because the causes of catastrophe are rooted in civilization itself and can not be avoided, no religious or political strategy is adequate to prevent considerable suffering, and because most people on the planet can be convinced to undergo the painful process of self-transformation and civilization transformation only when spurred by direct experience with suffering, we must suffer major catastrophes until a transformation is made or the old civilization collapses. We humans face, as Michael Grosso puts it, "the final choice." In *The Final Choice*, he writes that "the choice is between conforming to the lethal truth of the status quo and embracing the truths of human transformation."[27]

We must evolve if we are to survive. This means changing our politics, ethics, religion, and culture, but it means, first of all, changing ourselves. Based upon investigations of Psi, near-death experiences, visions, and more traditional science, Grosso's book concludes:

> The need to evolve has never before been so great. The evolution of human consciousness may be our only hope for survival. Technical progress has outstripped moral sensibility. . . .
>
> The lethal mixture of primitive psychism and government-backed high tech spells the need for a large-scale transformation of human consciousness. . . .
>
> Nothing short of a global change in consciousness is likely to avert this catastrophe [of nuclear war]. . . . Nothing short of a new reality principle, a kind of surrealpolitik (to counter the deadly logic of Realpolitik) will be enough to do the job. Indeed without . . . a morality based not upon prudent calculation but upon a deeply felt sense of human, of cosmic, solidarity . . . at least in a critical mass of humanity, the hands of the doomsday clock will sooner or later strike midnight.

To meet this challenge, Grosso argues that we must cultivate a "vision of the possible" and "forge the miracle of a new earth with our own deeds."[28]

The reigning politics and scientific civilization, based upon simple self-interest, is destroying the planet. We need "a reversal, not of the arms race alone but of the sense of reality that dominates the thought of the world . . . only a profound *inner* disarmament could impede the inertia of history." A new surrealpolitik must be based on three premises: "The transcendance of mere self-interest, unilateral affirmation of trust and a disposition to renounce power."[29] A compassionate politics of transformation would create such a change.

The evolutionary forces that have been at work in the twenty- billion-year history of the universe, and in the shorter period of human development, have not been sufficient to allow us an easy step from the Age of Industrialization into the New Aquarian Age. The politics of self-interest has not yet broadly been transformed into a politics of compassion and transformation.

A merger of religion, ethics, and politics is needed. But such a mixture has always been an explosive potion, leading to wars and repression as often as to benign results. The Crusades of the Middle Ages, the wars between Israel and the Arabs, and Iran under Ayatollah Khomeini are proof of that. Yet we must dare to merge them now. As Grosso puts it, we need "a transformation. A revolution. An evolution. A new consciousness. . . . Our assumption is that political change, apart from inner change, will in the long run not help. A new attitude, a new consciousness, a new rhythm of being is called for."[30]

Should we then look to established religions as our salvation? In the United States there has been a burst of political activity by churches and synagogues. The civil rights movement was spearheaded by activists in black churches and supported by Protestant, Catholic, and Jewish groups. Protestant denominations and religious agencies, such as Clergy and Laity Concerned, pressured to end the war in Vietnam. Fundamentalists in the 1970s revolted against liberal social trends and began their own countercampaign against abortion, pornography, and elimination of prayer in public schools. Catholic bishops have begun campaigns on rights of the unborn, the threat of nuclear war, and the effects of the U.S. economy on the poor. Most major religious groups now have a lobbying staff in Washington, D.C., and some have a large grassroots network to pressure government officials.

Whatever successes traditional religious groups have had in their adventures into the political arena, they will not be enough. Even if they further develop their "practical theologies," they will be unable to bring about major social transformations. Stephen D. Johnson and Joseph B. Tanney conclude in *The Political Role of Religion in the United States* that "success will probably take the form not of laws exactly as desired by religious leaders, but will be reflected in a greater awareness of the nation's moral traditions and of a stronger role for those values championed by the churches [and synagogues] in the inevitable compromises made by political leaders."[31] That is to say, the religious perspective will be heard in the political process, but it will be given no greater weight than the desires of other interest groups, many of which are politically much more powerful than religious organizations, for whom politics is a minor activity.

Ronald Pasquariello, Donald Shriver, and Alan Geyer in their analysis of why religious groups in the 1980s have been unable to achieve a coherent urban policy, jobs and housing for all, better health care, strengthened neighborhoods and a more just welfare system, conclude that churches have as many liabilities as assets in politics.

CHURCH ASSETS AND LIABILITIES IN URBAN POLICY

Assets	Liabilities
1. Humane values	1. Anti-political bias
2. Congregational presence	2. Congregational idolatry
3. Regional politics	3. Incongruous political boundaries
4. Racial inclusiveness	4. Racial separatism
5. Institutional experience	5. Preoccupation with church programs
6. Wealth	6. Capitalist elites
7. Educational institutions	7. Anti-intellectualism
8. Communications media	8. Narcissistic habits
9. Lay leadership	9. Church-domesticated laity
10. Urban pastoral experience	10. Demoralization of city pastors[32]

While churches and synagogues stress the humane values necessary for social change such as "the imperatives of justice and compassion for the poor and the oppressed," most congregations and most religious leaders have an anti-political bias which causes them to neglect issues of justice for the sake of "spirituality" or to focus on the relief of individual plight rather than solving endemic problems. "Christian education, missions, and even social action have, all too typically, been so conceived as to avoid controversial political issues, even when the very survival of city, nation, and world is at stake."[33]

A somewhat broader role is granted traditional religions by A. James Reichley in *Religion in American Public Life,* but he also stresses their limitations in the political arena.

From the standpoint of the public good, the most important services churches [and synagogues] offer to secular life in a free society is to nurture moral values that help humanize capitalism and give direction to democracy. Up to a point, participation by the churches [and synagogues] in the formation of public policy, particularly on issues with clear moral content, probably strengthens their ability to perform this nurturing function. If the churches [and synagogues] were to remain silent on issues like civil rights or nuclear war or abortion, they would soon lose moral credibility. But if the churches become too involved in the hurly-burly of routine politics, they will eventually appear to their members and to the general public as special pleaders for ideological causes or even as appendages to transitory political factions.[34]

The most that traditional religious groups can do politically is to nurture the values of our secular society which "help humanize" capitalism and democracy. But it is our capitalistic and democratic civilization that is creating the international crises, including the threat of nuclear holocaust—a little humanizing or softening their impact, a finger in the dike, which is about to break and flood the planet, is insufficient.

Three paths lie before us. First, the current crises already manifested upon the planet could serve as a "near-death experience" and inspire necessary personal, societal, and cultural transformation. As individuals are sometimes transformed by "near-death experiences," our society might also be revitalized, mobilized, and reestablished on better values than mere affluence and hedonism because of our collective brush with death. As Grosso put it, "the vivid premonition of catastrophe [which is clearly widely experienced upon the planet] might activate the reordering mechanisms of the deep psyche; we might then escape our bad fate and buy a lesson in enlightenment cheaply."[35] It does no harm and much good to strive for this form of transformation, letting the structures and norms of the old civilization collapse about us while we repair to new institutions made possible by a politics of compassion and transformation.

The second alternative is that we will not respond until the catastrophes are even more stark. Forced by "limited" nuclear war, resource scarcity, environmental crises, or international economic collapse we may turn in time to save a portion of human life and the planet itself from the final Armageddon. But the cost in misery and suffering will be very great. We will have to overcome massive obstacles to build a new civilization. Old institutions will have been destroyed, resources will have been squandered forever, and no outside resources will be available to help in reconstruction as they were after the bombing of Hiroshima and Nagasaki. Moreover, the psychological results (such as psychic numbing) of such a disaster would decrease, not increase, awareness; would encourage depersonalization, rather than compassion; and would limit our perception of the options available. Grosso concludes that the effect is more likely to be negative than positive. If we face truly severe crises like nuclear war, "the sheer immensity of the disaster would reverberate in the collective psyche of humankind. Evidence that the old consciousness . . . was *radically corrupt* would be apparent to all. The lesson will be written in letters brilliant enough for the blind to see: *the colossal burn-out of Western civilization.*"[36] Our old civilization would be destroyed and discredited. A return to barbarism or the collapse of our will to live is more likely after such a holocaust than is the birth of a better civilization.

The third and worst alternative would be a catastrophe which leads to extinction. But even here compassion and transformation are important. Grosso points out that when we are individually faced with knowledge of impending death, "the world [can] light up for [us]; the smallest things swell with significance, the doomed [person's] awareness changes radically, a conversion of consciousness takes place."[37]Especially in the face of an approaching apocalypse we must cherish life—taste it, feel it, live it fully. For we may be the last life on this planet. Each human life is precious; each must be cherished and saved from undue suffering. Each species must be preserved, for life on this planet will not come again. It is our last moment in which to become one with our brothers and sisters, with all sentient life, and with God.

Grosso suggests that a final strategy which may save the planet is creation of a network of Magi. Like Trevelyan and others favoring personal transformation, Grosso believes in a higher force which he calls the Mind at Large.

> In an age foreshadowing nuclear winter, we are all summoned to be magi, to form a network of magi, to hazard the desert and follow where stars lead. These lights that flash from the heaven of the Mind at Large inspire us to say farewell to the old, the life-denying self. . . . [The visions] help us to make the final choice, to take the leap beyond death to new life.

Grosso recognizes three different reactions to the impending crises: (1) the attempt at personal transformation seeking "to discover the source of peace within," (2) the response of peace-activists who lead grassroots political movements, and (3) an approach that embodies both. "It's plain that inner transformation without action will never set the banners of the New Age flying. Nor will our activists succeed in bringing peace into the world if they are not at peace with themselves." [38] As Robert Bellah and his coauthors write in *Habits of the Heart,* transformation must occur at many levels.[39] There must be personal transformations by many individuals and the development of broader social movements from existing networks and organizations. In short, we need inner and outer, personal and communal transformation. No other path leads through our current crises to a new and better civilization.

All these approaches—personal transformation, political leadership, politics of compassion, and civilization's transformation—provide components we need to overcome the problems we face personally and globally. Yet, by itself each falls short of providing the whole answer. Grosso and Bellah come closer to expressing how development at the personal and societal levels are related and essential, but the question of motivation still remains. Transformation is a painful process, and it does not seem that enough people are willing to undergo the pain or that transformed individuals will be able to coordinate their political efforts sufficiently before crises reach the stage of major calamities. The collective "near-death" experience on which Grosso pins his hopes has not been enough yet to force the necessary social transformations.

A New Earth

So we come at last to the inevitable conclusion in our search for a politics of compassion and transformation. The Bible says that if even a remnant leans upon God, they shall be saved, flourish, and fear no more. Add these two biblical quotations:

> For now I create new heavens and a new earth; and the past will not be remembered to people's minds. . . .
>
> I will rejoice in Jerusalem and be glad in my people; no more shall be heard in it the sound of weeping and the cry of distress. . . .
>
> They shall not hurt nor destroy on all my holy mountain, says the Lord.
>
> (Isaiah 65:17, 19, and 25)

> Then I saw a new heaven and a new earth; the first heaven and the first earth had disappeared now, and there was no longer any sea. I saw the holy city and the new Jerusalem, coming down from God. . . .
>
> Then the One sitting on the throne spoke: "Now I am making the whole creation new," he said. "Write this: That what I am saying is sure and will come true." And then he said, "It is already done!"
>
> (Revelations 21:1, 2, 5, and 6)

These Scriptures say to us: if there is a faithful remnant, then God can form a people and with these people will be created "a new earth."

Our spiritual journey begins with personal illumination and transformation. We individually become compassionate—at one and in harmony with our brothers and sisters, with our Mother Earth, and with God. We feel, breathe, and think with them.

Hildegard of Bingen describes her personal awakening this way: "When I was forty-two years and seven months old, a burning light of tremendous brightness coming down from heaven poured into my entire mind. Like a flame that does not burn but enkindles, it inflamed my entire heart and my entire breast, just like the sun that warms an object with its rays." Yet Hildegard defined "the ultimate act of illumination as compassion." She wrote: "I am flooded through with inner compassion; nothing—neither gold nor money, costly stones nor pearls—can hide me from the eyes of the poor who weep because they lack life's necessities."[40]

This compassion inevitably leads to the work of justice and social transformation. Yet, it does not come from without; neither is it a betrayal of personal transformation. Rather, compassion allows us to discover our connection with life and provides the motive for us to undertake our twin tasks of celebrating creation and justice-making.[41] Compassion, justice, and good works lead to the building of a new earth, which we create by uniting the divine powers of the universe in us. We become the "living stones" of the new Jerusalem which Hildegard says will be built upon "holy souls in the sight of peace."[42]

Put in the less mystical words of modern theologians, compassion brings us into community and leads to compassionate action. As Henri Nouwen and his coauthors declare in *Compassion,*

> Compassion asks us to go where it hurts, to enter into places of pain, to share in brokenness, fear, confusion, and anguish. Compassion challenges us to cry out with those in misery, to mourn with those who are lonely, to weep with those in tears. Compassion requires us to be weak with the weak, vulnerable with the vulnerable, and powerless with the powerless. Compassion means full immersion in the condition of being human.[43]

And they are echoed by Fran Peavey and her coauthors in *Heart Politics.* She wrote that "one of the most difficult parts of broadening my context has been coming to terms with the pain in the lives of people I have come to care about. . . . It has been painful for me to love people who are poor and down-and-out. It has meant I must somehow acknowledge that I can do very little to substantially change their situation. And yet I must help in the ways I can. As I become a more reliable ally of people different from me, I feel less guilt about our relationship. This, in turn, makes it easier for me to make connections with them."[44]

Because we live in dangerous times, there is no escaping interlocking international crises, which already have brought misery and death and which will lead to a series of catastrophes before the century is completed. Our existing postindustrial civilization, with its attendant economic, political, religious, and cultural institutions, is inadequate to cope with these crises. Already millions of people die of starvation, millions of Americans are homeless and hopeless; already other species are made extinct, and our natural resources are squandered. Because all life upon the planet is placed in jeopardy and suffering is already great, cries of anguish and fear can already be heard. The simple truth is that these crises will grow and that massive suffering will be the inevitable result. Contrary to all our hopes, there is no evidence that we will make fundamental changes until catastrophes actually occur. Yet, the Scriptures may prove true once again. A remnant may survive and from this remnant a "people of God" who have undergone painful personal transformation will arise. In the meantime we can build upon personal transformation, political leadership, and a politics of compassion to make survival of a remnant possible and to prepare the way for creation of a new earth when the new age dawns.

The first step is for us to hear these cries of pain and to face these crises. This can be achieved only by compassion. Compassion can be trivialized into mere sentimentality, but it can also open us to our connection with all life. Compassion can provide energy, wisdom, and strength. Personal transformation or enlightenment by itself is not a sufficient response to compassion. Rather, the four paths of compassion—positive, negative, creative, and transformative—require celebration of the beauty of creation, letting go our attachment to the negative aspects of our society and our personality, and the creation with God of a positive response. Through these steps we are led to seek justice and to transform our world.

Compassion can only be fully developed and our actions can only be fully effective in community. In scriptural language, a remnant must recognize itself as a "people of God." A new people must come together. The New Age network of Magi must be in touch with each other. Finding other members of the network, forming a new movement for societal transformation, becoming a "people" with common heritage and a common faith willing to concert our efforts in a common transforming mission is the task we face. Alone, we vibrate at too low a frequency; we are discouraged, despondent, and overcome by despair. Alone, we are afraid to risk too much for a dream we only dimly understand. We are left waiting for others to see the world as we see it. However, we are able to be inspired by one another. Now, new groups, congregations, communes, organizations, and communities are springing up around the globe. And they are actively searching for spiritual transformation and for justice. They already house the homeless, feed the hungry, provide sanctuary for refugees, fight against nuclear weapon proliferation, protect the environment, and seek more compassionate policies from existing institutions.

In developing our community we seek what Christians call "the communion of saints," similar to the relationship that Yogis experience with their gurus. As "people of God" we carry with us the life bred of thousands of years of human development and the resources of twenty billion years of cosmic evolution. Thus, we are not only custodians of Bach's Brandenberg Concerti, Beethoven's Quartets, Ravi Shankar's Indian Ragas, Shakespeare's Love Sonnets, the myths and legends of hundreds of cultures, the writings of all human philosophers, and the sacred teachings of all religions, but we are also inheritors of a human history that shows how humans have met previous challenges of civilization collapse and transformation. We have, most of all, the teachings of our Mother Earth herself.

Any personal transformation which allows our heart to open and any gathering together as a new people has a single object—the creation of a new earth. The purpose of our compassion and our politics is transformation. Nothing short of a new people living in a new way in a new civilization will allow our own survival and the reaching of our full potential as cocreators with God. In our postindustrial civilization we have thus far reached only the stage of *homo-faber* (maker of tools and products). Through our science and technology we unlocked certain mysteries of the universe and we have made things. But we are alienated from nature, from God, from each other, and from ourselves. Now, because of the planetary crises and the suffering they cause, our civilization must transform, and our planet must be healed and made whole. Instead of fabricators and tool makers we must become creators and healers. We already have the wisdom and the methods to make this transformation.

Religion and ethics let us discover and apply compassion. Politics, through the moments of compassionate analysis and philosophy, provides the tools of compassionate action. Compassionate action leads to transformation in which we become "the party of humanity."

Ultimately, we need a vision. The Bible presents images of a remnant, a people of God, building a new Jerusalem in which the suffering of the past is no more. My own image is of the sides of a building falling and a new temple rising from the midst of destruction. In this crystal temple, on the altar, is a glowing ball of energy. It is kept in existence by the energy sharing of every member of the community. Each member contributes his or her individual energy to this common sun, and each is healed and strengthened by the common energy. Every community on the planet will have such a temple, and the people of these future communities will be more sensitive, intuitive, open, and compassionate.

We cannot, individually, bring about such a future in the face of impending crises. No one of us can birth a crystal temple or a new civilization. But we can respond to the opportunity of becoming a new people. We can prepare ourselves, through the disciplines of body, emotions, mind, and spirit, to become warriors of compassionate politics and transformation. We can use our strength to oppose the prevailing trends, to lessen the suffering, to survive the coming crises, to open ourselves to compassion, and to participate in transformation. Give thanks for the life we have been given and the opportunity to live in these perilous times, for a long age of human history is ending and a new age is birthing.

AFTERWORD

Several early readers of this manuscript suggested that it seemed credible to them because they knew my past political involvement and my struggles on the spiritual path I have taken. At their urging I have included this personal afterword. It is not essential to understanding the book at an intellectual level, but it records my personal path toward a politics of compassion and transformation. For some readers it may help to know more about the author.

Although I have been a public person, leading political movements and serving as an elected official, I am by nature rather private. It is not that I purposely hide my private life, but I am shy, reticent, and quiet. Sometimes I succumb to a common psychological fear that if people really knew me, they wouldn't love me. As this book has grown it has become clearer that if I am to be taken seriously by readers who don't know me personally, I must share with them something of my life so that they will trust me enough to consider what I have to say. Given my background, if *I* could be convinced of what I write, then this book warrants careful consideration even if readers disagree with my conclusions.

There is another reason to share my story. To interpret what I am saying it may be important to know the journey that has brought me to this writing. When my experiences, passions, and personality are known it may be easier to understand what I am saying. This book can be easily misunderstood. Because it is about our collective life, death, and potential rebirth, readers deserve to know about me so that there may be less misunderstanding. So I provide here this brief psychological autobiography.

I was born in Houston, Texas, in 1940. Like everyone, I am product of a long, complicated family history. Both my parents came from large Anglo-Saxon families that had settled in Texas and Arkansas. My Grandfather, Will Simpson, was a farmer and horse tamer who committed suicide before I was born. My Grandfather Felts, who had a great impact on me, was a Nazarene preacher who rode the circuit of small churches in Oklahoma and Arkansas. There is a long history of preachers, teachers, frontiersmen, and Indian squaws in both families but more of businessmen and women in my parents' generation.

My mother was a member of the Methodist church and took me to Sunday school. My father preferred the golf course to Sunday worship. He was a Texas oilman with the drive and pride for which they are known. We were upper-middle-class but not rich. My parents' political views were characterized by tolerance, with mother being more liberal and father more conservative. My father held the bigoted views of the region and those Texas businessmen with whom he associated.

I grew up with the idealized view of the world common to a comfortable middle-class home in the 1940s and 1950s. My father left us when I was three to go to fight in World War II and returned a war hero when I was five. I received extra love and attention from my parents as I was an only child and I achieved early success with their support. I was an Eagle Scout by the time I was fourteen. I soon added the God and Country, Silver Explorer Award, and Order of the Arrow recognition from Scouting.

In my teenage years at junior high and high school I was a loner. I did well enough in grades to graduate with honors, well enough at golf and poker to hold my own at the country club, and I learned the social graces of bridge and dancing. I usually felt more at home with adults than with my peers. Like all fast-growing teenagers, I was shy and awkward. Scouting gave me an outlet, a chance to excel, and the opportunity of being a leader of other kids even when I was young.

By college I began developing my own distinctive religious and political path. I went to a military school, Texas A&M, set to become the nuclear physicist my parents believed would be a good career for me. My father had gone to A&M, which had trained him in petroleum engineering and in the arts of war. He had been a lieutenant colonel in the Battle of the Bulge in World War II. Naturally, he thought A&M would be perfect for me. After high school, I worked in the oil fields for my father's company for six months and then enrolled at A&M. All I knew about the school was that it had good sports teams and school spirit, and the students wore ROTC uniforms all the time. What I did not know was that A&M, in the practical everyday life within the Corps of Cadets, was anti-intellectual, inhumane, and antireligious. Nor did I know that I wasn't meant to be a nuclear physicist. My personal confrontations at A&M were to change me profoundly and to set my life on a different course.

By the time I entered Texas A&M I was equipped with a reasonably good education but had not discovered any profound truths from school. I was an avid reader but as much of science fiction and westerns as the "Great Books." I was a good swimmer and camper with a mystical oneness with the ocean and the wilderness. I had been friends with children of millionaires, but I had also been a golf caddy with poor blacks at the country club. I had only a sentimentalized religion. I had prayed with my Grandfather Felts at the dinner table and at bedtime, absorbed the usual Sunday School teachings, and served as a preacher myself at Scout camp. I liked the ceremonies of the DeMolays (a junior Masonic order) and the Order of the Arrow but could not see the mysteries behind them. I had a mythical view of myself as a westerner with Abe Lincoln ethics. Because my parents drank and my father went on drinking binges every six or seven years, I didn't drink. Nor did I even like coffee. I was a goody-goody, a Boy Scout.

I ended up at Texas A&M, which combined some of the worst aspects of a military academy and a fraternity gone bad. I did well enough in studies, learned military drills, followed the rules, stayed out of trouble, and went out for freshman cheerleader to be "one of the guys." But there was another side to my college life. I joined the campus YMCA and the campus Methodist church. Unlike the Corps, both treated me as a valuable human being; they fed my intellect and my idealism.

I was making a D in calculus but A's and B's in my other courses. When I took an aptitude test from the counseling service it was clear that I was meant to be in social sciences or social service, not in hard science. So I knew I would have to change majors and my future vocation. In the meantime, at the height of the segregation era, I was involved, through the YMCA, in interracial conferences in the South and was driving down on weekends to our sister black college, Prairie View A&M, to be with a black preacher, Reverend Lee Philips. The sit-in movement was just getting under way. By next year it would be in Texas and I would be a part of it.

But the ripping of my ties with A&M was more personal. In our dormitory a freshman decided to quit the academy midyear. The seniors were certain that he would "squeal" about the illegal hazing and that they would be in trouble. They convinced his classmates to punish him. Before he could get back from resigning from the Corps, they took all his papers and his clothes and threw them out his fourth floor dorm window. In a somewhat bizarre concession to conscience they carried his record player and records downstairs to the lawn.

Like all the cadets in our building, I saw it happen. But I wrote an editorial against it in the Wesley Foundation newsletter with brave declarations like "If this is what it means to be a man and an Aggie, I don't want to be either." Of course, the seniors were frightened that someone would see the editorial, so I was ostracized. No cadet was allowed to speak to me for weeks. But I survived and developed the strength to oppose prevailing social mores and opinions. This is an ability I would come to need later in life.

When the year came to an end, I decided to leave A&M and go to its archrival and infinitely better school, the University of Texas. There I experienced a virtual explosion of intellectual and emotional growth. I simultaneously grew in four different dimensions—religion, politics, love, and work. When I moved to the University of Texas, I moved into the Christian Faith and Life Community, a Protestant reform group that studied modern theologians like Tillich and Bultman and created its own worship services. It was an intentional community with covenants, reflection, and a sense of purpose. It sought to reform individuals, through them the local Protestant churches, and through these churches, the entire culture. There was really no place else in conservative Texas quite like it. More than anything else it taught me at what an intense level a community of people could live together and what a deep commitment such a group of people could sustain.

Supplementing the Christian Faith and Life Community was the student YMCA with which I had begun my journey to consciousness at Texas A&M. The YMCA/YWCA at the University of Texas was the meeting place and institutional sponsor of the sit-in and stand-in movement for racial integration. It was the subject of a laudatory newspaper column by Eleanor Roosevelt in the national press and a front-page series of "hatchet-jobs" in the *Dallas Morning News*. The student YMCA/YWCA served as a local support group translating general Christianity into social action, and the national student YMCA made me a national officer and sent me to Africa, Europe, the Soviet Union, and Japan. These exposures to foreign cultures and subsequent culture shock widened my understanding of the world. They made me fundamentally different from Americans who have not traveled abroad or those who have gone overseas only as casual tourists. The YMCA helped to make me a world citizen.

Growing up in Texas in the 1950s and 1960s, I learned to hold controversial social and political positions against intense opposition and even hatred. Within a few months of moving to the University of Texas, I joined the civil rights movement. At our first organizing meeting, a pipe bomb was set off in an attempt to end our movement. But it failed, only blowing a few bricks off the building. Gangs of high school toughs would ride by in cars shouting threats while we stood in demonstrations outside movie theaters we were trying to integrate. But I was never harmed or even arrested in the civil rights movement.

Texas was a state in which the few hundred "liberals" all knew each other. Certainly the hundred of us who participated in the civil rights demonstrations at movie theaters knew one another. There were not many black students at the university in those days, but blacks and liberal whites banded together to break the entrenched segregation patterns. And we succeeded.

Moving from protest movements to politics was easy. I became president of the local student YMCA/YWCA, a national YMCA officer, and a U.S. delegate to international meetings. I began a new student political party and helped elect a liberal-dominated student government. I became a part of the National Student Association, played a role electing others to national office, and was an effective delegate to international student meetings.

I switched my major from sociology to political science and graduated from the University of Texas with honors. I moved on to graduate school with every prospect of success. I learned to think—not just in the pragmatic calculations required for narrow politics— but also to consider the interplay of forces and ideas. Politics and the study of politics seemed glorious and exciting and I was on the winning side in student politics. It seemed in those years as if students, in cooperation with other progressive forces in society, would succeed in turning the country around. All things were possible. The marching, protests, music, and the voting were moving history. We were winning.

I was no longer an adolescent. I had become a man and I came to know love as an adult. I had dated in high school but mostly by having a regular bridge partner and going to formal dances. While at A&M I began "to fall in love." At the University of Texas I had several romances that lasted about a year each. I learned that I could love and be loved, which was perhaps the most important lesson of my college years. I also learned to take the risks that love requires.

After completing my B.A. in political science at the University of Texas in 1963, I enrolled as a graduate student in African studies at Indiana University. By then I had left formal church membership and attendance. The directly religious path would seem remote from my life from 1963 to 1980. I also became divorced from direct politics and political movements during graduate school, although I was studying politics academically. My love life flourished. Being a long way from my previous girlfriend in Texas, I soon fell in love in Indiana. I was married in the fall of 1964 to Mary Scott Head and would stay married for the next sixteen years.

I worked steadily toward my Ph.D. In 1966–67, my wife and I spent a year in Sierra Leone, West Africa, doing my dissertation research. This was my longest stay outside the United States. I studied the political evolution of two towns in Sierra Leone. I enjoyed being a close observer of another society and learned experientially that some of the assumptions I had been taught (such as social and economic development inevitably lead to democratic political development) were false. It was also important as a white to live for a year in a society in which I was a member of the minority race.

During our time in Africa, race riots came to U.S. cities. So my wife and I decided that we would move back to a U.S. city to contribute what we could to solving its problems. After returning to the United States and finishing my dissertation, I took a teaching job at the University of Illinois at Chicago where I still teach more than twenty years later.

Once in Chicago I became active in adult politics. In many ways I tried to make political movements my religion because Christian churches didn't seem to fit my needs. To reshape political movements more idealistically I often had to found new political organizations and continued to be a part of idealistic political movements.

Adult politics began for me with the 1968 McCarthy for president campaign. By the end of that campaign I was state campaign manager and had learned firsthand the craft of electoral politics even in our defeat. Since then, I have been a candidate or campaign official in dozens of successful electoral battles even against the once, all-powerful Chicago Democratic Machine.

Following the rout of the Kennedy-McCarthy-McGovern forces at the National Democratic Convention of 1968, I founded the Independent Precinct

Organization (IPO), which was far more participatory than existing political parties and was the very antithesis of the Chicago machine. In the decade that followed, IPO elected more than twenty local officials—aldermen, state legislators, and state Constitutional Convention delegates. We also directly affected the outcome of many higher elections. After ten years we merged with the Independent Voters of Illinois to become IVI-IPO, which continues to this day many of the traditions of independent politics in Chicago but it has not been as vibrant, as powerful, as idealistic, or as participatory as IPO in its early years.

Not entirely satisfied with the efforts of other officials who I helped to elect, I ran and was elected Forty-fourth Ward alderman in 1971. I was reelected in 1975 and served until 1979. Borrowing some of the tactics I had learned in the civil rights movement, I took nonviolent confrontation to City Hall and opposed Mayor Daley and his successor, Mayor Bilandic, face-to-face questioning nepotism, patronage, corruption, and machine politics in all its manifestations in Chicago.

I did more than this as alderman. I attempted to create an alternative to city government as IPO had been an alternative to political parties. In the Forty-fourth Ward I founded new forms of neighborhood government. Among the new institutions were the 44th Ward Assembly, Asemblea Abierta, Community Zoning Board, Traffic Review Commission, and Ward Service Office. By 1975 I led the opposition bloc of independent aldermen in the Chicago City Council. In 1979, having accomplished all that I believed was possible in City Council and in the Forty-fourth Ward, I voluntarily retired as alderman and as spokesperson for the antimachine forces in Chicago.

All this time I continued to teach and publish at the University of Illinois at Chicago. In 1972 I was promoted to associate professor with tenure. Over the years I have published more than fifty books, articles, films, and videotapes. I have taught more than twelve thousand students. Nonetheless, I have influenced more people in their political thinking by my political actions than by either my writing or my university teaching.

Despite my political and university successes, I began to face a series of major setbacks by 1979. My wife and I were divorced after sixteen years of marriage. We had grown apart over the years and simply weren't right as mates any more. I was devastated emotionally, and it took long months of healing before I began to recover. At one stage I considered suicide but as I grew close to former friends and had more contact with younger children, I began to regain a zest for life.

At this same time, the political institutions I had founded began to fall apart. We managed to save IPO from extinction by merger with the Independent Voters of Illinois. As IVI-IPO, it changed and adapted. The later Chicago reform movement led by Mayor Washington until his death even adopted participatory democracy as one of its goals. I helped write Mayor Washington's early campaign speeches and helped forge the alliance between black, Latino and white reformers in Chicago. I headed a division of the transition team after Mayor Washington was elected and continued to work with his administration until his death in 1987. Some of the early goals of the Independent political movement were achieved in city government under Mayor Washington but others were not implemented.

Just as IPO was eventually surplanted by other movements and organizations, the neighborhood government I had founded in the Forty-fourth Ward was completely destroyed two years after my retirement. When a Democratic machine alderman was elected to represent the ward, he ended the neighborhood government experiment. All that remains is the memory of what true neighborhood government meant in one Chicago community. The National Association of Neighborhoods, of which I had been a national officer and through which I had helped ten thousand neighborhood people to adopt a "National Neighborhood Platform," was on the verge of financial bankruptcy by the 1980s. Although it survived by federal government grants, it was weakened and divided into racial and political factions.

Other doors were closing. For two years I had attempted to obtain grants to return to Africa where my political research had begun in 1966. I thought that perhaps I could revive those experiences and start once again down a new path intellectually. Whereas I had easily obtained a Ford Foundation Grant in 1966, I failed to receive any of the five grants for which I applied in 1980–81. I believed that if I could only tour Sierra Leone, Liberia, and Nigeria to see for myself their failed experiments in democracy over the two decades of my absence that I would be able to complete my book, *Reinventing Democracy*. This would reopen and reorient my career as a political scientist.

When I failed to get the grants for overseas study, I tried to become the chair of a political science department or college president at a liberal arts college. After applying to four schools, I was not hired. My own department at the University of Illinois at Chicago voted to make me chair by fourteen to thirteen, but I was vetoed by the administration. I concluded that no university would accept me in an administrative position because I was politically too controversial.

Next I tried foundations. I applied to become executive director of the Wieboldt Foundation. Having worked with community organizations in Chicago for two decades and being a nationally recognized expert in neighborhood empowerment, it seemed like a natural post for me. As in the contest for chair of the University's Political Science Department, I came in second.

Divorce and dissolution of my political institutions destroyed the life I had built for myself since I had moved to Chicago. Yet this dissolution allowed me to rebuild a healthier life. In January 1981, I remarried and became part of a family with two stepdaughters. Because I had not had children previously, this took a considerable personal adjustment, but the larger family was a great blessing for me. My stepdaughters taught me to play, to nurture, and to see the world differently.

With the help and encouragement of my new family, I began again my spiritual journey. I began to learn yoga and meditation. I tried various techniques of self-discovery from psychotherapy and the Progoff Life Context Journal to past life regressions. I joined the Wellington Avenue United Church of Christ to which my new family belonged. Within the year I was serving as a liturgist and a church officer. The experience at the Wellington Avenue church was affirming and healing. As an adult, I grew quickly to the faith that had been mine as a youth.

Politically, I became active again. I joined in founding the Illinois Coalition Against Reagan Economics to fight against enlarged military expenditures and decreased funds for social programs. I worked with the Wellington Avenue United Church of Christ Sanctuary Project for Salvadoran and Guatemalan Refugees. I created an ad hoc group of religious, political, and community leaders to support adoption of the World Charter for Nature at the United Nations. I became active as an adviser in Harold Washington's mayoral campaign and wrote the Transition Team report which paved the way for his taking over the reins of government more effectively.

Having retired as alderman in 1979, having remarried and reorganized my life since 1981, I now made a major change. Attending my sister-in-law's wedding in the summer of 1982, I had the simple vision of myself in the place of the priest conducting the service. After meditating over the vision for several weeks, I decided it was a "call" to become a minister and returned to school to get the necessary formal training. While continuing as a political science professor at the University of Illinois at Chicago, I enrolled in September 1982 at McCormick Theological Seminary.

I began to combine religion and politics. In addition to my work at the Wellington Avenue church, I joined the teaching faculty at the Institute in Creation-Centered Spirituality where I taught, with Matthew Fox, a Catholic theologian, a course entitled "Towards a Politics of Compassion," and I began to team-teach a similar course at McCormick Theological Seminary.

At first, I tried to reject the idea of being a minister. After all I was forty-two years old, secure and established in my university position. But I developed in seminary a "dual competency" in religion and politics. In June 1984, I graduated with a master of divinity degree. During seminary I did preliminary drafts of this book to integrate the new material from the study of religion with the political knowledge I already possessed.

I began to understand that a minister is primarily a shaman—one who is in touch with the *holy* and helps others become in touch with the *holy*. This is not learned from books but from "religious" experience.

Before my seminary education was completed, I was divorced again. Once again I lost my family. This time I knew emotionally what to expect, but that made it no more pleasant. I had already begun to do work with a therapist in an attempt to save my marriage. With my divorce I continued in therapy for over a year. Through analysis and work with dreams and meditations, I began to be both more aware and more open about my feelings. As I struggled to become more whole and as I began to heal myself, I came to understand, as Henri Nouwen writes in *The Wounded Healer,* that we cannot heal or minister to others, we cannot compassionately share their pain, unless we have been wounded ourselves.

In July 1984, I was ordained minister of urban mission by the Wellington Avenue United Church of Christ. My formal "call" is "to enable Wellington Avenue Church along with other...religious agencies...to develop and engage in effective and faithful mission." The congregation, with the approval of our denomination, commissioned me not only to work with them to devise mission strategies and to administer sacraments but also to work with other religious agencies to perform "a more effective and faithful witness, ministry, and mission of the church." They explicitly recognized the impending social crises and the new skills needed to confront them. While I continued my job at the University of Illinois at Chicago, I undertook several new "jobs" to carry out my joint role as minister and political scientist.

In July 1984, I became executive director of the Institute on the Church in Urban-Industrial Society (ICUIS). ICUIS had been dormant with no staff or operations for two years; under my leadership we grew to a staff of seven. We began with the Presbyterians, Methodists, Episcopals, and United Church of Christ as national denomination sponsors. During my term, we added the North American Contact Group of the World Council of Churches-Urban Rural Mission, the American Baptist Church, and the Unitarian Universalists Association. This was our official purpose:

ICUIS is an ecumenical agency for strengthening the mission of the church in urban-industrial society.

It monitors effective grass-roots urban strategies and programs of local congregations and religious organizations. It facilitates contact and communication among these local groups so that they can learn from each other, can better collaborate their work, and can inspire similar programs in other churches.

ICUIS seeks to support people engaged in urban and economic justice ministries by stimulating theological reflection, and providing analyses of program possibilities, information on spiritual disciplines and direct assistance.

We saw ourselves as furthering "urban ministry," "public ministry," and "justice ministries."

ICUIS had a contract with the Urban Academy of Chicago (an ecumenical agency of local judicatories of denominations and a dozen seminaries) to design seminary courses and weekend workshops. Under Urban Academy aegis we developed a core faculty of thirty seminary professors, religious leaders, pastors, and community organizers who met monthly to try and shape a common curriculum and understanding of "public ministry." For the Urban Academy, ICUIS also designed a major workshop on hunger, homelessness, and joblessness and another on disarmament, sanctuary, Central America, and South Africa.

During the same brief period while I was executive director, ICUIS was also reorganizing its files, preparing to microfilm its extensive archives, reorganizing its board of directors, and more carefully redefining its own mission. In many ways ICUIS was successful. In other ways we failed. We held successful workshops and distributed several thousand workbooks on model church and synagogue programs fighting hunger, homelessness, and unemployment as well as working on the issues of divestment in South Africa, nuclear weapon free zones, and sanctuary for Central American refugees. In Chicago we provided technical assistance to a number of congregations and seminaries undertaking social justice projects. We also provided technical assistance to religious agencies in the Playskool lawsuit, affirmative action lawsuit, and the successful campaign to pass the Chicago Nuclear Weapon Free Zone Ordinance. We helped staff a National Congress on Urban Ministry, developed new seminary courses on public ministry, and held a national leadership training course in urban ministry attended by representatives from eight denominations, from Catholics to Unitarians. We helped Latino churches develop a food pantry system for the Hispanic community in Chicago, and Operation PUSH become the first black sanctuary church for Central American and South African refugees.

We were successful in promoting these social justice projects, but we became controversial. When it became clear that the board of directors would not allow us to be directly involved in future social justice projects, I resigned as executive director at ICUIS, serving first as program director, then as acting executive director, as program consultant, and then leaving the agency altogether. "Urban ministry" became more narrowly defined at ICUIS and budget cuts reduced the staff from seven to three. I began to do more of my social justice work as chair of the Peace, Poverty, Hunger Network of the Illinois Conference of the United Church of Christ, which in 1988 changed its name to the Justice and Peace Network. While I was chair it grew in membership, effectiveness, staff, and budget. It became the effective social justice action group for the Illinois Conference.

In 1979 and 1980 I had visited Greece and Italy and became more interested in the history of these birthplaces of Western democracy. I also thought more deeply about the evolution and decline of Greek and Roman civilizations. As part of my religious quest I went to India in the summer of 1985 to see Indian religious leaders like Sathya Sai Baba and to learn the history of Indian civilization. I have also returned four times to the Sivanda Yoga Retreat in the Bahamas since 1981. These contacts with other civilizations, cultures, and religions continued my personal growth.

Over the several years of my involvement with ICUIS and its sister agencies, I worked with many urban ministry staff members and attended several national conferences and consultations. As chair of the Peace, Poverty, Hunger Network, I was one of ten United Church of Christ leaders chosen to go on the denomination's human rights fact-finding mission to the Middle East in October 1986. There we found three of the holiest sites in the world crowded together within two blocks of each other in the old city of Jerusalem: the ancient Jewish Temple ("Wailing Wall"), the Muslim "Dome of the Rock" (where God appeared to Mohammed), and the site of Jesus' crucifixion. We also found the most likely location for beginning World War III! We encountered a war of two "rights." Palestinians have a right to a homeland, to be a people, and to have a future. Jews have a right to safe haven from persecution, to be a people, and to have a future. Both rights are jeopardized by continued Israeli occupation of the occupied territories, by continued Palestinian terrorism, and by the continuing war between Israel and the Arab nations that surround it. We found human rights violations under international human rights standards on both sides of the conflict and a U.S. foreign policy that aggravates rather than alleviates the conflict. This journey made real for me the intractability of worldwide crises we face.

In my personal life I spent several years recovering from my second divorce and married for a third time in the spring of 1987. Once again my new family had two stepchildren to enlighten me with their innocence and wisdom. This book is dedicated to my family who have brought me once more a new life. My wife is not only a talented actress, but she is also able to love with a powerful and healing passion. The fact that my new family is Jewish and that I remain an ordained Christian minister helps to stretch our religious lives. The religious dimension of our Jewish-Christian family is even clearer to me since my journey to Israel.

In April 1987, I became executive director of Metro Chicago Clergy and Laity Concerned. Its board of directors, of which I had been a member for several years, was dedicated to leading struggles for Justice and Peace, rather than to avoiding controversy. This made CALC an ideal agency for me. However, I was able to take on this new responsibility (in addition to my university teaching and my demanding writing schedule) only because of the support I received from my new family. At each stage of my life I have needed support at home to expand my activities in the outer world. The danger for me is always that I will overextend my external activities and neglect my inner growth and my family. It requires a constant struggle to achieve balance between the inner and outer dimensions.

At CALC we have been effective in extending the Chicago Nuclear Weapon Free Zone to include the unincorporated areas of Cook County and six suburban towns. We helped to organize the largest Soweto Day demonstrations against South African apartheid in Chicago's history. We organized a successful boycott of Citibank in coordination with national religious groups to force its divestment of South African holdings. We have worked to end city of Chicago contracts with Illinois companies doing business in South Africa. We pressured U.S. Senator Alan Dixon to vote against contra aid and we signed a "People's Appeal for Peace" with Russian Religious Leaders as a basis of our continuing legislative work for Nuclear Test Ban legislation in Congress.

In addition to the political successes at CALC, I was nominated for a Fulbright Fellowship to return to West Africa with my family to study the African struggle for democracy. Once again, however, I did not get the fellowship. But I did get a small grant to create a new method of recording city council roll call votes in Chicago. These City Council studies are now regularly released to the press. And I have just published a major book on Chicago politics and government, *Chicago's Future in a Time of Change.* So there have been advances in my academic career despite setbacks.

Yet my successes in religion, politics, and the university have exacted a price. From the added stress I have gained weight and lost the physical fitness I had only a few years ago. I have fallen off in my practice of the disciplines of compassion although I have begun jogging, yoga, swimming, and meditation again in some measure. Stress has meant a higher cholesterol count and other sure signs of ill health.

My personal struggle for balance continues. It cannot be permanently won but must be found anew at each phase of my life. It requires a continual recommitment. Advances in the public or exterior life require a deepening interior life just as tall trees require deep roots. The implicate order of my life, in love, religion, politics, and teaching continues to unfold. Having transformed my life many times already, I seek to be transformed once more. The fourfold path of compassion still lies ahead.

In any case, this is the personal history that caused me to write *The Politics of Compassion and Transformation.* I have studied and practiced politics nearly three decades, and have continued my personal, religious journey even longer. I have learned from Eastern and Western teachers and from the cultures of four continents. I have experienced personal successes and suffered personal defeats. All these experiences have gone into this writing which was spurred and given special urgency by the vision of the collapse of our civilization. Five years have been spent reassembling what I knew about politics and learning more about ethics and religion. I gratefully acknowledge that much of the writing occurred during 1985–86 when I received a grant from the Humanities Institute of the University of Illinois at Chicago.

I fully recognize in writing about a changeable future that errors will occur. I could merely be projecting fears of my own aging and death on a broader canvas, but intuitive and rational evidence as well as our collective experiences make my analysis more convincing. I firmly believe that we must merge religion, ethics, and politics by means of the fourfold path of compassion if we are to experience either the individual or cultural transformation necessary for our survival in this new "authentic dark age."

My professional reputation as a political scientist will be more harmed than helped by this book. My personal heresies revealed here will limit any advancement as an ordained minister. But writing it has helped clarify my own thinking, allowed me to face my fears, developed the intellectual and spiritual disciplines I need personally, and synthesized my disparate experiences. I hope it may help you join the network of Magi who may yet preserve life and create a new civilization. Whatever errors I have committed in the text will make no difference if this account of compassion, politics, and transformation contributes to a new people awakening, discovering themselves, and fulfilling their mission.

Whatever the ultimate fate of our civilization, we are the privileged participants in a saga that began at least sixteen billion years ago and which will continue at least six billion more years before our sun will self-destruct. We sense even now the pregnant void out of which we and our universe were created. We have the freedom to make a special contribution by honoring this past, by living fully in the present, and by daring to join in the unfolding of creation.

To those readers whom I will never meet, once more I send greetings and love. May the flame within you burn ever brighter and may your energy flame forth to create the crystal temple. Send your blessings to those of us who live in this troubled time and pray that we may all be empowered to create a better future.

Acknowledgments

This project has taken several years and has been an integral part of my life's journey. My journey is described in the *Afterword*, but there are a number of people whose contributions I especially wish to acknowledge.

My former wife, Bea Briggs, introduced me to yoga and the Eastern religious traditions. She also encouraged me to join the Wellington Avenue church and supported my decision to study for the ministry. This book is one of the results.

Faculty at the Institute in Creation-Centered Spirituality taught me about compassion in its manifold forms. My teachers and colleagues at the institute included Matthew Fox, John Giannini, Barbara Clow, and Brian Swimme. Each has been important in my life.

Faculty members at McCormick Theological Seminary read early versions of this manuscript and provided many suggestions that have been incorporated. Carl Dudley served as my adviser and coordinated my independent study program at the seminary that allowed me to integrate what I knew about politics with what I was learning about religion. Other faculty who critically read the early manuscript were Jack Stotts, Lew Mudge, and Bob Whorley. During this period I also studied with David Tracy at the University of Chicago Divinity School.

In order to develop the seminary papers into a book I needed the time to write and an interdisciplinary audience. Both were provided when I was awarded a fellowship at the Humanities Institute at the University of Illinois at Chicago during the 1985–86 school year. The comments, questions, and encouragement of the Institute Fellows were important in transforming the early drafts, and we were able to put some beliefs into practice by questioning the long-term goal and mission of the University itself. Several other faculty at the University of Illinois at Chicago provided critical advice, particularly on Chapter 2. The most important were Professor Ike Balbas who improved the reasoning and arguments, Professor Lansine Kaba who taught me about Islamic religion and traditions, and Professor Clinton Stockwell who read the entire manuscript and made many helpful suggestions.

I was fortunate to be able to enrich this book with real life experiences. First, I served as executive director of the Institute on the Church in Urban-Industrial Society from 1984–86 and as dean of the faculty at the Urban Academy where I taught "politics of compassion" to seminary students. These positions allowed me to observe urban ministry at the local, national, and international level. Second, I made pilgrimages to India and to the Sivananda Ashram in the Bahamas to study Eastern religions directly.

Finally, I became executive director of Metro Chicago Clergy and Laity Concerned and a member of the National CALC Executive Committee in 1987. As executive director of an interfaith, social justice action agency trying to cope with the crises outlined in this book I understand how difficult it is to change current conditions. But I am grateful for these opportunities to develop my own compassion and to be transformed by these organizations and their leaders.

The students who have taken "Politics of Compassion" courses from me at the Institute in Creation-Centered Spirituality, Seminary Consortium of Urban Pastoral Education, Urban Academy, and the University of Illinois at Chicago have helped to reshape every chapter of this book. Likewise, the congregations at Peoples Church, Wellington Avenue United Church of Christ, and Third Unitarian Church heard the original sermons, which became key sections of the book. The support and reactions of these congregations taught me what to keep and what to change. They also proved by their deeds that local congregations can make a difference.

I am grateful to the Office of Publication Services at the University of Illinois at Chicago who designed the cover, typeset, and corrected the text. The powerful drawings on the cover and in the text were done by my friend, Sue Ennis.

But, most of all, birth of this book was made possible by my family to whom it is dedicated. Kate and August Donley, my stepchildren, put up with my absences and my distractions. My concern for them and their generation made the book more real and concrete. My wife, Sarajane Avidon, gave me the love I needed to be able to write and rewrite the book. She has read aloud every chapter so we could do the endless corrections together. She even compiled the index for me. Without my family this book could not have been born.

NOTES

Chapter 1: A New Beginning

1. William Ophuls, *Ecology and the Politics of Scarcity* (San Francisco: Freeman, 1977), 48–49, and Robert Heilbroner, *The Human Prospect* (New York: Norton, 1980), 33, 62. Other analyses that consider the different dimensions of these crises include Audrey Smock, ed., *Christian Faith and Economic Life* (New York: United Church of Christ, 1987), chap. 7, and Fritjof Capra, *The Turning Point: Science, Society, and the Rising Culture* (New York: Bantam, 1983), chap. 1.

2. Culler Schippe, *A World Hungry* (Los Angeles: Franciscan Communications Center, 1975), 1.

3. Michael Parenti, *Democracy for the Few,* 3d ed. (New York: St. Martin's Press, 1980), chap. 2.

4. Joan Dolmes, "The Decline in Hunger-Related Deaths" (San Francisco: The Hunger Project, 1984), 2.

5. Ophuls, 48–60.

6. Heilbroner, 62.

7. Jonathan Schell, *The Fate of the Earth* (New York: Knopf, 1982), 209. For levels of military expenditures see Ruth Leger Sivard, *World Military and Social Expenditures 1985* (Washington, D.C.: World Priorities, 1986).

8. Heilbroner, 42–43.

9. R. P. Turco, O. B. Toon, T. P. Ackerman, J. B. Pollack, and Carl Sagan, "Nuclear Winter: Global Consequences of Multiple Nuclear Explosions," *Science,* Vol. 222, No. 4630, 23 Dec. 1983.

10. "Nuclear Winter Ideas puts 'Freeze' on War," *Chicago Tribune,* 9 Sept. 1984.

11. Heilbroner, 72. Data on extinction of species is also now more widely reported. See, for instance, the UPI story "Extinction 'spasm' is on big kill," *Chicago Tribune,* 7 Dec. 1986.

12. Edward Cornish, president of the World Future Society, has written that an increase of 2 to 4 degrees centigrade might have these beneficial effects: "Canadian and Russian farmers might be able to grow more crops if their lands became balmier. Northern winters would be milder, and

people in places like New England and North Dakota would save on fuel." Cornish also writes that "the 'greenhouse effect' is not something we need be alarmed about. . . . We have more pressing problems confronting us these days. . . . It is conceivable that highly effective new ways to remove carbon dioxide from the atmosphere will be discovered." See Edward Cornish, "Let's Not Panic Over Earth's Warming, Yet," *Chicago Sun-Times,* 8 Dec. 1985, 82. For counter predictions on the rising seas and lakes see Eric Eckholm, "Problems Will Seep Far Inland," *Chicago Tribune,* 16 March 1986, and Howard Witt, "Lake Michigan," *Chicago Tribune,* 1 June, 1986. For predictions of an increase in global temperatures from three to eight degrees by 2030 and recommendations to combat the Greenhouse Effect see Ronald Kotulak, "Greenhouse Effect Spurs Global Fears," *Chicago Tribune,* 1 July, 1988.

13. Tom Hayden, *The American Future: New Visions Beyond Old Frontiers* (Boston: South End Press, 1980), 58.

14. Joe Holland and Peter Henriot, *Social Analysis: Linking Faith and Justice* (Maryknoll, New York: Orbis and Center of Concern, 1963), xii, xiii, and xvii.

15. Sigmund Freud, *Civilization and Its Discontents* (New York: Norton, 1961; originally published 1930), 69.

16. Ibid., 92.

17. Joanna Macy, *Despair and Personal Power in the Nuclear Age* (Philadelphia: New Society Publishers, 1983), 13.

18. Ibid., 22–23.

19. Robert Jay Lifton and Nicholas Humphrey, eds., *In a Dark Time: Images for Survival* (Cambridge: Harvard University Press, 1984), 123.

20. Ibid., 135.

21. Quoted in Ibid., 136.

22. David Kinsley, *The Sword and the Flute: Kali and Krsna: Dark Visions of the Terrible and the Sublime in Hindu Mythology* (Berkeley: University of California Press, 1975), 1, 142–44.

23. Erika Cheetham, *The Further Prophecies of Nostradamus: 1985 and Beyond* (London: Corgi Books, 1985), 160, 174, 205, 210.

24. Ibid.

25. For predictions of other current prophets of doom, see Cheetham, chap. 10. See also Jeane Dixon, *My Life and Prophecies* (New York: William Morrow, 1969), chaps. 9 and 10.

26. William Butler Yeats, "The Second Coming," *Selected Poems and Two*

Plays of William Butler Yeats, ed. M.L. Rosenthal (New York: Collier Books, 1962), 91.

27. Some of the more thoughtful science fiction books that treat the end of our civilization and the time that follows include Thea Plym Alexander, *2150 A.D.* (Tempe, Ariz.: MACRO, 1971); Walter Miller, Jr., *A Canticle for Liebowitz* (New York: Bantam, 1959); George Stewart, *Earth Abides* (Greenwich, Conn.: Fawcett, 1949); Kate Wilhelm, *Where Late the Sweet Birds Sang* (New York: Pocket Books, 1976).

28. Arthur M. Schlesinger, Jr., *The Cycles of American History* (Boston: Houghton Mifflin, 1986), 15–16.

29. Capra, 5.

30. Ibid., 15–16.

31. Ibid., 419.

32. Michael Howard, "Imperial Cycles: Bucks, Bullets and Bust," a review of Paul Kennedy, *The Rise and Fall of the Great Powers* (New York: Random House, 1988), *New York Times Book Review,* 10 Jan. 1988, 28.

33. George Gallup, Jr., with William Proctor, *Forecast 2000* (New York: William Morrow, 1984).

34. Other books that I recommend on the politics of compassion and transformation include Jack Nelson-Pallmeyer, *The Politics of Compassion* (Maryknoll, N.Y.: Orbis, 1986) and Fran Peaney with Myra Levy and Charles Varon, *Heart Politics* (Philadelphia: New Society Publishers, 1986). For a fuller discussion of political action and how the study of politics might focus on political action, see George Beam and Dick Simpson, *Political Action: The Key to Understanding Politics* (Athens, Ohio: Swallow/Ohio University Press, 1984). For further readings on the general connection between politics and religion see the articles and bibliography in *CoEvolution Quarterly,* 39 (Fall 1983).

Chapter 2: Resolving the Dilemmas in Religion, Ethics, and Politics

1. The parallelism of the crisis in the three disciplines was clarified for me in discussions with Isaac Balbus of the University of Illinois at Chicago. A discussion of the crisis in political science is to be found in Charles Taylor, "Interpretation and the Sciences of Man," in *Understanding and Social Inquiry,* ed. Fred Dallmayr and Thomas A. McCarthy (Notre Dame: University of Notre Dame Press, 1977), 101–31.

2. Eric Patridge, *Origins: A Short Etymological Dictionary of Modern*

English (New York: Macmillan, 1966). The Oxford English Dictionary questions the etymological derivation but gives as the first usage the "state of life bound by monastic vows." See *The Compact Edition of the Oxford English Dictionary* (Oxford, England: Oxford University Press, 1971).

3. Ken Wilber, *A Sociable God: Toward a New Understanding of Religion* (Boulder, Col.: New Science Library, 1984).

4. David Tracy, "Religion" (Class lecture, University of Chicago, 6 Nov. 1983).

5. Langdon Gilkey, *Naming the Whirlwind: The Renewal of God-Language* (Indianapolis: Bobbs-Merrill, 1969), 295.

6. William James, *The Varieties of Religious Experience* (New York: Penguin, 1982), 31; first published in 1902.

7. Friedrich Schleiermacher, *The Christian Faith* (Edinburgh: T. & T. Clark, 1928), 131–34.

8. David Tracy, *Blessed Rage for Order* (New York: Seabury, 1978), 92.

9. Quoted in David Tracy, "Religion and Human Rights in the Public Realm," *Daedalus*, Vol. 112, No. 4, (Fall 1983), 237–54.

10. Clifford Geertz, "Religion As a Cultural System," in *The Religious Situation: 1968,* ed. Donald Cutler (Boston: Beacon, 1968), 643; cited in Tracy, *Blessed Rage for Order,* 92.

11. Tracy, *Blessed Rage for Order,* 93.

12. Class notes from David Tracy lectures at the University of Chicago, 1983.

13. Paul Tillich, *The Shaking of the Foundations* (New York: Scribner, 1948), 57, 59.

14. Robert Bellah, *The Broken Covenant* (New York: Seabury, 1975), ix. See also Robert Bellah, "Civil Religion in America," *Daedalus* (Winter, 1967), 9, 20.

15. Jean-Jacques Rousseau, *The Social Contract* (New York: New American Library, 1974), 113; also quoted in Michael Harrington, *The Politics at God's Funeral: The Spiritual Crisis of Western Civilization* (New York: Penguin, 1983), 36.

16. G. W. F. Hegel, *Werke in Zwanzig Banden* (Frankfurt-am-Main: Suhrkamp, 1969), XII, 141; quoted in Harrington, 61.

17. See Emile Durkheim, *The Elementary Forms of the Religious Life* (New York: Free Press, 1965; originally published in 1915). See also Harrington, 134–36.

18. Peter Berger, *The Sacred Canopy: Elements of a Sociological Theory of Religion* (Garden City, New York: Doubleday, 1967), 33.

19. T. Harry Williams, ed., *Abraham Lincoln: Selected Speeches, Messages, and Letters* (New York: Holt, Rinehart, & Winston, 1957), 283.

20. Richard Nixon, quoted in Robert Jewett, *The Captain America Complex* (Santa Fe: Bear & Company, 1984), 185.

21. Harrington, 172, 198.

22. Matthew Fox, *Meditations with Meister Eckhart* (Santa Fe: Bear & Company, 1983), 111.

23. *Webster's New World Dictionary*, College ed. (Cleveland: The World Publishing Company, 1968) and *The Compact Edition of the Oxford English Dictionary*.

24. Matthew Fox, *A Spirituality Named Compassion* (Minneapolis: Winston, 1979), chap. 1.

25. Ibid.

26. Matthew Fox, *Original Blessing: A Primer in Creation Spirituality* (Santa Fe: Bear & Company, 1983), 288.

27. Walpola Sri Rahula, *What the Buddha Taught* (New York: Grove, 1974), 47, 75; first published in 1959. See also Lucien Stryk, ed., *World of the Buddha* (New York: Grove Press, 1986). Especially the Introduction and chap. 3.

28. Ibid., xv–xvi, 77; See also William Johnston, *Silent Music: The Science of Meditation* (San Francisco: Harper & Row, 1976), chap. 7.

29. I am indebted to Professor Lansine Kaha, Director of Black Studies at the University of Ilinois at Chicago for teaching me about the deeper meaning of Islam, *Jihad,* and the Islamic notion of compassion. The quotation is from Alfred Guillaume, *Islam* (New York: Penguin, 1954), 64.

30. Ibid., 67.

31. Ibid., 148.

32. Kenneth Cragg, *The Wisdom of the Sufis* (New York: New Directions, 1976), 80.

33. Fox, *Meditations with Meister Eckhart,* 30.

34. Gabriele Uhlein, *Meditations with Hildegard of Bingen* (Santa Fe: Bear & Company, 1982), 35.

35. Fox, *Meditations with Meister Eckhart,* 48.

36. Sue Woodruff, *Meditations with Mechtild of Magdeburg* (Santa Fe: Bear & Company, 1982), 58, 71.

37. Fox, *Meditations with Meister Eckhart,* 49, 45, 54.

38. Woodruff, 83.

39. Fox, *Meditations with Meister Eckhart,* 80.

40. Uhlein, 111.

41. Fox, *Meditations with Meister Eckhart,* 120, 102.

42. William Frankena, *Ethics,* 2d ed. (Englewood Cliff, N.J.: Prentice-Hall, 1973).

43. Alasdair MacIntyre, *After Virtue: A Study in Moral Theory* (Notre Dame: University of Notre Dame Press, 1981), 6–8.

44. Ibid., 51.

45. Ibid., 12.

46. Rahula, 80.

47. Dietrich Bonhoeffer, *Ethics* (New York: Macmillan, 1955), 55; cited in Heinrich Ott, *Reality and Faith: The Theological Legacy of Dietrich Bonhoeffer* (Philadelphia: Fortress Press, 1972), 172.

48. Ott, 272.

49. Dietrich Bonhoeffer, *Letters and Papers from Prison* (S.C.M. Press, 1967), 201; first published in 1951; cited in Ott, 17.

50. James Gustafson, *Ethics from a Theocentric Perspective,* Vol. 1, *Theology and Ethics* (Chicago: University of Chicago Press, 1981), 88, 89, 112.

51. Ibid., 327.

52. E. Clinton Gardner, *Biblical Faith and Social Ethics* (New York: Harper and Row, 1960), 162.

53. Ibid., 163.

54. Ibid., 165.

55. Carol Gilligan, *In a Different Voice: Psychological Theory and Women's Development* (Cambridge: Harvard University Press, 1982), 2, 19.

56. Nell Noddings, *Caring: A Feminist Approach to Ethics and Moral Education* (Berkeley: University of California Press, 1984), 1, 5.
57. Ibid., 9, 30, 14, 13.

58. Ibid., 131.

59. Owen J. Flanagan, Jr. and Jonathan E. Adler, "Impartiality and Particularity," *Social Research,* 50 (Autumn 1983): 585.

60. John Broughton, "Women's Rationality and Men's Virtues: A Critique of Gender Dualism in Gilligan's Theory of Moral Development," *Social Research,* 50 (Autumn 1983): 614.

61. Matthew Fox and Brian Swimme, *Manifesto for a Global Civilization* (Santa Fe: Bear & Company, 1982), 28–30.

62. Jose Miguez Bonino, *Toward a Christian Political Ethics* (Philadelphia: Fortress Press, 1983), 107.

63. See George Beam and Dick Simpson, *Political Action: The Key to Understanding Politics* (Athens, Ohio: Swallow/Ohio University Press, 1984), chap. 5.

64. Dick Simpson, ed., *Declaration on the Study of Politics* (Chicago: Swallow Press, 1976).

65. Leo Strauss, *What Is Political Philosophy?* (New York: Free Press of Glencoe, 1959), 11–12.

66. *The Republic of Plato,* translated with introduction and notes by Francis McDonald Cornford (New York: Oxford University Press, 1945), 226.

67. Jacques Maritain, *On the Use of Philosophy: Three Essays* (Princeton, N.J.: Princeton University Press, 1961), 3, 57.

68. John Plamenatz, *Man and Society: Political and Social Theory* (New York: McGraw-Hill, 1963), Vol. I, xiii.

69. John Rawls, *A Theory of Justice* (Cambridge: Harvard University Press, 1971), chap. 4. For a useful discussion of Rawls, Dworkin, and Nozick, see Alasdair MacIntyre, chap. 17.

70. Robert Nozick, *Anarchy, State, and Utopia* (New York: Basic Books, 1974), 151.

71. Beam and Simpson, 57.

72. George Mendenhall, *The Tenth Generation* (Baltimore: Johns Hopkins University Press, 1973), 217–20.

73. The process of action was suggested to me by Carl Dudley in a course we taught together at McCormick Theological Seminary in 1984. See also Dick Simpson and George Beam, *Strategies for Change* (Chicago: Swallow Press, 1976).

74. Reinhold Niebuhr, *Moral Man and Immoral Society: A Study in Ethics and Politics* (New York: Scribner, 1960).

75. Harvey Cox, *Religion in the Secular City: Toward a Postmodern Theology* (New York: Simon and Schuster, 1984), 154.

76. Marvin Maurer, "The World View of the Religious Society of Friends (Quakers)," *American Political Science Association,* 3–6 Sept. 1987.

Chapter 3: Teachers of Compassionate Politics

1. Paul Tillich, "The Depth of Existence," in *The Shaking of the Foundations* (New York: Scribner's, 1948), 52, 53, 58–59.

2. Matthew Fox, *Meditations with Meister Eckhart* (Santa Fe: Bear & Company, 1982), 102, 109.

3. Matthew Fox, *A Spirituality Named Compassion* (Minneapolis: Winston, 1979), 24, vi.

4. B. D. Napier, "Prophet, Prophetism," in *Interpreter's Dictionary of the Bible* (New York: Abingdon Press, 1962), 896–919.

5. Walter Brueggemann, *The Prophetic Imagination* (Philadelphia: Fortress Press, 1978), 16–17. Very different interpretations of Moses can be found in Emil Bock, *Moses: From the Mysteries of Egypt to the Judges of Israel* (New York: Inner Traditions International, 1986) and Aaron Wildavsky, *The Nursing Father: Moses as a Political Leader* (University, Alabama: University of Alabama Press, 1984).

6. John Yoder, *The Politics of Jesus* (Grand Rapids: Eerdmans, 1972), 62–63, 39.

7. Albert Nolan, *Jesus Before Christianity* (Maryknoll, N.Y.: Orbis, 1982), 27; first published in 1976 in Claremont, South Africa, by David Philip Publishing.

8. This list of Jesus' political principles are compiled from Yoder, from Nolan, and from Richard Cassidy, *Jesus, Politics, and Society* (Maryknoll, N.Y.: Orbis, 1983); originally published by Orbis in 1978.

9. Cassidy, 61–62.

10. Fox, *Meditations*, 3.

11. These paths are developed from Eckhart's writings by Matthew Fox. For the fullest explication of the paths and their consequences, see Matthew Fox, *Original Blessing: A Primer in Creation Spirituality* (Santa Fe: Bear & Company, 1983).

12. Fox, *Meditations*, 6–7.

13. Ibid., 34.

14. Ibid., 70.

15. Ibid., 77.

16. Sri Swami Sivananda, *Practice of Karma Yoga*, 4th ed. (Shivanandanagar, India: The Divine Life Society, 1980), 53.

17. Rahavan Iyer, *The Moral and Political Thoughts of Mahatma Gandhi* (Oxford: Oxford University Press, 1973), 150. For additional

information on the life and teachings of Gandhi I especially recommend his autobiography, the film *Gandhi,* and the opera "Satyagraha."

18. M. K. Gandhi, *Mohan-Mala: A Gandhian Rosary,* comp. R. K. Prabhu (Ahmedabab, India: Navajivan Publishing House, 1949), 2, 26.

19. Robert O. Ballou, ed., *The Bible of the World* (New York: Viking, 1939), 60. A more modern translation of the passages of the Bhagavad Gita is available in J. A. B. van Buitenen, *The Bhagavadgita in the Mahabharata: A Bilingual Edition* (Chicago: University of Chicago Press, 1981). In this edition this passage would be rendered:

> He who thinks that this being is a killer and he who imagines that it is killed do neither of them know. It is not killed nor does it kill.
>
> It is never born nor does it die;
> Nor once that it is will it ever not be;
> Unborn, unending, eternal and ancient
> It is not killed when the body is killed.

20. Ibid., 61.

21. M. K. Gandhi, *An Autobiography: The Story of My Experiments with Truth* (Boston: Beacon, 1957), xii–xiv; first published in Gujarati in 1927 and 1929.

22. Iyer, 179–80.

23. Bhagwan Shri Patanjali, *Aphorisms of Yoga* (London: Faber, 1973), 51–58; first published in 1938.

24. Iyer, 253.

25. Ballou, 63–64.

26. Susanne Rudolph and Lloyd Rudolph, *Gandhi: The Traditional Roots of Charisma* (Chicago: University of Chicago Press, 1983), viii; originally published in 1967.

27. Rabindranath Tagore, quoted in B. K. Ahluwalia and Shashi Ahluwalia, *Tagore and Gandhi* (New Delhi: Pankaj Publications, 1981), 17.

28. Rudolph and Rudolph, 7.

29. Hanes Walton, Jr., *The Political Philosophy of Martin Luther King, Jr.* (Westport, Conn.: Greenwood Press, 1971), xxxvi, 34, 31.

30. Ibid., 32.

31. Ibid., 47.

32. Martin Luther King, Jr., *Where Do We Go from Here: Chaos or*

Community? (New York: Bantam, 1967), 67; originally published by Harper & Row, 1967.

33. Martin Luther King, Jr., *Why We Can't Wait* (New York: Signet, 1964), 81–82.

34. David J. Garrow, *Bearing the Cross: Martin Luther King, Jr., and the Southern Christian Leadership Conference* (New York: William Morrow, 1980). This is the most comprehensive biography of King yet written. I also recommend the film *King: From Montgomery to Memphis* as the best documentary film on his life and the movement he led.

35. N. Kasturi, *Sathya Sai Baba Speaks: Discourses Given by Bhagavan Sri Sathya Sai Baba* (Prasanthi Nilayam, India: Sri Sathya Sai Books, 1981), 10:5. The spelling of sathya is another English transliteration of the Hindu word for absolute truth, which Gandhi and others spell in English as satya.

36. Quoted in *Service Opportunities: Newsletter of the Sathya Sai American Service Organization* (July 1985): 1.

37. Quoted in ibid.

38. Kasturi, 10:8.

39. Ram Das and Paul Gorman, *How Can I Help?* (New York: Knopf, 1985), 19.

40. Quoted in *Service Opportunities*, 1.

41. Kasturi, 10: 32–33.

42. International Subud Committee, "Bapak Speaks to Candidates" (Kent, England: Subud Publications, n.d.), 1.

43. International Subud Committee, "A Selection of Appropriate Extracts from Bapak's Writings and Talks" (Kent, England: Subud Publications, 1982), 9; first published in 1969.

44. Chogyam Trungpa, *Shambhala: The Sacred Path of the Warrior* (Boulderd: Shambhala, 1984), 28.

45. Ibid., 109, 126.

46. Dorothy Day, *The Long Loneliness* (New York: Harper & Row, 1981), vii, viii, 11; originally published in 1952.

47. Ibid., 39.

48. Ibid., 137.

49. Ibid., 149, 220.

50. Ibid., 214–15.

51. Ibid., 243.

52. Ibid., 285–86.

Chapter 4: The Call to Justice and Compassion

1. This section was developed from a paper by Richard Luecke of the Community Renewal Society of Chicago for the Urban Academy. It was quoted in Dick Simpson and Clinton Stockwell, eds., *Justice Ministries: Fighting against Hunger, Homelessness, and Joblessness* (Chicago, ICUIS, 1985), 5.

2. B. D. Napier, "Prophet, Prophetism," *International Dictionary of the Bible* (New York: Abingdon Press, 1962), 896, 899, 897.

3. Rabbi Abraham Heschel, *The Wisdom of Heschel,* selected by Ruth Marcus Goodhill, (New York: Farran, Straus and Giroux, 1975), 279, 283, 295. See also the complete text of Rabbi Abraham Heschel, *The Prophets* (New York: Harper & Row, 1962).

4. Walter Brueggemann, *The Prophetic Imagination* (Philadelphia: Fortress Press, 1978), 16, 49–51.

5. Ibid., 28, 45.

6. Byron Sherwin, *Abraham Joshua Heschel* (Atlanta: John Knox Press, 1979), 50.

7. Richard Neuhaus, "What the Fundamentalists Want" (Washington, D. C.: Ethics and Public Policy Center, 1985), Reprint no. 61; originally published in *Commentary* May 1985.

8. Richard Fenn, "A New Sociology of Religion," *Journal for the Scientific Study of Religion* (March 1977): 17; quoted in Harvey Cox, *Religion in the Secular City* (New York: Simon & Schuster, 1984), 12.

9. Neuhaus, 43.

10. Ibid., 44, 45, 46.

11. Jerry Falwell, quoted in Cox, 36. See also *Time Magazine,* 2 Sept. 1985, 48–61.

12. Jim Wallis, *Agenda for a Biblical People* (New York: Harper & Row, 1976), 50.

13. Ibid., 64, 43, 37.

14. Ibid., 134.

15. Friedrich Schleiermacher, *The Christian Faith* (Edinburgh: T. & T. Clark, 1928).

16. David Tracy, *Blessed Rage for Order* (New York: Seabury, 1978), 26.

17. David Tracy, *The Analogical Imagination* (New York: Crossroads, 1981), xi, 5.

18. Elmer Johnson to John Cooper of the American Enterprise Institute, 16 June 1981.

19. John H. Leith, ed., *Creeds of Churches,* 3rd ed. (Atlanta: John Knox Press, 1982), 697.

20. Ibid., 699–703.

21. Robert Bellah, *The Broken Covenant* (New York: Seabury, 1975), 2. See also Robert Jewett, *The Captain America Complex* (Santa Fe: Bear & Company, 1985).

22. Lewis Mudge, *Why Is the Church in the World?* (Philadelphia: Board of Christian Education of the United Presbyterian Church in the U.S.A., 1967), 17, 64, 66–67.

23. H. Richard Niebuhr, *Christ and Culture* (New York: Harper & Row, 1975; First published in 1951), chap. 3, 87–89.

24. Ibid., 86, 108, 112.

25. Dietrich Bonhoeffer, *Ethics* (New York: Macmillan, 1955), 136–37.

26. Robert M. Brown, *Theology in a New Key: Responding to Liberation Themes* (Philadelphia: Westminster, 1978), 60.

27. Gustavo Gutierrez, quoted in Brown, 61–62.

28. Jose Miguez Bonino, *Doing Theology in a Revolutionary Situation* (Philadelphia: Fortress, 1975), 81, xxvi.

29. Cox, 108.

30. Ibid., 129.

31. Ernesto Cardenal, *The Gospel of Solentiname* (Maryknoll, N.Y.: Orbis, 1976), vii–ix.

32. Ibid., 26–32.

33. Rosemary Reuther, *Sexism and God-Talk: Toward a Feminist Theology,* (Boston: Beacon, 1983), 18–19.

34. Tissa Balasuriya, *Planetary Theology* (Maryknoll, New York: Orbis, 1984), 13–15, 151–52.

35. Ibid., 253–54.

36. Matthew Fox and Brian Swimme, *Manifesto for a Global Civilization* (Santa Fe: Bear & Company, 1982), 25.

37. Thomas Berry, "Twelve Principles . . ."(unpublished papers, Riverdale, New York: Riverdale Center of Religious Research, 1985), 1.

38. Thomas Berry, "The Spirituality of the Earth" (unpublished papers), 1, 7.

39. Thomas Berry, "Ecological Age" (unpublished papers), 9.

40. Berry, "Twelve Principles," 1–2.

41. Brian Swimme, *The Universe Is a Green Dragon* (Santa Fe: Bear & Company, 1985), 32, 35.

42. Ibid., 58–59, 81.

43. Ibid., 171.

44. See Tracy's *Blessed Rage* and *Analogical Imagination*.

45. Tracy, *Analogical Imagination*, 57–58.

46. National Conference of Catholic Bishops,"The Challenge of Peace: God's Promises and Our Response" (A Pastoral Letter on War and Peace, 3 May 1983), ii, iii, v–vi.

47. Catholic Bishops, paragraphs 83–96.

48. Ibid., paragraph 333.

49. The United Methodist Council of Bishops, *In Defense of Creation: The Nuclear Crises and a Just Peace* (Nashville, TN: Graded Press, 1986), 14, 15, 92.

50. Quoted in Dick Simpson and Clinton Stockwell, eds., *Justice Ministries: The Struggle for Peace, Justice, Sanctuary* (Chicago: ICUIS, 1985), 17. See Susan Thistlewaite, ed., *A Just Peace Church* (New York: United Church Press, 1986), chap. 3.

51. *Justice Ministries*, 23.

52. *Minutes of the Fifteenth General Synod, United Church of Christ* (St. Louis: Church Leadership Resources, 1985), 48.

53. Ibid., 49.

54. Ibid., 50.

55. "Declaration of Wellington United Church of Christ As a Nuclear Free Zone," in *Justice Ministries: The Struggle for Peace, Justice, Sanctuary*, 175.

56. *Journal of Proceedings of the City Council of the City of Chicago* (12 March 1986), 28523.

57. The quotations are taken from "Excerpt from Draft of Bishops' Letter on Catholic Social teaching and the U.S. Economy," cited in *Justice Ministries: Fighting against Hunger, Homelessness, Joblessness*, 10. The complete text was published in *Origins: National Catholic Documentary Service* 14 (15 Nov. 1984).

58. *Justice Ministries: Fighting against Hunger, Homelessness, Joblessness,* 10–11.

59. Ibid., 12.

60. Eugene Kennedy, *Re-imagining American Catholicism* (New York: Vintage, 1985), 64–65.

61. Great Lakes/Appalachian Project on the Economic Crisis, "Doing Theology in the Economic Crisis," cited in *Justice Ministries: Fighting against Hunger, Homelessness, Joblessness,* 16.

62. *Justice Ministries; Fighting against Hunger, Homelessness, Joblessness,* 17–18.

63. United Church of Christ, *Christian Faith and Economic Life: A Study Paper* (New York: United Church Board for World Ministries, 1987).

64. *CALC Report,* Vol. 8, No. 6, 18–19.

65. Reprinted in *Justice Ministries: Fighting against Hunger, Homelessness, Joblessness,* 157.

66. Ibid., 157–58.

67. See "Toymaker Cuts Deal with City on Closing," *Chicago Tribune,* 29 Jan. 1985, and "City, Developer, Near Pact to Reopen Playskool Plant," *Crain's Chicago Business,* 22–28 Sept. 1986, 1.

68. "Brief of Amici Curiae in Opposition to the United States' Motion for Prospective Modification of Decrees," in *United States of America v. City of Chicago,* note 11. Copies available from the Chicago Chapter of the ACLU.

69. Quoted in *1986 Handbook of Denominational Statements on Urban Mission and Ministry* (Chicago: ICUIS, 1986), 7, 8.

70. Ibid., 15, 16.

71. Ibid., 25.

72. Ibid., 41.

73. Resolution adopted at the April 1986 Congress on Urban Ministry sponsored by the Seminary Consortium for Urban Pastoral Education. *SCUPE Report,* 7 (June 1986), 5.

74. Archbishop Weakland, quoted in Kennedy, 19.

75. "The Karios Document" (Closter, N.J.: Theology in Global Context Program, 1986), 3; also quoted in part in *BASTA!* February 1986, 19.

76. *BASTA!* 20.

77. "The Karios Document," 10.

78. *BASTA!* 21.

79. "The Karios Document," 22.

80. *BASTA!* 21.

81. Jacques Ellul, *Presence of the Kingdom* (New York: Seabury, 1967), 48–49; quoted in Wallis, 131.

82. These terms are further developed in Jewett.

Chapter 5: Becoming Religious: The Interior Work Necessary for Exterior Action

1. Richard Foster, *Celebration of Discipline* (New York: Harper & Row, 1978), 3.

2. Bhagwan Shree Rajneesh, *Yoga: The Alpha and the Omega* (Poona, India; Rajneesh Foundation, 1976), 174.

3. Swami Vishnudevananda, *The Complete Illustrated Book of Yoga* (New York: Simon & Schuster, 1972), 12; first published by Julian Press, 1960.

4. Frances Moore Lappé, *Diet for a Small Planet* (New York: Ballantine, 1971), xviii. See also Frances Moore Lappé and Joseph Collins, *Food First* (New York: Ballantine, 1979), 3.

5. Frances Moore Lappé, *Diet for a Small Planet: Tenth Anniversary Edition* (New York: Ballantine, 1982), 9, 69–71, 85, 121–39.

6. Frank Waters, *The Man Who Killed the Deer* (Chicago: Swallow Press, 1969), 23–24.

7. Swami Vishnudevananda, 222–23.

8. Foster, 47, 43, 48.

9. Ibid., 51.

10. See Bhagwan Shri Patanjali, *Aphorisms of Yoga* (London: Faber and Faber, 1979), 51; first published in 1938. The paths are summarized in Samskrti and Veda, *Hatha Yoga* (Honesdale, Penn: Himalayan Institute, 1977), ix. A number of books set forth the basic hatha yoga exercises. In addition to the other yoga books cited in this chapter I would recommend Lucy Lidell, et al., *The Sivananda Companion to Yoga* (New York: Simon & Schuster, 1983).

11. Rajneesh, 7–9.

12. Samskrti and Veda, ix–x.

13. Vishnudevananda, 5, 13, 68.

14. Samskrti and Veda, 60.

15. Ibid.

16. Usharbudh Arya, *Philosophy of Hatha Yoga,* 2d ed. (Honesdale, Penn.: Himalayan Institute, 1985), 102, 119.

17. Samskrti and Veda, 106.

18. Arya, 77.

19. Ibid., 77–78.

20. Rachel Carr, *The Yoga Way to Release Tension* (New York: Harper & Row, 1974), 30.

21. Quoted in Carr, 29.

22. A chart of the number of calories burned in various exercises by people with different weights may be found, among other places, in *The Heartland: Health News,* 6, no. 2 (February 1986): 2.

23. Sandra Bartky, "The Modernization of Patriarchal Power," *Women Studies Newsletter* (Winter 1986): 15.

24. Foster, 14, 15.

25. Ibid., 15.

26. Dietrich Bonhoeffer, *Life Together* (New York: Harper & Row, 1954), 32.

27. Lawrence LeShan, *How to Meditate: A Guide to Self Discovery* (New York: Bantam, 1981), 1; first published in 1974.

28. Sri Swami Sivananda, *Concentration and Meditation* (Shivanandanagar, India: Divine Life Society, 1975), 84–85, 87.

29. Swami Muktananda, *Meditate* (Albany: SUNY Press, 1980), 16, 24.

30. Ibid., 25–26.

31. LeShan, 24–25.

32. Foster, 21–22.

33. Muktananda, 42.

34. Gurudev Siddha Peeth, "Instructions on Meditation," published brochure, 1974.

35. Muktananda, 43.

36. LeShan, 93.

37. William Johnston, *Silent Music* (San Francisco: Harper & Row, 1976), 17–18, 37, 55.

38. Ibid., 67, 72.

39. Ibid., 86.

40. Bonhoeffer, 88.

41. Johnston, 174.

42. *The Cloud of Unknowing*, introduction and translation by Ira Progoff (New York: Dell, 1957), 24, 71, 27, 35.

43. *The Cloud of Unknowing*, 151.

44. *The Cloud of Unknowing*, 120.

45. *The Secret of the Golden Flower*, translated by Richard Wilhelm with a commentary by C. J. Jung (New York: Harcourt Brace Jovanovich, 1962), 17, 21; first published in 1931.

46. *The Secret of the Golden Flower*, 40, 122, 65. For more information on Eastern meditation techniques see Mantak Chia, *Awaken Healing Energy Through the Tao* (New York: Aurora Press, 1983), which describes health-related forms of Taoist meditation. For a survey of the teachings of Tibetan Yoga see W. Y. Evans-Wentz, *Tibetan Yoga and Secret Doctrines* (London: Oxford University Press, 1982); first published in 1935.

47. Sigmund Freud, *The Origin and Development of Psycho-analysis* (Chicago: Henry Regnery, 1955), 6, 14. This was originally printed in the *American Journal of Psychology,* 21 (April 1910): 3–63.

48. Ibid., 28.

49. Joseph Campbell, ed. *The Portable Jung* (New York: Penguin Books, 1976), xxvi.

50. Jung, "Aion: Phenomenology of the Self," in *The Portable Jung,* 145.

51. *The Portable Jung,* 145, xxi.

52. C. G. Jung, *Memories, Dreams, Reflections,* recorded and edited by Aniela Jaffe (New York: Vintage, 1965), 233.

53. Jung, *Aion* (Princeton: Princeton University Press, 1959), 31.

54. John Giannini, "Jung's Social and Economic Psychology," *Transformation: The Bulletin of the C. G. Jung Center* (May 1982); 1.

55. John Sanford, *The Kingdom Within* (New York: Paulist Press, 1970), 27, 33–35.

56. C. G. Jung, *The Undiscovered Self* (New York: New American Library, 1960), 96.

57. Ibid., 121.

58. Ira Progoff, *Jung's Psychology and Its Social meaning* (New York: Grove, 1955), 138–39.

59. Volodyrayer Odajnizk, *Jung and Politics* (New York: New York University Press, 1976), 39.

60. Progoff, 219–20.

61. Odajnizk, 65–66.

62. Ira Progoff, *At a Journal Workshop: The Basic Text and Guide for Using the Intensive Journal Process* (New York: Dialogue House, 1975), 3, 10–11.

63. Ibid., 65.

64. Ibid., 81.

65. Foster, 30, 34, 36.

66. From *Gates of the House: The New Union Home Prayerbook* (New York: Central Conference of American Rabbis, 1977), 56.

67. From *Gates of Repentance: The New Union Prayerbook for the Days of Awe* (New York: Central Conference of American Rabbis, 1978), 497–98, 521–22.

68. Matthew Fox, *Meditations with Meister Eckhart* (Santa Fe: Bear & Co., 1982), 34.

69. N. Kasturi, *Sathya Sai Baba Speaks* (Prasanthi Nilayam, India: Sri Sathya Sai Books, 1981), 10: 109.

70. M. K. Gandhi, *Prayer,* comp. and ed. Chandra Kant Kaji (Ahmedabad, India: Navajivan Publishing, 1977), 7, 9, 27–29.

71. Ibid., 31, 32.

72. Anthony de Mello, *Sadhana: A Way to God: Christian Exercises in Eastern Form* (New York: Doubleday, 1984), 107. Father Andrew Skotnicki in Chicago maintains that there is a fourth part to this process which is "contemplation," and thus we are led back to meditation in the Eastern sense at the end of the prayer.

73. Bonhoeffer, 84–85.

74. See de Mello, 107–9.

75. Ibid., 126.

76. Robert Fritz, *The Path of Least Resistance* (Salem, Mass.: DMA, Inc., 1984), xii, x.

77. Picasso, quoted in Fritz, 67 (emphasis is mine).

78. Fritz, 68.

79. For the specifics of these techniques, see Robert Fritz, *DMA Basic Course Manual* (Salem, Mass.: DMA, Inc., 1982).

80. Bonhoeffer, 86.

81. See de Mello, 137–38, 140.

82. Charles Elliott, *Praying the Kingdom: Towards a Political Spirituality* (New York: Paulist Press, 1985), 30–31, 145.

83. Foster, 138–39.

84. Ibid., 140, 148.

85. John Sanford, *Ministry Burnout* (New York: Paulist Press, 1982), 5–15.

86. William Stringfellow, *The Politics of Spirituality* (Philadelphia, Westminster Press, 1984), 40, 41.

87. Sanford, 85.

88. Ram Dass and Paul Gorman, *How Can I Help?* (New York: Knopf, 1985), 210, 211.

89. There are, of course, many other disciplines of body, mind, emotion, and spirit that one can develop. Some seem even more radical or exotic than the ones discussed in this chapter. For a demonstration of the power and uses of "past life regressions" see Barbara Hand Clow, *Eye of the Centaur: A Visionary Guide into Past Lives* (St. Paul: Llewellyn, 1986). For an introduction to "channeling" and other methods of "activating your life purpose" see Meredith Lady Young, *Language of the Soul: Applying Universal Principles for Self-Empowerment* (Walpole, NH: Stillpoint, 1987).

Chapter 6: Compassionate Action

1. L. S. Stavrianos, *The Promise of the Coming Dark Age* (New York: W. H. Freeman, 1976), 3, 15.

2. Mayor Harold Washington, "Chicago's Future," Speech no. 7 in The Future of Chicago series, ed. Dick Simpson and David Gullo (Chicago: University of Illinois at Chicago, 1984), 4. Reprinted in Dick Simpson, ed., *Chicago's Future in a Time of Change* (Champaign, Ill: Stipes, 1988), 64.

3. Denise Griebler, "Sanctuary at Wellington UCC: An Assessment," in *Justice Ministries: The Struggle for Peace, Justice, Sanctuary,* ed. Dick Simpson and Clinton Stockwell (Chicago: ICUIS, 1985), 114, 97.

4. Ibid., 113.

5. Chicago Religious Task Force on Central America, "Sanctuary: A Justice Ministry," reprinted in *Justice Ministries: The Struggle for Peace, Justice, Sanctuary,* 90.

6. Renny Golden and Michael McConnell, *Sanctuary: The New Underground Railroad* (Maryknoll, N.Y.: Orbis, 1986), 49–51.

7. Ibid., 17, 59.

8. Ibid., 93–94.

9. This description is taken from Dick Simpson and Joey Sylvester, "Caravan: A Spiritual Journey," originally published in *Bear and Company Magazine* 3 (1984); reprinted in *Justice Ministries: The Struggle for Peace, Justice, Sanctuary,* 103–9.

10. The National Immigration and Alien Rights Project of the American Civil Liberties Union, "Salvadorans in the U.S.: The Case for Extended Voluntary Departure," (A report issued in April 1984).

11. *Sanctuary,* 135.

12. Ibid., 131, 178–79, 187, 188, 193.

13. City of Chicago, *President Reagan's Proposed 1987 Budget Impact on Chicago* (Chicago: City Office of Budget and Management, 1986), 1. Reprinted in Simpson, *Chicago's Future in a Time of Change,* 510.

14. *Justice Ministries: The Struggle for Peace, Justice, Sanctuary,* 156, 173.

15. Ibid., 173–74.

16. Ibid., 175.

17. Dick Simpson, "Birthing a Nuclear Free World," Sermon, Wellington Avenue United Church of Christ, 30 Sept. 1984.

18. *Justice Ministries: The Struggle for Peace, Justice, Sanctuary,* 168.

19. Metro Chicago Clergy and Laity Concerned, "Nuclear Weapon Free Zone Packet," 1986.

20. City of Chicago, Department of Economic Development, 1, 3.

21. David Orr, Press Statement, 14 Jan. 1986.

22. Metro Chicago Clergy and Laity Concerned, Press Release, 14 Jan. 1986.

23. Dick Simpson, "Spreading the Light," Sermon, Third Unitarian Church, Chicago, 12 Jan. 1986.

24. Mayor's Task Force on Hunger, City of Chicago, November 1984.

25. David Burnham, "A Servant in the Streets," *Reader* 13 (29 June 1984): 1, 25.

26. Ibid., 25.

27. Ibid.

28. James Harper (Candidate for the Ordained Ministry of the United Church

of Christ). "Statement of Beliefs." Unpublished paper written for ordination, 1983, 11.

29. Ibid., 11, 13.

30. Burnham, 26.

31. Dick Simpson, "Wellington Shelter Report," May 1986, 2–3.

32. Dick Simpson and Clinton Stockwell, eds., *Justice Ministries: Fighting against Hunger, Homelessness, Joblessness* (Chicago: ICUIS, 1985), 144.

33. See Pierre de Vise, "Chicago's Widening Color Gap," in *Chicago's Future in a Time of Change,* 66–91.

34. Merrill Goozner, "What Ails Post-Industrial Chicago?" *Crain's Chicago Business* 9 (24 Oct.–2 Nov. 1986), 1, 69.

35. David Roozen, William McKinney and Jackson Carroll, *Varieties of Religious Presence* (New York: Pilgrim Press, 1984), 249.

36. Another book that describes activist congregations is David S. King, *No Church is an Island* (New York: Pilgrim Press, 1980).

37. The story was told originally by Ruth Isabel Seabury and is quoted in King, 2–3.

38. Hugh Lewin, *A Community of Clowns: Testimonies of People in Urban Rural Mission* (Geneva, Switzerland: World Council of Churches, 1987), 8.

39. Ibid., 282.

40. Ibid., 290.

41. Ibid., 292.

42. See George D. Younger, *From New Creation to Urban Crisis: A History of Action Training Ministries* (Chicago: Center for the Scientific Study of Religion, 1987).

Chapter 7: A New People

1. Lucien Stryk, *Encounter with Zen: Writings on Poetry and Zen* (Athens, Ohio: Swallow/Ohio University Press, 1981), 57–62.

2. Quoted in Ibid., 88.

3. George Trevelyan, *A Vision of the Aquarian Age* (Walpole, N.H.: Stillpoint, 1984), 160, 2, 16, 17.

4. Ibid., 27, 72–73.

5. Ibid., 153.

6. Ibid., 160–61.

7. Ibid., 171.

8. William Stringfellow, *The Politics of Spirituality* (Philadelphia: Westminster, 1984), 32.

9. Ibid., 84.

10. For instance, José Argüelles in *The Mayan Factor: Path Beyond Technology* (Santa Fe: Bear & Company, 1987), argues that we are passing through a galactic beam from which we will emerge and quickly evolve after A.D. 2012.

11. Riane Eisler, *The Chalice and the Blade: Our History, Our Future* (San Francisco: Harper & Row, 1987), chap. 1–4, 169, 188, 198–99.

12. Robert Tucker, *Politics As Leadership* (Columbia, Mo.: University of Missouri Press, 1982), 15, 20.

13. On "cutting the issue" and the importance of defining the situation, see also E. E. Schattschneider, *Semi-Sovereign People* (Hinsdale, Ill.: Dryden Press, 1960), chap. 1 and 4; and Saul Alinsky, *Rules for Radicals* (New York: Random House, 1971), 130–36.

14. Tucker, 114, 123.

15. Ibid., 130, 131, 134.

16. Ibid., 154.

17. Dag Hammarskjold, *Markings* translated from the Swedish by Leif Sjoberg and W. H. Auden (New York: Knopf, 1977).

18. Robert Muller, *New Genesis: Shaping a Global Spirituality* (New York: Doubleday, 1982), 173–74.

19. Ibid., 183.

20. Jonathan Porritt, *Seeing Green: The Politics of Ecology Explained* (London: Basil Blackwell, 1986), 216–17.

21. Charlene Spretnak and Fritjof Capra, *Green Politics: The Global Promise* (Santa Fe: Bear & Company, 1986), chap. 10. See also Charlene Spretnak, *The Spiritual Dimension of Green Politics* (Santa Fe: Bear & Company, 1986).

22. Jack Nelson-Pallmeyer, *The Politics of Compassion* (Maryknoll, N.Y.: Orbis, 1986), 29, 16.

23. Ibid., 30, 34.

24. Ibid., 109–15.

25. Ibid., 114, 117.

26. See Walter Dean Burnham, *Critical Elections and the Mainsprings of American Politics* (New York: Norton, 1970); and James Sundquist, *Dynamics of the Party System* (Washington, D.C.: Brookings, 1973).

27. Michael Grosso, *The Final Choice* (Walpole, N.H.: Stillpoint, 1985), 245.

28. Ibid., 243–44.

29. Ibid., 256, 258.

30. Ibid., 293.

31. Stephen D. Johnson and Joseph B. Tanney, *The Political Role of Religion in the United States* (Boulder, Col.: Westview, 1986), 342.

32. Ronald D. Pasquariello, Donald Shriver, Jr., and Alan Geyer, *Redeeming the City: Theology, Politics and Urban Policy* (New York: Pilgrim, 1982), 146.

33. Ibid., 146–47.

34. A. James Reichley, *Religion in American Public Life* (Washington, D.C.: Brookings, 1985), 359.

35. Grosso, 301.

36. Ibid., 297, 301.

37. Ibid., 291.

38. Ibid., 314, 337.

39. Robert Bellah et al., *Habits of the Heart: Individualism and Commitment in American Life* (New York: Harper & Row, 1985), 286.

40. Matthew Fox, *Illuminations of Hildegard of Bingen* (Santa Fe: Bear & Company, 1985), 9, 20, 24.

41. Ibid., 45.

42. Ibid., 76.

43. Donald McNeill, Douglas Morrison, and Henri Nouwen, *Compassion: A Reflection on the Christian Life,* (New York: Doubleday, 1983), 4.

44. Fran Peavey with Myra Levy and Charles Varon, *Heart Politics* (Philadelphia: New Society Publishers, 1986), 138.

INDEX